NINJA FOODI
SMART XL GRILL COOKBOOK
FOR BEGINNERS

Over 500 Easy, Delicious and Healthy Recipes to Fry,
Bake, Grill and Roast for Your Smart XL Grill

Cinna Weyllen

Table of Content

Chapter 4 Appetizers and Snacks 51

Chapter 5 Poultry 65

Chapter 6 Meats   **83**

Chapter 7 Fish and Seafood 100

Chapter 8 Desserts 116

Introduction

The Inspiration Behind This Cookbook

One of my all-time favourite foods is Beef Stew. It's a great meal to batch cook for those busy nights, but it's also what I make for my kids when they're sick. Beef stew is not only hearty and delicious, but it reminds me of my childhood in a way that could bring me to tears.

Now, before my Ninja Foodi... Let me tell you how I used to make Beef Stew. First, I would pat dry the beef cubes and season them - this step is a no brainer. Next, I would heat a frying pan on high with some oil and slowly sear the beef, in batches so I didn't overcrowd the pan. This takes a long time and produces a lot of smoke, not to mention, used a lot of oil. Next I would fill my slow cooker with stock and vegetables. This worked great but took all day to cook and created a lot of dishes to clean.

With the Ninja Foodi, I can sear, simmer, roast and braise all in one easy-to-clean appliance. The pre-programmed buttons make it so easy, even my kids can make beef stew in it now! This is one of the only tabletop appliances on the market that gets hot enough to sear meat properly, so the first thing I made with my Ninja Foodi was beef stew.

What Makes The Ninja Foodi so Great?

Allow me to walk you through how I make beef stew since getting my Ninja Foodi. I open a package of meat, season it, and add it to the Ninja foodie and set it to "sear." In minutes, the temperature has reached 500F so I set a timer after placing the lid on (so there's virtually no smoke at all,) and then come back when the timer has gone off to add the stock and fresh veggies.... And voila! In just one hour I have tender, flavourful, juicy, hearty, healthy beef stew!

But it's more than just beef stew! I use my Ninja Foodi for just about everything now, which is why I wanted to create this cookbook (with more than 500 recipes!) to show you how you too can revolutionize the way you cook. You and your family will save time and be healthier in the end - it's really a win-win! (You might also end up feeling like a world class chef in the end, because everything in this book is so tasty!)

Along with saving money on my energy bill and saving me tons of time around dinner time, this appliance also helped make me and my family healthier! I used to add a lot of oil to the surface of meat before cooking, to prevent it from sticking. I was fed up with losing half a chicken breast on the barbeque so then I started baking them, which didn't offer a lot of flavour. I also used a lot of oil on things like grilled bread, fish or vegetables. But with the air crisp setting on this machine, you don't need to use any oil whatsoever... which has had an incredible impact on my health. If you're not concerned about oil, this machine will still allow you to enjoy more of the foods that fit into your meal plan – for keto or paleo diets, the Ninja Foodi is a great addition to your kitchen, because of how conveniently you can cook such a variety of proteins.

Making The Most of Your Ninja Foodi

The Ninja Foodi has 6 function buttons which completely replaced my toaster, toaster oven, deep fryer, oven, stovetop, microwave and even my outdoor barbeque! With this device I can roast a chicken, a whole fish or any of my favourite oven meals. I can quickly heat up a piece of pizza of toast. I can air crisp chicken wings or fish sticks for the kids. I can bake a cake or fresh bread. I can dehydrate apple chips or kale chips. I can broil garlic bread or grilled cheese. And probably most impressively... I can grill with no smoke or fire hazards year round indoors!! Now you try to name an appliance that can do all of that!?!?!

Now you may be wondering – "But is this thing really as good as my barbeque?" The answer is YES and once you try just a few of the recipes from this cook, you will see for yourself. So far I have grilled everything from shrimp skewers to corn on the cob, to loaded baked potatoes, to hot dogs and yes, even the perfect medium rare steak. The Ninja Foodi comes with a thermometer probe that is inserted into the center of a seasoned steak, to alert you when it's reached your desire doneness. Once the internal temperature of the steak reaches that temperature, you open the lid and have the perfectly cooked dinner. It really is that easy! Alongside your steak, you can also enjoy perfectly roasted vegetables and potatoes, and you can even enjoy a fresh baked apple pie for dessert... all from your Ninja Foodi!

One of the best parts of this machine though, is that it reaches a temperature of 500F – this is almost unheard of for a tabletop interior grill. This high temperature allows me to properly sear my food (especially steaks, chicken or fish) and really allows it to get those tasty grill marks. But this device does more than just sear, as I've told you... because of its unique cyclonic technology, it also circulates the air around your food continuously, which cooks food perfectly, every time.

Now Let's Get Cooking!

The Ninja Foodi system changed everything about how I cook and eat, and I cannot wait for you to see, through the recipes in this cookbook, how revolutionary this appliance will be for your lifestyle and cooking routine. I've included 500 recipes in this book to show you exactly what this appliance can do; but really, there is nothing this machine can't cook. Everything from breads and pastries, to French fries and chicken wings, to home-style chicken and perfect steaks... The Ninja Foodi has been a game changer in my life, and if you're about to read this cookbook, it will change your life too!

Chapter 1 Breakfasts

Banana Chips with Peanut Butter

Prep time: 10 minutes | Cook time: 8 hours | Makes 1 cup

2 bananas, sliced into ¼-inch rounds
2 tablespoons creamy peanut butter

1. In a medium bowl, toss the banana slices with the peanut butter, until well coated. If the peanut butter is too thick and not mixing well, add 1 to 2 tablespoons of water.
2. Place the banana slices flat on the Crisper Basket. Arrange them in a single layer, without any slices touching each another.
3. Place the basket in the pot and close the hood.
4. Select DEHYDRATE, set the temperature to 135ºF (57ºC), and set the time to 8 hours. Select START/STOP.
5. When cooking is complete, remove the basket from the pot. Transfer the banana chips to an airtight container and store at room temperature.

Sourdough Croutons

Prep time: 5 minutes | Cook time: 6 minutes | Makes 4 cups

4 cups cubed sourdough bread, 1-inch cubes
1 tablespoon olive oil
1 teaspoon fresh
thyme leaves
¼ teaspoon salt
Freshly ground black pepper, to taste

1. Combine all ingredients in a bowl.
2. Insert the Crisper Basket and close the hood. Select AIR CRISP, set the temperature to 400ºF (204ºC), and set the time to 6 minutes. Select START/STOP to begin preheating.
3. Toss the bread cubes and transfer to the basket. Close the hood and AIR CRISP for 6 minutes, shaking the basket once or twice while they cook.
4. Serve warm.

Potato Bread Rolls

Prep time: 15 minutes | Cook time: 20 minutes | Serves 5

5 large potatoes, boiled and mashed
Salt and ground black pepper, to taste
½ teaspoon mustard seeds
1 tablespoon olive oil
2 small onions, chopped
2 sprigs curry leaves
½ teaspoon turmeric powder
2 green chilis, seeded and chopped
1 bunch coriander, chopped
8 slices bread, brown sides discarded

1. Insert the Crisper Basket and close the hood. Select AIR CRISP, set the temperature to 400ºF (204ºC), and set the time to 15 minutes. Select START/STOP to begin preheating.
2. Put the mashed potatoes in a bowl and sprinkle on salt and pepper. Set to one side.
3. Fry the mustard seeds in olive oil over a medium-low heat in a skillet, stirring continuously, until they sputter.
4. Add the onions and cook until they turn translucent. Add the curry leaves and turmeric powder and stir. Cook for a further 2 minutes until fragrant.
5. Remove the skillet from the heat and combine with the potatoes. Mix in the green chilies and coriander.
6. Wet the bread slightly and drain of any excess liquid.
7. Spoon a small amount of the potato mixture into the center of the bread and enclose the bread around the filling, sealing it entirely. Continue until the rest of the bread and filling is used up. Brush each bread roll with some oil and transfer to the basket.
8. Close the hood and AIR CRISP for 15 minutes, gently shaking the Crisper Basket at the halfway point to ensure each roll is cooked evenly.
9. Serve immediately.

Egg and Sausage Stuffed Breakfast Pockets

Prep time: 15 minutes | Cook time: 23 minutes | Serves 4

1 (6-ounce / 170-g) package ground breakfast sausage, crumbled
3 large eggs, lightly beaten
1/3 cup diced red bell pepper
1/3 cup thinly sliced scallions (green part only)
Sea salt, to taste
Freshly ground black pepper, to taste
1 (16-ounce / 454-g) package pizza dough
All-purpose flour, for dusting
1 cup shredded Cheddar cheese
2 tablespoons canola oil

1. Select ROAST, set the temperature to 375ºF (191ºC), and set the time to 15 minutes. Select START/STOP to begin preheating.
2. When the unit beeps to signify it has preheated, place the sausage directly in the pot. Close the hood, and ROAST for 10 minutes, checking the sausage every 2 to 3 minutes, breaking apart larger pieces with a wooden spoon.
3. After 10 minutes, pour the eggs, bell pepper, and scallions into the pot. Stir to evenly incorporate with the sausage. Close the hood and let the eggs roast for the remaining 5 minutes, stirring occasionally. Transfer the sausage and egg mixture to a medium bowl to cool slightly. Season with salt and pepper.
4. Insert the Crisper Basket and close the hood. Select AIR CRISP, set the temperature to 350ºF (177ºC), and set the time to 8 minutes. Select START/STOP to begin preheating.
5. Meanwhile, divide the dough into four equal pieces. Lightly dust a clean work surface with flour. Roll each piece of dough into a 5-inch round of even thickness. Divide the sausage-egg mixture and cheese evenly among each round. Brush the outside edge of the dough with water. Fold the dough over the filling, forming a half circle. Pinch the edges of the dough together to seal in the filling. Brush both sides of each pocket with the oil.
6. When the unit beeps to signify it has preheated, place the breakfast pockets in the basket. Close the hood and AIR CRISP for 6 to 8 minutes, or until golden brown.

Nut and Seed Muffins

Prep time: 15 minutes | Cook time: 10 minutes | Makes 8 muffins

1/2 cup whole-wheat flour, plus 2 tablespoons
1/4 cup oat bran
2 tablespoons flaxseed meal
1/4 cup brown sugar
1/2 teaspoon baking soda
1/2 teaspoon baking powder
1/4 teaspoon salt
1/2 teaspoon cinnamon
1/2 cup buttermilk
2 tablespoons melted butter
1 egg
1/2 teaspoon pure vanilla extract
1/2 cup grated carrots
1/4 cup chopped pecans
1/4 cup chopped walnuts
1 tablespoon pumpkin seeds
1 tablespoon sunflower seeds
Cooking spray

Special Equipment:
16 foil muffin cups, paper liners removed

1. Select BAKE, set the temperature to 330ºF (166ºC), and set the time to 10 minutes. Select START/STOP to begin preheating.
2. In a large bowl, stir together the flour, bran, flaxseed meal, sugar, baking soda, baking powder, salt, and cinnamon.
3. In a medium bowl, beat together the buttermilk, butter, egg, and vanilla. Pour into flour mixture and stir just until dry ingredients moisten. Do not beat.
4. Gently stir in carrots, nuts, and seeds.
5. Double up the foil cups so you have 8 total and spritz with cooking spray.
6. Put 4 foil cups in the pot and divide half the batter among them.
7. Close the hood and BAKE for 10 minutes, or until a toothpick inserted in center comes out clean.
8. Repeat step 7 to bake remaining 4 muffins.
9. Serve warm.

Bacon and Broccoli Bread Pudding

Prep time: 15 minutes | Cook time: 48 minutes | Serves 2 to 4

½ pound (227 g) thick cut bacon, cut into ¼-inch pieces
3 cups brioche bread, cut into ½-inch cubes
2 tablespoons butter, melted
3 eggs
1 cup milk
½ teaspoon salt
Freshly ground black pepper, to taste
1 cup frozen broccoli florets, thawed and chopped
1½ cups grated Swiss cheese

1. Insert the Crisper Basket and close the hood. Select AIR CRISP, set the temperature to 400ºF (204ºC), and set the time to 10 minutes. Select START/STOP to begin preheating.
2. Put the bacon in the basket. Close the hood and AIR CRISP for 8 minutes until crispy, shaking the basket a few times to help it cook evenly. Remove the bacon and set it aside on a paper towel.
3. AIR CRISP the brioche bread cubes for 2 minutes to dry and toast lightly.
4. Butter a cake pan. Combine all the remaining ingredients in a large bowl and toss well. Transfer the mixture to the buttered cake pan, cover with aluminum foil and refrigerate the bread pudding overnight, or for at least 8 hours.
5. Remove the cake pan from the refrigerator an hour before you plan to bake and let it sit on the countertop to come to room temperature.
6. Select BAKE, set the temperature to 330ºF (166ºC), and set the time to 40 minutes. Select START/STOP to begin preheating.
7. Place the covered cake pan directly in the pot. Fold the ends of the aluminum foil over the top of the pan. Close the hood and BAKE for 20 minutes. Remove the foil and bake for an additional 20 minutes. If the top browns a little too much before the custard has set, simply return the foil to the pan. The bread pudding has cooked through when a skewer inserted into the center comes out clean.
8. Serve warm.

Spinach Omelet

Prep time: 10 minutes | Cook time: 10 minutes | Serves 1

1 teaspoon olive oil
3 eggs
Salt and ground black pepper, to taste
1 tablespoon ricotta
cheese
¼ cup chopped spinach
1 tablespoon chopped parsley

1. Grease a baking pan with olive oil.
2. Select BAKE, set the temperature to 330ºF (166ºC), and set the time to 10 minutes. Select START/STOP to begin preheating.
3. In a bowl, beat the eggs with a fork and sprinkle salt and pepper.
4. Add the ricotta, spinach, and parsley and then transfer to the baking pan. Place the pan directly in the pot.
5. Close the hood and BAKE for 10 minutes or until the egg is set.
6. Serve warm.

Fast Coffee Donuts

Prep time: 5 minutes | Cook time: 6 minutes | Serves 6

¼ cup sugar
½ teaspoon salt
1 cup flour
1 teaspoon baking powder
¼ cup coffee
1 tablespoon aquafaba
1 tablespoon sunflower oil

1. In a large bowl, combine the sugar, salt, flour, and baking powder.
2. Add the coffee, aquafaba, and sunflower oil and mix until a dough is formed. Leave the dough to rest in and the refrigerator.
3. Insert the Crisper Basket and close the hood. Select AIR CRISP, set the temperature to 400ºF (204ºC), and set the time to 6 minutes. Select START/STOP to begin preheating.
4. Remove the dough from the fridge and divide up, kneading each section into a doughnut.
5. Put the doughnuts in the basket. Close the hood and AIR CRISP for 6 minutes.
6. Serve immediately.

Bacon and Egg Stuffed Peppers

Prep time: 10 minutes | Cook time: 15 minutes | Serves 4

1 cup shredded
Cheddar cheese
4 slices bacon,
cooked and chopped
4 bell peppers,
seeded and tops
removed

4 large eggs
Sea salt, to taste
Freshly ground black
pepper, to taste
Chopped fresh
parsley, for garnish

1. Insert the Crisper Basket and close the hood. Select AIR CRISP, set the temperature to 390ºF (199ºC), and set the time to 15 minutes. Select START/STOP to begin preheating.
2. Meanwhile, divide the cheese and bacon between the bell peppers. Crack one of the eggs into each bell pepper, and season with salt and pepper.
3. When the unit beeps to signify it has preheated, place each bell pepper in the basket. Close the hood and AIR CRISP for 10 to 15 minutes, until the egg whites are cooked and the yolks are slightly runny.
4. Remove the peppers from the basket, garnish with parsley, and serve.

Mushroom and Onion Frittata

Prep time: 10 minutes | Cook time: 10 minutes | Serves 4

4 large eggs
¼ cup whole milk
Sea salt, to taste
Freshly ground black
pepper, to taste
½ bell pepper,

seeded and diced
½ onion, chopped
4 cremini
mushrooms, sliced
½ cup shredded
Cheddar cheese

1. In a medium bowl, whisk together the eggs and milk. Season with the salt and pepper. Add the bell pepper, onion, mushrooms, and cheese. Mix until well combined.
2. Select BAKE, set the temperature to 400ºF (204ºC), and set the time to 10 minutes. Select START/STOP to begin preheating.
3. Meanwhile, pour the egg mixture into the baking pan, spreading evenly.

4. When the unit beeps to signify it has preheated, place the pan directly in the pot. Close the hood and BAKE for 10 minutes, or until lightly golden.

Egg and Avocado Burrito

Prep time: 10 minutes | Cook time: 3 to 5 minutes | Serves 4

4 low-sodium whole-
wheat flour tortillas
Filling:
1 hard-boiled egg,
chopped
2 hard-boiled egg
whites, chopped
1 ripe avocado,
peeled, pitted, and
chopped
1 red bell pepper,

chopped
1 (1.2-ounce / 34-
g) slice low-sodium,
low-fat American
cheese, torn into
pieces
3 tablespoons low-
sodium salsa, plus
additional for serving
(optional)

Special Equipment:
4 toothpicks (optional), soaked in water for at least 30 minutes

1. Insert the Crisper Basket and close the hood. Select AIR CRISP, set the temperature to 390ºF (199ºC), and set the time to 5 minutes. Select START/STOP to begin preheating.
2. Make the filling: Combine the egg, egg whites, avocado, red bell pepper, cheese, and salsa in a medium bowl and stir until blended.
3. Assemble the burritos: Arrange the tortillas on a clean work surface and place ¼ of the prepared filling in the middle of each tortilla, leaving about 1½-inch on each end unfilled. Fold in the opposite sides of each tortilla and roll up. Secure with toothpicks through the center, if needed.
4. Transfer the burritos to the Crisper Basket. Close the hood and AIR CRISP for 3 to 5 minutes, or until the burritos are crisp and golden brown.
5. Allow to cool for 5 minutes and serve with salsa, if desired.

Cinnamon Toast with Strawberries

Prep time: 15 minutes | Cook time: 10 minutes | Serves 4

1 (15-ounce / 425-g) can full-fat coconut milk, refrigerated overnight
½ tablespoon powdered sugar
1½ teaspoons vanilla extract, divided
1 cup halved strawberries
1 tablespoon maple syrup, plus more for garnish
1 tablespoon brown sugar, divided
¾ cup lite coconut milk
2 large eggs
½ teaspoon ground cinnamon
2 tablespoons unsalted butter, at room temperature
4 slices challah bread

1. Turn the chilled can of full-fat coconut milk upside down (do not shake the can), open the bottom, and pour out the liquid coconut water. Scoop the remaining solid coconut cream into a medium bowl. Using an electric hand mixer, whip the cream for 3 to 5 minutes, until soft peaks form.
2. Add the powdered sugar and ½ teaspoon of the vanilla to the coconut cream, and whip it again until creamy. Place the bowl in the refrigerator.
3. Insert the Grill Grate and close the hood. Select GRILL, set the temperature to MAX, and set the time to 15 minutes. Select START/STOP to begin preheating.
4. While the unit is preheating, combine the strawberries with the maple syrup and toss to coat evenly. Sprinkle evenly with ½ tablespoon of the brown sugar.
5. In a large shallow bowl, whisk together the lite coconut milk, eggs, the remaining 1 teaspoon of vanilla, and cinnamon.
6. When the unit beeps to signify it has preheated, place the strawberries on the Grill Grate. Gently press the fruit down to maximize grill marks. Close the hood and GRILL for 4 minutes without flipping.
7. Meanwhile, butter each slice of bread on both sides. Place one slice in the egg mixture and let it soak for 1 minute. Flip the slice over and soak it for another minute. Repeat with the remaining bread slices. Sprinkle each side of the toast with the remaining ½ tablespoon of brown sugar.
8. After 4 minutes, remove the strawberries from the grill and set aside. Decrease the temperature to HIGH. Place the bread on the Grill Grate; close the hood and GRILL for 4 to 6 minutes until golden and caramelized. Check often to ensure desired doneness.
9. Place the toast on a plate and top with the strawberries and whipped coconut cream. Drizzle with maple syrup, if desired.

Grilled Sausage Mix

Prep time: 5 minutes | Cook time: 22 minutes | Serves 4

8 mini bell peppers
2 heads radicchio, each cut into 6 wedges
Canola oil, for brushing
Sea salt, to taste
Freshly ground black pepper, to taste
6 breakfast sausage links
6 hot or sweet Italian sausage links

1. Insert the Grill Grate and close the hood. Select GRILL, set the temperature to MAX, and set the time to 22 minutes. Select START/STOP to begin preheating.
2. While the unit is preheating, brush the bell peppers and radicchio with the oil. Season with salt and black pepper.
3. When the unit beeps to signify it has preheated, place the bell peppers and radicchio on the Grill Grate; close the hood and GRILL for 10 minutes, without flipping.
4. Meanwhile, poke the sausages with a fork or knife and brush them with some of the oil.
5. After 10 minutes, remove the vegetables and set aside. Decrease the temperature to LOW. Place the sausages on the Grill Grate; close the hood and GRILL for 6 minutes.
6. Flip the sausages. Close the hood and GRILL for 6 minutes more. Remove the sausages from the Grill Grate.
7. Serve the sausages and vegetables on a large cutting board or serving tray.

Honey-Lime Glazed Grilled Fruit Salad

Prep time: 10 minutes | Cook time: 4 minutes | Serves 4

½ pound (227 g) strawberries, washed, hulled and halved
1 (9-ounce / 255-g) can pineapple chunks, drained, juice reserved
2 peaches, pitted and sliced
6 tablespoons honey, divided
1 tablespoon freshly squeezed lime juice

1. Insert the Grill Grate and close the hood. Select GRILL, set the temperature to MAX, and set the time to 4 minutes. Select START/STOP to begin preheating.
2. While the unit is preheating, combine the strawberries, pineapple, and peaches in a large bowl with 3 tablespoons of honey. Toss to coat evenly.
3. When the unit beeps to signify it has preheated, place the fruit on the Grill Grate. Gently press the fruit down to maximize grill marks. Close the hood and GRILL for 4 minutes without flipping.
4. Meanwhile, in a small bowl, combine the remaining 3 tablespoons of honey, lime juice, and 1 tablespoon of reserved pineapple juice.
5. When cooking is complete, place the fruit in a large bowl and toss with the honey mixture. Serve immediately.

Cornflakes Toast Sticks

Prep time: 10 minutes | Cook time: 6 minutes | Serves 4

2 eggs
½ cup milk
⅛ teaspoon salt
½ teaspoon pure vanilla extract
¾ cup crushed cornflakes
6 slices sandwich bread, each slice cut into 4 strips
Maple syrup, for dipping
Cooking spray

1. Insert the Crisper Basket and close the hood. Select AIR CRISP, set the temperature to 390ºF (199ºC), and set the time to 6 minutes. Select START/STOP to begin preheating.
2. In a small bowl, beat together the eggs, milk, salt, and vanilla.
3. Put crushed cornflakes on a plate or in a shallow dish.
4. Dip bread strips in egg mixture, shake off excess, and roll in cornflake crumbs.
5. Spray both sides of bread strips with oil.
6. Put bread strips in Crisper Basket in a single layer.
7. Close the hood and AIR CRISP for 6 minutes or until golden brown.
8. Repeat steps 5 and 6 to AIR CRISP remaining French toast sticks.
9. Serve with maple syrup.

PB&J

Prep time: 5 minutes | Cook time: 6 minutes | Serves 4

½ cup cornflakes, crushed
¼ cup shredded coconut
8 slices oat nut bread or any whole-grain, oversize bread
6 tablespoons peanut butter
2 medium bananas, cut into ½-inch-thick slices
6 tablespoons pineapple preserves
1 egg, beaten
Cooking spray

1. Insert the Crisper Basket and close the hood. Select AIR CRISP, set the temperature to 360ºF (182ºC), and set the time to 6 minutes. Select START/STOP to begin preheating.
2. In a shallow dish, mix the cornflake crumbs and coconut.
3. For each sandwich, spread one bread slice with 1½ tablespoons of peanut butter. Top with banana slices. Spread another bread slice with 1½ tablespoons of preserves. Combine to make a sandwich.
4. Using a pastry brush, brush top of sandwich lightly with beaten egg. Sprinkle with about 1½ tablespoons of crumb coating, pressing it in to make it stick. Spray with cooking spray.
5. Turn sandwich over and repeat to coat and spray the other side. Place the sandwiches in the Crisper Basket.
6. Close the hood and AIR CRISP for 6 minutes or until coating is golden brown and crispy.
7. Cut the cooked sandwiches in half and serve warm.

Spinach with Scrambled Eggs

Prep time: 10 minutes | Cook time: 10 minutes | Serves 2

2 tablespoons olive oil
4 eggs, whisked
5 ounces (142 g) fresh spinach, chopped
1 medium tomato, chopped

1 teaspoon fresh lemon juice
½ teaspoon coarse salt
½ teaspoon ground black pepper
½ cup of fresh basil, roughly chopped

1. Grease a baking pan with the oil, tilting it to spread the oil around.
2. Select BAKE, set the temperature to 280ºF (138ºC), and set the time to 10 minutes. Select START/STOP to begin preheating.
3. In the pan, mix the remaining ingredients, apart from the basil leaves, whisking well until everything is completely combined.
4. Place the pan directly in the pot. Close the hood and BAKE for 10 minutes.
5. Top with fresh basil leaves before serving.

Buttermilk Biscuits

Prep time: 5 minutes | Cook time: 5 minutes | Makes 12 biscuits

2 cups all-purpose flour, plus more for dusting the work surface
1 tablespoon baking powder
¼ teaspoon baking soda

2 teaspoons sugar
1 teaspoon salt
6 tablespoons cold unsalted butter, cut into 1-tablespoon slices
¾ cup buttermilk

1. Spray the Crisper Basket with olive oil.
2. Insert the Crisper Basket and close the hood. Select BAKE, set the temperature to 360ºF (182ºC), and set the time to 5 minutes. Select START/STOP to begin preheating.
3. In a large mixing bowl, combine the flour, baking powder, baking soda, sugar, and salt and mix well.
4. Using a fork, cut in the butter until the mixture resembles coarse meal.
5. Add the buttermilk and mix until smooth.

6. Dust more flour on a clean work surface. Turn the dough out onto the work surface and roll it out until it is about ½ inch thick.
7. Using a 2-inch biscuit cutter, cut out the biscuits. Put the uncooked biscuits in the greased Crisper Basket in a single layer.
8. Close the hood and BAKE for 5 minutes. Transfer the cooked biscuits from the grill to a platter.
9. Cut the remaining biscuits. Bake the remaining biscuits.
10. Serve warm.

Avocado Quesadillas

Prep time: 10 minutes | Cook time: 11 minutes | Serves 4

4 eggs
2 tablespoons skim milk
Salt and ground black pepper, to taste
Cooking spray
4 flour tortillas

4 tablespoons salsa
2 ounces (57 g) Cheddar cheese, grated
½ small avocado, peeled and thinly sliced

1. Select BAKE, set the temperature to 270ºF (132ºC), and set the time to 8 minutes. Select START/STOP to begin preheating.
2. Beat together the eggs, milk, salt, and pepper.
3. Spray a baking pan lightly with cooking spray and add egg mixture.
4. Place the pan directly in the pot. Close the hood and BAKE for 8 minutes, stirring every 1 to 2 minutes, until eggs are scrambled to the liking. Remove and set aside.
5. Spray one side of each tortilla with cooking spray. Flip over.
6. Divide eggs, salsa, cheese, and avocado among the tortillas, covering only half of each tortilla.
7. Fold each tortilla in half and press down lightly. Increase the temperature of the grill to 390ºF (199ºC).
8. Put 2 tortillas in Crisper Basket and AIR CRISP for 3 minutes or until cheese melts and outside feels slightly crispy. Repeat with remaining two tortillas.
9. Cut each cooked tortilla into halves. Serve warm.

Lush Vegetable Omelet

Prep time: 10 minutes | Cook time: 13 minutes | Serves 2

2 teaspoons canola oil
4 eggs, whisked
3 tablespoons plain milk
1 teaspoon melted butter
1 red bell pepper, seeded and chopped
1 green bell pepper, seeded and chopped
1 white onion, finely chopped
½ cup baby spinach leaves, roughly chopped
½ cup Halloumi cheese, shaved
Kosher salt and freshly ground black pepper, to taste

1. Select BAKE, set the temperature to 350ºF (177ºC), and set the time to 13 minutes. Select START/STOP to begin preheating.
2. Grease a baking pan with canola oil.
3. Put the remaining ingredients in the baking pan and stir well.
4. Place the pan directly in the pot. Close the hood and BAKE for 13 minutes.
5. Serve warm.

English Pumpkin Egg Bake

Prep time: 10 minutes | Cook time: 10 minutes | Serves 2

2 eggs
½ cup milk
2 cups flour
2 tablespoons cider vinegar
2 teaspoons baking powder
1 tablespoon sugar
1 cup pumpkin purée
1 teaspoon cinnamon powder
1 teaspoon baking soda
1 tablespoon olive oil

1. Select BAKE, set the temperature to 300ºF (149ºC), and set the time to 10 minutes. Select START/STOP to begin preheating.
2. Crack the eggs into a bowl and beat with a whisk. Combine with the milk, flour, cider vinegar, baking powder, sugar, pumpkin purée, cinnamon powder, and baking soda, mixing well.
3. Grease a baking pan with oil. Add the mixture to the pan. Place the pan directly in the pot. Close the hood and BAKE for 10 minutes.
4. Serve warm.

Grit and Ham Fritters

Prep time: 15 minutes | Cook time: 20 minutes | Serves 6 to 8

4 cups water
1 cup quick-cooking grits
¼ teaspoon salt
2 tablespoons butter
2 cups grated Cheddar cheese, divided
1 cup finely diced ham
1 tablespoon chopped chives
Salt and freshly ground black pepper, to taste
1 egg, beaten
2 cups panko bread crumbs
Cooking spray

1. Bring the water to a boil in a saucepan. Whisk in the grits and ¼ teaspoon of salt, and cook for 7 minutes until the grits are soft. Remove the pan from the heat and stir in the butter and 1 cup of the grated Cheddar cheese. Transfer the grits to a bowl and let them cool for 10 to 15 minutes.
2. Stir the ham, chives and the rest of the cheese into the grits and season with salt and pepper to taste. Add the beaten egg and refrigerate the mixture for 30 minutes.
3. Put the panko bread crumbs in a shallow dish. Measure out ¼-cup portions of the grits mixture and shape them into patties. Coat all sides of the patties with the panko bread crumbs, patting them with the hands so the crumbs adhere to the patties. You should have about 16 patties. Spritz both sides of the patties with cooking spray.
4. Insert the Crisper Basket and close the hood. Select AIR CRISP, set the temperature to 400ºF (204ºC), and set the time to 12 minutes. Select START/STOP to begin preheating.
5. Place the fritters in the basket. Close the hood and AIR CRISP for 8 minutes. Using a flat spatula, flip the fritters over and AIR CRISP for another 4 minutes.
6. Serve hot.

Mushroom and Squash Toast

Prep time: 10 minutes | Cook time: 10 minutes | Serves 4

1 tablespoon olive oil
1 red bell pepper, cut into strips
2 green onions, sliced
1 cup sliced button or cremini mushrooms
1 small yellow squash, sliced
2 tablespoons softened butter
4 slices bread
½ cup soft goat cheese

1. Brush the Crisper Basket with the olive oil.
2. Insert the Crisper Basket and close the hood. Select AIR CRISP, set the temperature to 350ºF (177ºC), and set the time to 7 minutes. Select START/STOP to begin preheating.
3. Put the red pepper, green onions, mushrooms, and squash inside the basket and give them a stir. Close the hood and AIR CRISP for 7 minutes or the vegetables are tender, shaking the basket once throughout the cooking time.
4. Remove the vegetables and set them aside.
5. Spread the butter on the slices of bread and transfer to the basket, butter-side up. Close the hood and AIR CRISP for 3 minutes.
6. Remove the toast from the grill and top with goat cheese and vegetables. Serve warm.

Ham and Corn Muffins

Prep time: 10 minutes | Cook time: 6 minutes | Makes 8 muffins

¾ cup yellow cornmeal
¼ cup flour
1½ teaspoons baking powder
¼ teaspoon salt
1 egg, beaten
2 tablespoons canola oil
½ cup milk
½ cup shredded sharp Cheddar cheese
½ cup diced ham

1. Select BAKE, set the temperature to 390ºF (199ºC), and set the time to 6 minutes. Select START/STOP to begin preheating.
2. In a medium bowl, stir together the cornmeal, flour, baking powder, and salt.
3. Add the egg, oil, and milk to dry ingredients and mix well.
4. Stir in shredded cheese and diced ham.
5. Divide batter among 8 parchment paper-lined muffin cups.
6. Put 4 filled muffin cups in the pot. Close the hood and BAKE for 5 minutes.
7. Reduce temperature to 330ºF (166ºC) and bake for 1 minute or until a toothpick inserted in center of the muffin comes out clean.
8. Repeat steps 6 and 7 to bake remaining muffins.
9. Serve warm.

Banana Bread

Prep time: 10 minutes | Cook time: 22 minutes | Makes 3 loaves

3 ripe bananas, mashed
1 cup sugar
1 large egg
4 tablespoons (½ stick) unsalted butter, melted
1½ cups all-purpose flour
1 teaspoon baking soda
1 teaspoon salt

1. Coat the insides of 3 mini loaf pans with cooking spray.
2. In a large mixing bowl, mix the bananas and sugar.
3. In a separate large mixing bowl, combine the egg, butter, flour, baking soda, and salt and mix well.
4. Add the banana mixture to the egg and flour mixture. Mix well.
5. Divide the batter evenly among the prepared pans.
6. Select BAKE, set the temperature to 310ºF (154ºC), and set the time to 22 minutes. Select START/STOP to begin preheating.
7. Set the mini loaf pans into the pot.
8. Close the hood and BAKE for 22 minutes. Insert a toothpick into the center of each loaf; if it comes out clean, they are done.
9. When the loaves are cooked through, remove the pans from the Crisper Basket. Turn out the loaves onto a wire rack to cool.
10. Serve warm.

Grilled Egg and Arugula Pizza

Prep time: 10 minutes | Cook time: 8 minutes | Serves 2

2 tablespoons all-purpose flour, plus more as needed
½ store-bought pizza dough (about 8 ounces / 227 g)
1 tablespoon canola oil, divided
1 cup fresh ricotta cheese
4 large eggs
Sea salt, to taste
Freshly ground black pepper, to taste
4 cups arugula, torn
1 tablespoon extra-virgin olive oil
1 teaspoon freshly squeezed lemon juice
2 tablespoons grated Parmesan cheese

1. Insert the Grill Grate and close the hood. Select GRILL, set the temperature to MAX, and set the time to 7 minutes. Select START/STOP to begin preheating.
2. While the unit is preheating, dust a clean work surface with flour. Place the dough on the floured surface and roll it into a 9-inch round of even thickness. Dust your rolling pin and work surface with additional flour, as needed, to ensure the dough does not stick.
3. Brush the surface of the rolled-out dough evenly with ½ tablespoon of canola oil. Flip the dough over and brush with the remaining ½ tablespoon oil. Poke the dough with a fork 5 or 6 times across its surface to prevent air pockets from forming during cooking.
4. When the unit beeps to signify it has preheated, place the dough on the Grill Grate. Close the hood and GRILL for 4 minutes.
5. After 4 minutes, flip the dough, then spoon teaspoons of ricotta cheese across the surface of the dough, leaving a 1-inch border around the edges.
6. Crack one egg into a ramekin or small bowl. This way you can easily remove any shell that may break into the egg and keep the yolk intact. Imagine the dough is split into four quadrants. Pour one egg into each. Repeat with the remaining 3 eggs. Season the pizza with salt and pepper.
7. Close the hood and continue cooking for the remaining 3 to 4 minutes until the egg whites are firm.
8. Meanwhile, in a medium bowl, toss together the arugula, oil, and lemon juice, and season with salt and pepper.
9. Transfer the pizza to a cutting board and let it cool. Top it with the arugula mixture, drizzle with olive oil, if desired, and sprinkle with Parmesan cheese. Cut into pieces and serve.

Breakfast Tater Tot Casserole

Prep time: 5 minutes | Cook time: 17 to 19 minutes | Serves 4

4 eggs
1 cup milk
Salt and pepper, to taste
12 ounces (340 g) ground chicken sausage
1 pound (454 g) frozen tater tots, thawed
¾ cup grated Cheddar cheese
Cooking spray

1. Whisk together the eggs and milk in a medium bowl. Season with salt and pepper to taste and stir until mixed. Set aside.
2. Place a skillet over medium-high heat and spritz with cooking spray. Place the ground sausage in the skillet and break it into smaller pieces with a spatula or spoon. Cook for 3 to 4 minutes until the sausage starts to brown, stirring occasionally. Remove from heat and set aside.
3. Select BAKE, set the temperature to 400ºF (204ºC), and set the time to 15 minutes. Select START/STOP to begin preheating.
4. Coat a baking pan with cooking spray.
5. Arrange the tater tots in the baking pan. Place the pan directly in the pot. Close the hood and BAKE for 15 minutes. Stir in the egg mixture and cooked sausage. Bake for another 6 minutes.
6. Scatter the cheese on top of the tater tots. Continue to bake for 2 to 3 minutes more until the cheese is bubbly and melted.
7. Let the mixture cool for 5 minutes and serve warm.

Crustless Broccoli Quiche

Prep time: 5 minutes | Cook time: 10 minutes | Serves 4

1 cup broccoli florets
¾ cup chopped roasted red peppers
1¼ cups grated Fontina cheese
6 eggs
¾ cup heavy cream
½ teaspoon salt
Freshly ground black pepper, to taste
Cooking spray

1. Select AIR CRISP, set the temperature to 325ºF (163ºC), and set the time to 10 minutes. Select START/STOP to begin preheating.
2. Spritz a baking pan with cooking spray
3. Add the broccoli florets and roasted red peppers to the pan and scatter the grated Fontina cheese on top.
4. In a bowl, beat together the eggs and heavy cream. Sprinkle with salt and pepper. Pour the egg mixture over the top of the cheese. Wrap the pan in foil.
5. Place the pan directly in the pot. Close the hood and AIR CRISP for 8 minutes. Remove the foil and continue to cook another 2 minutes until the quiche is golden brown.
6. Rest for 5 minutes before cutting into wedges and serve warm.

Banana and Oat Bread Pudding

Prep time: 10 minutes | Cook time: 16 to 20 minutes | Serves 4

2 medium ripe bananas, mashed
½ cup low-fat milk
2 tablespoons maple syrup
2 tablespoons peanut butter
1 teaspoon vanilla
extract
1 teaspoon ground cinnamon
2 slices whole-grain bread, cut into bite-sized cubes
¼ cup quick oats
Cooking spray

1. Select AIR CRISP, set the temperature to 350ºF (177ºC), and set the time to 20 minutes. Select START/STOP to begin preheating.
2. Spritz a baking pan lightly with cooking spray.

3. Mix the bananas, milk, maple syrup, peanut butter, vanilla, and cinnamon in a large mixing bowl and stir until well incorporated.
4. Add the bread cubes to the banana mixture and stir until thoroughly coated. Fold in the oats and stir to combine.
5. Transfer the mixture to the baking pan. Wrap the baking pan in aluminum foil.
6. Place the pan directly in the pot. Close the hood and AIR CRISP for 10 to 12 minutes until heated through.
7. Remove the foil and cook for an additional 6 to 8 minutes, or until the pudding has set.
8. Let the pudding cool for 5 minutes before serving.

Cheesy Hash Brown Casserole

Prep time: 15 minutes | Cook time: 30 minutes | Serves 4

3½ cups frozen hash browns, thawed
1 teaspoon salt
1 teaspoon freshly ground black pepper
3 tablespoons butter, melted
1 (10.5-ounce / 298-
g) can cream of chicken soup
½ cup sour cream
1 cup minced onion
½ cup shredded sharp Cheddar cheese
Cooking spray

1. Put the hash browns in a large bowl and season with salt and black pepper. Add the melted butter, cream of chicken soup, and sour cream and stir until well incorporated. Mix in the minced onion and cheese and stir well.
2. Select BAKE, set the temperature to 325ºF (163ºC), and set the time to 30 minutes. Select START/STOP to begin preheating.
3. Spray a baking pan with cooking spray.
4. Spread the hash brown mixture evenly into the baking pan.
5. Place the pan directly in the pot. Close the hood and BAKE for 30 minutes until browned.
6. Cool for 5 minutes before serving.

Sausage and Cheese Quiche

Prep time: 5 minutes | Cook time: 25 minutes | Serves 4

12 large eggs
1 cup heavy cream
Salt and black pepper, to taste
12 ounces (340 g)
sugar-free breakfast sausage
2 cups shredded Cheddar cheese
Cooking spray

1. Select BAKE, set the temperature to 375ºF (191ºC), and set the time to 25 minutes. Select START/STOP to begin preheating.
2. Coat a casserole dish with cooking spray.
3. Beat together the eggs, heavy cream, salt and pepper in a large bowl until creamy. Stir in the breakfast sausage and Cheddar cheese.
4. Pour the sausage mixture into the prepared casserole dish. Place the dish directly in the pot. Close the hood and BAKE for 25 minutes, or until the top of the quiche is golden brown and the eggs are set.
5. Remove from the grill and let sit for 5 to 10 minutes before serving.

Cheesy Breakfast Casserole

Prep time: 10 minutes | Cook time: 14 minutes | Serves 4

6 slices bacon
6 eggs
Salt and pepper, to taste
Cooking spray
½ cup chopped green bell pepper
½ cup chopped onion
¾ cup shredded Cheddar cheese

1. Place the bacon in a skillet over medium-high heat and cook each side for about 4 minutes until evenly crisp. Remove from the heat to a paper towel-lined plate to drain. Crumble it into small pieces and set aside.
2. Whisk the eggs with the salt and pepper in a medium bowl.
3. Select BAKE, set the temperature to 400ºF (204ºC), and set the time to 8 minutes. Select START/STOP to begin preheating.
4. Spritz a baking pan with cooking spray.

5. Place the whisked eggs, crumbled bacon, green bell pepper, and onion in the prepared pan. Place the pan directly in the pot. Close the hood and BAKE for 6 minutes.
6. Scatter the Cheddar cheese all over and bake for 2 minutes more.
7. Allow to sit for 5 minutes and serve on plates.

Tomato-Corn Frittata with Avocado Dressing

Prep time: 10 minutes | Cook time: 20 minutes | Serves 2 or 3

½ cup cherry tomatoes, halved
Kosher salt and freshly ground black pepper, to taste
6 large eggs, lightly beaten
½ cup corn kernels, thawed if frozen
¼ cup milk
1 tablespoon finely chopped fresh dill
½ cup shredded Monterey Jack cheese

Avocado Dressing:
1 ripe avocado, pitted and peeled
2 tablespoons fresh lime juice
¼ cup olive oil
1 scallion, finely chopped
8 fresh basil leaves, finely chopped

1. Put the tomato halves in a colander and lightly season with salt. Set aside for 10 minutes to drain well. Pour the tomatoes into a large bowl and fold in the eggs, corn, milk, and dill. Sprinkle with salt and pepper and stir until mixed.
2. Select BAKE, set the temperature to 300ºF (149ºC), and set the time to 20 minutes. Select START/STOP to begin preheating.
3. Pour the egg mixture into a baking pan. Place the pan directly in the pot. Close the hood and BAKE for 15 minutes.
4. Scatter the cheese on top. Increase the grill temperature to 315ºF (157ºC) and continue to cook for another 5 minutes, or until the frittata is puffy and set.
5. Meanwhile, make the avocado dressing: Mash the avocado with the lime juice in a medium bowl until smooth. Mix in the olive oil, scallion, and basil and stir until well incorporated.
6. Let the frittata cool for 5 minutes and serve alongside the avocado dressing.

Spinach, Leek and Cheese Frittata

Prep time: 10 minutes | Cook time: 20 to 23 minutes | Serves 2

4 large eggs
4 ounces (113 g) baby bella mushrooms, chopped
1 cup (1 ounce / 28-g) baby spinach, chopped
½ cup (2 ounces / 57-g) shredded Cheddar cheese
⅓ cup (from 1 large) chopped leek, white part only
¼ cup halved grape tomatoes
1 tablespoon 2% milk
¼ teaspoon dried oregano
¼ teaspoon garlic powder
½ teaspoon kosher salt
Freshly ground black pepper, to taste
Cooking spray

1. Select BAKE, set the temperature to 300ºF (149ºC), and set the time to 23 minutes. Select START/STOP to begin preheating.
2. Lightly spritz a baking pan with cooking spray.
3. Whisk the eggs in a large bowl until frothy. Add the mushrooms, baby spinach, cheese, leek, tomatoes, milk, oregano, garlic powder, salt, and pepper and stir until well blended. Pour the mixture into the prepared baking pan.
4. Place the pan directly in the pot. Close the hood and BAKE for 20 to 23 minutes, or until the center is puffed up and the top is golden brown.
5. Let the frittata cool for 5 minutes before slicing to serve.

Olives, Kale, and Pecorino Baked Eggs

Prep time: 5 minutes | Cook time: 10 to 12 minutes | Serves 2

1 cup roughly chopped kale leaves, stems and center ribs removed
¼ cup grated pecorino cheese
¼ cup olive oil
1 garlic clove, peeled
3 tablespoons whole almonds
Kosher salt and freshly ground black pepper, to taste
4 large eggs
2 tablespoons heavy cream
3 tablespoons chopped pitted mixed olives

1. Place the kale, pecorino, olive oil, garlic, almonds, salt, and pepper in a small blender and blitz until well incorporated.
2. Select BAKE, set the temperature to 300ºF (149ºC), and set the time to 12 minutes. Select START/STOP to begin preheating.
3. One at a time, crack the eggs in a baking pan. Drizzle the kale pesto on top of the egg whites. Top the yolks with the cream and swirl together the yolks and the pesto.
4. Place the pan directly in the pot. Close the hood and BAKE for 10 to 12 minutes, or until the top begins to brown and the eggs are set.
5. Allow the eggs to cool for 5 minutes. Scatter the olives on top and serve warm.

Fried Potatoes with Peppers and Onions

Prep time: 10 minutes | Cook time: 35 minutes | Serves 4

1 pound (454 g) red potatoes, cut into ½-inch dices
1 large red bell pepper, cut into ½-inch dices
1 large green bell pepper, cut into ½-inch dices
1 medium onion, cut into ½-inch dices
1½ tablespoons extra-virgin olive oil
1¼ teaspoons kosher salt
¾ teaspoon sweet paprika
¾ teaspoon garlic powder
Freshly ground black pepper, to taste

1. Insert the Crisper Basket and close the hood. Select AIR CRISP, set the temperature to 350ºF (177ºC), and set the time to 35 minutes. Select START/STOP to begin preheating.
2. Mix together the potatoes, bell peppers, onion, oil, salt, paprika, garlic powder, and black pepper in a large mixing and toss to coat.
3. Transfer the potato mixture to the Crisper Basket. Close the hood and AIR CRISP for 35 minutes, or until the potatoes are nicely browned. Shake the basket three times during cooking.
4. Remove from the basket to a plate and serve warm.

Western Omelet

Prep time: 5 minutes | Cook time: 18 to 21 minutes | Serves 2

¼ cup chopped bell pepper, green or red
¼ cup chopped onion
¼ cup diced ham
1 teaspoon butter
4 large eggs
2 tablespoons milk
⅛ teaspoon salt
¾ cup shredded sharp Cheddar cheese

1. Select AIR CRISP, set the temperature to 390ºF (199ºC), and set the time to 6 minutes. Select START/STOP to begin preheating.
2. Put the bell pepper, onion, ham, and butter in a baking pan and mix well. Place the pan directly in the pot.
3. Close the hood and AIR CRISP for 1 minute. Stir and continue to cook for an additional 4 to 5 minutes until the veggies are softened.
4. Meanwhile, whisk together the eggs, milk, and salt in a bowl.
5. Pour the egg mixture over the veggie mixture.
6. Reduce the grill temperature to 360ºF (182ºC) and BAKE for 13 to 15 minutes more, or until the top is lightly golden browned and the eggs are set.
7. Scatter the omelet with the shredded cheese. Bake for another 1 minute until the cheese has melted.
8. Let the omelet cool for 5 minutes before serving.

Veggie Frittata

Prep time: 10 minutes | Cook time: 8 to 12 minutes | Serves 4

½ cup chopped red bell pepper
⅓ cup grated carrot
⅓ cup minced onion
1 teaspoon olive oil
1 egg
6 egg whites
1/3 cup 2% milk
1 tablespoon shredded Parmesan cheese

1. Select BAKE, set the temperature to 350ºF (177ºC), and set the time to 12 minutes. Select START/STOP to begin preheating.
2. Mix together the red bell pepper, carrot, onion, and olive oil in a baking pan and stir to combine.
3. Place the pan directly in the pot. Close the hood and BAKE for 4 to 6 minutes, or until the veggies are soft. Stir once during cooking.
4. Meantime, whisk together the egg, egg whites, and milk in a medium bowl until creamy.
5. When the veggies are done, pour the egg mixture over the top. Scatter with the Parmesan cheese.
6. Bake for an additional 4 to 6 minutes, or until the eggs are set and the top is golden around the edges.
7. Allow the frittata to cool for 5 minutes before slicing and serving.

Bacon and Egg Bread Cups

Prep time: 10 minutes | Cook time: 8 to 12 minutes | Serves 4

4 (3-by-4-inch) crusty rolls
4 thin slices Gouda or Swiss cheese mini wedges
5 eggs
2 tablespoons heavy cream
3 strips precooked bacon, chopped
½ teaspoon dried thyme
Pinch salt
Freshly ground black pepper, to taste

1. Select BAKE, set the temperature to 330ºF (166ºC), and set the time to 12 minutes. Select START/STOP to begin preheating.
2. On a clean work surface, cut the tops off the rolls. Using your fingers, remove the insides of the rolls to make bread cups, leaving a ½-inch shell. Place a slice of cheese onto each roll bottom.
3. Whisk together the eggs and heavy cream in a medium bowl until well combined. Fold in the bacon, thyme, salt, and pepper and stir well.
4. Scrape the egg mixture into the prepared bread cups.
5. Place the bread cups directly in the pot. Close the hood and BAKE for 8 to 12 minutes, or until the eggs are cooked to your preference.
6. Serve warm.

Maple Walnut Pancake

Prep time: 10 minutes | Cook time: 20 minutes | Serves 4

3 tablespoons melted butter, divided
1 cup flour
2 tablespoons sugar
1½ teaspoons baking powder
¼ teaspoon salt
1 egg, beaten

¾ cup milk
1 teaspoon pure vanilla extract
½ cup roughly chopped walnuts
Maple syrup or fresh sliced fruit, for serving

1. Select BAKE, set the temperature to 330ºF (166ºC), and set the time to 20 minutes. Select START/STOP to begin preheating.
2. Grease a baking pan with 1 tablespoon of melted butter.
3. Mix together the flour, sugar, baking powder, and salt in a medium bowl. Add the beaten egg, milk, the remaining 2 tablespoons of melted butter, and vanilla and stir until the batter is sticky but slightly lumpy.
4. Slowly pour the batter into the greased baking pan and scatter with the walnuts.
5. Place the pan directly in the pot. Close the hood and BAKE for 20 minutes until golden brown and cooked through.
6. Let the pancake rest for 5 minutes and serve topped with the maple syrup or fresh fruit, if desired.

Mixed Berry Dutch Baby Pancake

Prep time: 10 minutes | Cook time: 12 to 16 minutes | Serves 4

1 tablespoon unsalted butter, at room temperature
1 egg
2 egg whites
½ cup 2% milk
½ cup whole-wheat pastry flour

1 teaspoon pure vanilla extract
1 cup sliced fresh strawberries
½ cup fresh raspberries
½ cup fresh blueberries

1. Select BAKE, set the temperature to 330ºF (166ºC), and set the time to 16 minutes. Select START/STOP to begin preheating.
2. Grease a baking pan with the butter.

3. Using a hand mixer, beat together the egg, egg whites, milk, pastry flour, and vanilla in a medium mixing bowl until well incorporated.
4. Pour the batter into the pan. Place the pan directly in the pot. Close the hood and BAKE for 12 to 16 minutes, or until the pancake puffs up in the center and the edges are golden brown.
5. Allow the pancake to cool for 5 minutes and serve topped with the berries.

Asparagus and Cheese Strata

Prep time: 10 minutes | Cook time: 14 to 19 minutes | Serves 4

6 asparagus spears, cut into 2-inch pieces
1 tablespoon water
2 slices whole-wheat bread, cut into ½-inch cubes
4 eggs
3 tablespoons whole milk

2 tablespoons chopped flat-leaf parsley
½ cup grated Havarti or Swiss cheese
Pinch salt
Freshly ground black pepper, to taste
Cooking spray

1. Select BAKE, set the temperature to 330ºF (166ºC), and set the time to 19 minutes. Select START/STOP to begin preheating.
2. Add the asparagus spears and 1 tablespoon of water in a baking pan. Place the pan directly in the pot. Close the hood and BAKE for 3 to 5 minutes until crisp-tender. Remove the asparagus from the pan and drain on paper towels. Spritz the pan with cooking spray.
3. Place the bread and asparagus in the pan.
4. Whisk together the eggs and milk in a medium mixing bowl until creamy. Fold in the parsley, cheese, salt, and pepper and stir to combine. Pour this mixture into the baking pan.
5. Place the pan directly in the pot. Close the hood and BAKE for 11 to 14 minutes, or until the eggs are set and the top is lightly browned.
6. Let cool for 5 minutes before slicing and serving.

Chicken Breakfast Sausages

Prep time: 15 minutes | Cook time: 8 to 12 minutes | Makes 8 patties

1 Granny Smith apple, peeled and finely chopped
2 tablespoons apple juice
2 garlic cloves, minced
1 egg white

1/3 cup minced onion
3 tablespoons ground almonds
1/8 teaspoon freshly ground black pepper
1 pound (454 g) ground chicken breast

1. Insert the Crisper Basket and close the hood. Select AIR CRISP, set the temperature to 330ºF (166ºC), and set the time to 12 minutes. Select START/STOP to begin preheating.
2. Combine all the ingredients except the chicken in a medium mixing bowl and stir well.
3. Add the chicken breast to the apple mixture and mix with your hands until well incorporated.
4. Divide the mixture into 8 equal portions and shape into patties. Arrange the patties in the Crisper Basket. You may need to work in batches depending on the size of your Crisper Basket.
5. Close the hood and AIR CRISP for 8 to 12 minutes, or until a meat thermometer inserted in the center of the chicken reaches at least 165ºF (74ºC).
6. Remove from the grill to a plate and repeat with the remaining patties.
7. Let the chicken cool for 5 minutes and serve warm.

Soufflé

Prep time: 10 minutes | Cook time: 22 minutes | Serves 4

1/3 cup butter, melted
1/4 cup flour
1 cup milk
1 ounce (28 g) sugar
4 egg yolks

1 teaspoon vanilla extract
6 egg whites
1 teaspoon cream of tartar
Cooking spray

1. In a bowl, mix the butter and flour until a smooth consistency is achieved.
2. Pour the milk into a saucepan over medium-low heat. Add the sugar and allow to dissolve before raising the heat to boil the milk.
3. Pour in the flour and butter mixture and stir rigorously for 7 minutes to eliminate any lumps. Make sure the mixture thickens. Take off the heat and allow to cool for 15 minutes.
4. Select BAKE, set the temperature to 320ºF (160ºC), and set the time to 15 minutes. Select START/STOP to begin preheating.
5. Spritz 6 soufflé dishes with cooking spray.
6. Put the egg yolks and vanilla extract in a separate bowl and beat them together with a fork. Pour in the milk and combine well to incorporate everything.
7. In a smaller bowl mix the egg whites and cream of tartar with a fork. Fold into the egg yolks-milk mixture before adding in the flour mixture. Transfer equal amounts to the 6 soufflé dishes.
8. Put the dishes in the grill. Close the hood and BAKE for 15 minutes.
9. Serve warm.

Coconut Brown Rice Porridge with Dates

Prep time: 5 minutes | Cook time: 23 minutes | Serves 1 or 2

½ cup cooked brown rice
1 cup canned coconut milk
¼ cup unsweetened shredded coconut
¼ cup packed dark brown sugar
4 large Medjool dates, pitted and roughly
chopped
½ teaspoon kosher salt
¼ teaspoon ground cardamom
Heavy cream, for serving (optional)

1. Select BAKE, set the temperature to 375ºF (191ºC), and set the time to 23 minutes. Select START/STOP to begin preheating.
2. Place all the ingredients except the heavy cream in a baking pan and stir until blended.
3. Place the pan directly in the pot. Close the hood and BAKE for 23 minutes until the porridge is thick and creamy. Stir the porridge halfway through the cooking time.
4. Remove from the grill and ladle the porridge into bowls.
5. Serve hot with a drizzle of the cream, if desired.

Banana Churros with Oatmeal

Prep time: 15 minutes | Cook time: 15 minutes | Serves 2

For the Churros:
1 large yellow banana, peeled, cut in half lengthwise, then cut in half widthwise
2 tablespoons whole-wheat pastry flour
⅛ teaspoon sea salt
2 teaspoons oil (sunflower or melted
coconut)
1 teaspoon water
Cooking spray
1 tablespoon coconut sugar
½ teaspoon cinnamon

For the Oatmeal:
¾ cup rolled oats
1½ cups water

To make the churros
1. Put the 4 banana pieces in a medium-size bowl and add the flour and salt. Stir gently. Add the oil and water. Stir gently until evenly mixed. You may need to press some coating onto the banana pieces.
2. Spray the Crisper Basket with the oil spray. Put the banana pieces in the Crisper Basket and AIR CRISP for 5 minutes. Remove, gently turn over, and AIR CRISP for another 5 minutes or until browned.
3. In a medium bowl, add the coconut sugar and cinnamon and stir to combine. When the banana pieces are nicely browned, spray with the oil and place in the cinnamon-sugar bowl. Toss gently with a spatula to coat the banana pieces with the mixture.

To make the oatmeal
1. While the bananas are cooking, make the oatmeal. In a medium pot, bring the oats and water to a boil, then reduce to low heat. Simmer, stirring often, until all the water is absorbed, about 5 minutes. Put the oatmeal into two bowls.
2. Top the oatmeal with the coated banana pieces and serve immediately.

Chocolate Banana Bread with White Chocolate

Prep time: 10 minutes | Cook time: 30 minutes | Serves 4

¼ cup cocoa powder
6 tablespoons plus 2 teaspoons all-purpose flour, divided
½ teaspoon kosher salt
¼ teaspoon baking soda
1½ ripe bananas
1 large egg, whisked

¼ cup vegetable oil
½ cup sugar
3 tablespoons buttermilk or plain yogurt (not Greek)
½ teaspoon vanilla extract
6 tablespoons chopped white chocolate
6 tablespoons chopped walnuts

1. Select BAKE, set the temperature to 310°F (154°C), and set the time to 30 minutes. Select START/STOP to begin preheating.
2. Mix together the cocoa powder, 6 tablespoons of the flour, salt, and baking soda in a medium bowl.
3. Mash the bananas with a fork in another medium bowl until smooth. Fold in the egg, oil, sugar, buttermilk, and vanilla, and whisk until thoroughly combined. Add the wet mixture to the dry mixture and stir until well incorporated.
4. Combine the white chocolate, walnuts, and the remaining 2 tablespoons of flour in a third bowl and toss to coat. Add this mixture to the batter and stir until well incorporated. Pour the batter into a baking pan and smooth the top with a spatula.
5. Place the pan directly in the pot. Close the hood and BAKE for 30 minutes. Check the bread for doneness: If a toothpick inserted into the center of the bread comes out clean, it's done.
6. Remove from the grill and allow to cool on a wire rack for 10 minutes before serving.

Apple and Walnut Muffins

Prep time: 15 minutes | Cook time: 10 minutes | Makes 8 muffins

1 cup flour
⅓ cup sugar
1 teaspoon baking powder
¼ teaspoon baking soda
¼ teaspoon salt
1 teaspoon cinnamon
¼ teaspoon ginger
¼ teaspoon nutmeg
1 egg

2 tablespoons pancake syrup, plus 2 teaspoons
2 tablespoons melted butter, plus 2 teaspoons
¾ cup unsweetened applesauce
½ teaspoon vanilla extract
¼ cup chopped walnuts
¼ cup diced apple

1. Select BAKE, set the temperature to 330°F (166°C), and set the time to 10 minutes. Select START/STOP to begin preheating.
2. In a large bowl, stir together the flour, sugar, baking powder, baking soda, salt, cinnamon, ginger, and nutmeg.
3. In a small bowl, beat egg until frothy. Add syrup, butter, applesauce, and vanilla and mix well.
4. Pour egg mixture into dry ingredients and stir just until moistened.
5. Gently stir in nuts and diced apple.
6. Divide batter among 8 parchment paper-lined muffin cups.
7. Put 4 muffin cups in the pot. Close the hood and BAKE for 10 minutes.
8. Repeat with remaining 4 muffins or until toothpick inserted in center comes out clean.
9. Serve warm.

Posh Orange Rolls

Prep time: 15 minutes | Cook time: 8 minutes | Makes 8 rolls

3 ounces (85 g) low-fat cream cheese
1 tablespoon low-fat sour cream or plain yogurt
2 teaspoons sugar
¼ teaspoon pure vanilla extract
¼ teaspoon orange extract

1 can (8 count) organic crescent roll dough
¼ cup chopped walnuts
¼ cup dried cranberries
¼ cup shredded, sweetened coconut
Butter-flavored cooking spray

Orange Glaze:
½ cup powdered sugar
1 tablespoon orange juice

¼ teaspoon orange extract
Dash of salt

1. Cut a circular piece of parchment paper slightly smaller than the bottom of the Crisper Basket. Set aside.
2. In a small bowl, combine the cream cheese, sour cream or yogurt, sugar, and vanilla and orange extracts. Stir until smooth.
3. Insert the Crisper Basket and close the hood. Select AIR CRISP, set the temperature to 300ºF (149ºC), and set the time to 8 minutes. Select START/STOP to begin preheating.
4. Separate crescent roll dough into 8 triangles and divide cream cheese mixture among them. Starting at wide end, spread cheese mixture to within 1 inch of point.
5. Sprinkle nuts and cranberries evenly over cheese mixture.
6. Starting at wide end, roll up triangles, then sprinkle with coconut, pressing in lightly to make it stick. Spray tops of rolls with butter-flavored cooking spray.
7. Put parchment paper in Crisper Basket, and place 4 rolls on top, spaced evenly.
8. Close the hood and AIR CRISP for 8 minutes, until rolls are golden brown and cooked through.
9. Repeat steps 7 and 8 to AIR CRISP remaining 4 rolls. You should be able to use the same piece of parchment paper twice.
10. In a small bowl, stir together ingredients for glaze and drizzle over warm rolls. Serve warm.

Chapter 2 Wraps and Sandwiches

Sweet Potato and Black Bean Burritos

Prep time: 15 minutes | Cook time: 1 hour | Makes 6 burritos

2 sweet potatoes, peeled and cut into a small dice
1 tablespoon vegetable oil
Kosher salt and ground black pepper, to taste
6 large flour tortillas
1 (16-ounce / 454-g) can refried black beans, divided
1½ cups baby spinach, divided
6 eggs, scrambled
¾ cup grated Cheddar cheese, divided
¼ cup salsa
¼ cup sour cream
Cooking spray

1. Insert the Crisper Basket and close the hood. Select AIR CRISP, set the temperature to 400ºF (204ºC), and set the time to 10 minutes. Select START/STOP to begin preheating.
2. Put the sweet potatoes in a large bowl, then drizzle with vegetable oil and sprinkle with salt and black pepper. Toss to coat well.
3. Place the sweet potatoes in the basket. Close the hood and AIR CRISP for 10 minutes or until lightly browned. Shake the basket halfway through.
4. Unfold the tortillas on a clean work surface. Divide the black beans, spinach, sweet potatoes, scrambled eggs, and cheese on top of the tortillas.
5. Fold the long side of the tortillas over the filling, then fold in the shorter side to wrap the filling to make the burritos.
6. Work in batches, wrap the burritos in the aluminum foil and put in the basket.
7. Adjust the temperature to 350ºF (177ºC). Close the hood and AIR CRISP for 20 minutes. Flip the burritos halfway through.
8. Remove the burritos from the grill and put back to the grill. Spritz with cooking spray and AIR CRISP for 5 more minutes or until lightly browned. Repeat with remaining burritos.
9. Remove the burritos from the grill and spread with sour cream and salsa. Serve immediately.

Classic Sloppy Joes

Prep time: 10 minutes | Cook time: 17 to 19 minutes | Makes 4 large sandwiches or 8 sliders

1 pound (454 g) very lean ground beef
1 teaspoon onion powder
$\frac{1}{3}$ cup ketchup
¼ cup water
½ teaspoon celery seed
1 tablespoon lemon juice
1½ teaspoons brown sugar
1¼ teaspoons low-sodium Worcestershire sauce
½ teaspoon salt (optional)
½ teaspoon vinegar
⅛ teaspoon dry mustard
Hamburger or slider buns, for serving
Cooking spray

1. Insert the Crisper Basket and close the hood. Select ROAST, set the temperature to 390ºF (199ºC), and set the time to 12 minutes. Select START/STOP to begin preheating.
2. Spray the Crisper Basket with cooking spray.
3. Break raw ground beef into small chunks and pile into the basket. Close the hood and ROAST for 5 minutes. Stir to break apart and roast for 3 minutes. Stir and roast for 2 to 4 minutes longer, or until meat is well done.
4. Remove the meat from the grill, drain, and use a knife and fork to crumble into small pieces.
5. Give your Crisper Basket a quick rinse to remove any bits of meat.
6. Place all the remaining ingredients, except for the buns, in a baking pan and mix together. Add the meat and stir well.
7. Adjust the temperature to 330ºF (166ºC). Place the pan directly in the pot. Close the hood and BAKE for 5 minutes. Stir and bake for 2 minutes.
8. Scoop into buns. Serve hot.

Cheesy Greens Sandwich

Prep time: 15 minutes | Cook time: 10 to 13 minutes | Serves 4

1½ cups chopped mixed greens
2 garlic cloves, thinly sliced
2 teaspoons olive oil
2 slices low-sodium low-fat Swiss cheese
4 slices low-sodium whole-wheat bread
Cooking spray

1. Select AIR CRISP, set the temperature to 400ºF (204ºC), and set the time to 5 minutes. Select START/STOP to begin preheating.
2. In a baking pan, mix the greens, garlic, and olive oil. Place the pan directly in the pot. Close the hood and AIR CRISP for 4 to 5 minutes, stirring once, until the vegetables are tender. Drain, if necessary.
3. Make 2 sandwiches, dividing half of the greens and 1 slice of Swiss cheese between 2 slices of bread. Lightly spray the outsides of the sandwiches with cooking spray. Transfer to the pan.
4. Place the pan directly in the pot. Close the hood and BAKE for 6 to 8 minutes, turning with tongs halfway through, until the bread is toasted and the cheese melts.
5. Cut each sandwich in half and serve.

Cream Cheese Wontons

Prep time: 5 minutes | Cook time: 6 minutes | Serves 4

2 ounces (57 g) cream cheese, softened
1 tablespoon sugar
16 square wonton wrappers
Cooking spray

1. Spritz the Crisper Basket with cooking spray.
2. Insert the Crisper Basket and close the hood. Select AIR CRISP, set the temperature to 350ºF (177ºC), and set the time to 6 minutes. Select START/STOP to begin preheating.
3. In a mixing bowl, stir together the cream cheese and sugar until well mixed. Prepare a small bowl of water alongside.
4. On a clean work surface, lay the wonton wrappers. Scoop ¼ teaspoon of cream cheese in the center of each wonton wrapper. Dab the water over the wrapper edges. Fold each wonton wrapper diagonally in half over the filling to form a triangle.
5. Arrange the wontons in the Crisper Basket. Spritz the wontons with cooking spray. Close the hood and AIR CRISP for 6 minutes, or until golden brown and crispy. Flip once halfway through to ensure even cooking.
6. Divide the wontons among four plates. Let rest for 5 minutes before serving.

Chicken and Yogurt Taquitos

Prep time: 15 minutes | Cook time: 12 minutes | Serves 4

1 cup cooked chicken, shredded
¼ cup Greek yogurt
¼ cup salsa
1 cup shredded
Mozzarella cheese
Salt and ground black pepper, to taste
4 flour tortillas
Cooking spray

1. Spritz the Crisper Basket with cooking spray.
2. Insert the Crisper Basket and close the hood. Select AIR CRISP, set the temperature to 380ºF (193ºC), and set the time to 12 minutes. Select START/STOP to begin preheating.
3. Combine all the ingredients, except for the tortillas, in a large bowl. Stir to mix well.
4. Make the taquitos: Unfold the tortillas on a clean work surface, then scoop up 2 tablespoons of the chicken mixture in the middle of each tortilla. Roll the tortillas up to wrap the filling.
5. Arrange the taquitos in the basket and spritz with cooking spray.
6. Close the hood and AIR CRISP for 12 minutes or until golden brown and the cheese melts. Flip the taquitos halfway through.
7. Serve immediately.

Pork Momos

Prep time: 20 minutes | Cook time: 10 minutes per batch | Serves 4

2 tablespoons olive oil
1 pound (454 g) ground pork
1 shredded carrot

1 onion, chopped
1 teaspoon soy sauce
16 wonton wrappers
Salt and ground black pepper, to taste

1. Insert the Crisper Basket and close the hood. Select AIR CRISP, set the temperature to 320ºF (160ºC), and set the time to 10 minutes. Select START/STOP to begin preheating.
2. Heat the olive oil in a nonstick skillet over medium heat until shimmering.
3. Add the ground pork, carrot, onion, soy sauce, salt, and ground black pepper and sauté for 10 minutes or until the pork is well browned and carrots are tender.
4. Unfold the wrappers on a clean work surface, then divide the cooked pork and vegetables on the wrappers. Fold the edges around the filling to form momos. Nip the top to seal the momos.
5. Arrange the momos in the basket and spritz with cooking spray. Close the hood and AIR CRISP for 10 minutes or until the wrappers are lightly browned. Work in batches to avoid overcrowding.
6. Serve immediately.

Crispy Crab and Cream Cheese Wontons

Prep time: 10 minutes | Cook time: 10 minutes per batch | Serves 6 to 8

24 wonton wrappers, thawed if frozen
Cooking spray

For the Filling:
5 ounces (142 g) lump crabmeat, drained and patted dry
4 ounces (113 g) cream cheese, at room temperature
2 scallions, sliced

1½ teaspoons toasted sesame oil
1 teaspoon Worcestershire sauce
Kosher salt and ground black pepper, to taste

1. Spritz the Crisper Basket with cooking spray.

2. Insert the Crisper Basket and close the hood. Select AIR CRISP, set the temperature to 350ºF (177ºC), and set the time to 10 minutes. Select START/STOP to begin preheating.
3. In a medium-size bowl, place all the ingredients for the filling and stir until well mixed. Prepare a small bowl of water alongside.
4. On a clean work surface, lay the wonton wrappers. Scoop 1 teaspoon of the filling in the center of each wrapper. Wet the edges with a touch of water. Fold each wonton wrapper diagonally in half over the filling to form a triangle.
5. Arrange the wontons in the Crisper Basket. Spritz the wontons with cooking spray. Work in batches, 6 to 8 at a time. Close the hood and AIR CRISP for 10 minutes, or until crispy and golden brown. Flip once halfway through.
6. Serve immediately.

Bacon and Bell Pepper Sandwich

Prep time: 10 minutes | Cook time: 6 minutes | Serves 4

⅓ cup spicy barbecue sauce
2 tablespoons honey
8 slices cooked bacon, cut into thirds
1 red bell pepper, sliced

1 yellow bell pepper, sliced
3 pita pockets, cut in half
1¼ cups torn butter lettuce leaves
2 tomatoes, sliced

1. Insert the Crisper Basket and close the hood. Select ROAST, set the temperature to 350ºF (177ºC), and set the time to 6 minutes. Select START/STOP to begin preheating.
2. In a small bowl, combine the barbecue sauce and the honey. Brush this mixture lightly onto the bacon slices and the red and yellow pepper slices.
3. Put the peppers into the Crisper Basket. Close the hood and ROAST for 4 minutes. Then shake the basket, add the bacon, and ROAST for 2 minutes or until the bacon is browned and the peppers are tender.
4. Fill the pita halves with the bacon, peppers, any remaining barbecue sauce, lettuce, and tomatoes, and serve immediately.

Tuna Muffin Sandwich

Prep time: 8 minutes | Cook time: 4 to 8 minutes | Serves 4

1 (6-ounce / 170-g) can chunk light tuna, drained	minced
¼ cup mayonnaise	3 English muffins, split with a fork
2 tablespoons mustard	3 tablespoons softened butter
1 tablespoon lemon juice	6 thin slices Provolone or Muenster cheese
2 green onions,	

1. Select BAKE, set the temperature to 390ºF (199ºC), and set the time to 4 minutes. Select START/STOP to begin preheating.
2. In a small bowl, combine the tuna, mayonnaise, mustard, lemon juice, and green onions. Set aside.
3. Butter the cut side of the English muffins. Place in a baking pan, butter-side up. Place the pan directly in the pot.
4. Close the hood and BAKE for 2 to 4 minutes, or until light golden brown. Remove the muffins from the grill.
5. Top each muffin with one slice of cheese and return to the grill. Bake for 2 to 4 minutes or until the cheese melts and starts to brown.
6. Remove the muffins from the grill, top with the tuna mixture, and serve.

Cheesy Shrimp Sandwich

Prep time: 10 minutes | Cook time: 5 to 7 minutes | Serves 4

1¼ cups shredded Colby, Cheddar, or Havarti cheese	mayonnaise
1 (6-ounce / 170-g) can tiny shrimp, drained	2 tablespoons minced green onion
3 tablespoons	4 slices whole grain or whole-wheat bread
	2 tablespoons softened butter

1. Insert the Crisper Basket and close the hood. Select AIR CRISP, set the temperature to 400ºF (204ºC), and set the time to 7 minutes. Select START/STOP to begin preheating.
2. In a medium bowl, combine the cheese, shrimp, mayonnaise, and green onion, and mix well.
3. Spread this mixture on two of the slices of bread. Top with the other slices of bread to make two sandwiches. Spread the sandwiches lightly with butter. Transfer to the basket.
4. Close the hood and AIR CRISP for 5 to 7 minutes, or until the bread is browned and crisp and the cheese is melted.
5. Cut in half and serve warm.

Turkey Sliders with Chive Mayo

Prep time: 10 minutes | Cook time: 15 minutes | Serves 6

12 burger buns	Cooking spray

For the Turkey Sliders:

¾ pound (340 g) turkey, minced	chopped scallions
1 tablespoon oyster sauce	1 tablespoon chopped fresh cilantro
¼ cup pickled jalapeno, chopped	1 to 2 cloves garlic, minced
2 tablespoons	Sea salt and ground black pepper, to taste

For the Chive Mayo:

1 tablespoon chives	Zest of 1 lime
1 cup mayonnaise	1 teaspoon salt

1. Insert the Crisper Basket and close the hood. Select AIR CRISP, set the temperature to 365ºF (185ºC), and set the time to 15 minutes. Select START/STOP to begin preheating.
2. Spritz the Crisper Basket with cooking spray.
3. Combine the ingredients for the turkey sliders in a large bowl. Stir to mix well. Shape the mixture into 6 balls, then bash the balls into patties.
4. Arrange the patties in the basket and spritz with cooking spray. Close the hood and AIR CRISP for 15 minutes or until well browned. Flip the patties halfway through.
5. Meanwhile, combine the ingredients for the chive mayo in a small bowl. Stir to mix well.
6. Smear the patties with chive mayo, then assemble the patties between two buns to make the sliders. Serve immediately.

Turkey, Leek, and Pepper Hamburger

Prep time: 10 minutes | Cook time: 20 minutes | Serves 4

1 cup leftover turkey, cut into bite-sized chunks
1 leek, sliced
1 Serrano pepper, deveined and chopped
2 bell peppers, deveined and chopped
2 tablespoons Tabasco sauce
½ cup sour cream
1 heaping tablespoon fresh cilantro, chopped
1 teaspoon hot paprika
¾ teaspoon kosher salt
½ teaspoon ground black pepper
4 hamburger buns
Cooking spray

1. Select BAKE, set the temperature to 385ºF (196ºC), and set the time to 20 minutes. Select START/STOP to begin preheating.
2. Spritz a baking pan with cooking spray.
3. Mix all the ingredients, except for the buns, in a large bowl. Toss to combine well.
4. Pour the mixture in the baking pan. Place the pan directly in the pot. Close the hood and BAKE for 20 minutes, or until the turkey is well browned and the leek is tender.
5. Assemble the hamburger buns with the turkey mixture and serve immediately.

Chicken Pita Sandwich

Prep time: 10 minutes | Cook time: 9 to 11 minutes | Serves 4

2 boneless, skinless chicken breasts, cut into 1-inch cubes
1 small red onion, sliced
1 red bell pepper, sliced
1/3 cup Italian salad
dressing, divided
½ teaspoon dried thyme
4 pita pockets, split
2 cups torn butter lettuce
1 cup chopped cherry tomatoes

1. Insert the Crisper Basket and close the hood. Select BAKE, set the temperature to 380ºF (193ºC), and set the time to 11 minutes. Select START/STOP to begin preheating.
2. Place the chicken, onion, and bell pepper in the Crisper Basket. Drizzle with 1 tablespoon of the Italian salad dressing, add the thyme, and toss.
3. Close the hood and BAKE for 9 to 11 minutes, or until the chicken is 165ºF (74ºC) on a food thermometer, stirring once during cooking time.
4. Transfer the chicken and vegetables to a bowl and toss with the remaining salad dressing.
5. Assemble sandwiches with the pita pockets, butter lettuce, and cherry tomatoes. Serve immediately.

Thai Pork Sliders

Prep time: 10 minutes | Cook time: 14 minutes | Makes 6 sliders

1 pound (454 g) ground pork
1 tablespoon Thai curry paste
1½ tablespoons fish sauce
¼ cup thinly sliced scallions, white and green parts
2 tablespoons minced
peeled fresh ginger
1 tablespoon light brown sugar
1 teaspoon ground black pepper
6 slider buns, split open lengthwise, warmed
Cooking spray

1. Spritz the Crisper Basket with cooking spray.
2. Insert the Crisper Basket and close the hood. Select AIR CRISP, set the temperature to 375ºF (191ºC), and set the time to 14 minutes. Select START/STOP to begin preheating.
3. Combine all the ingredients, except for the buns in a large bowl. Stir to mix well.
4. Divide and shape the mixture into six balls, then bash the balls into six 3-inch-diameter patties.
5. Arrange the patties in the basket and spritz with cooking spray. Close the hood and AIR CRISP for 14 minutes or until well browned. Flip the patties halfway through.
6. Assemble the buns with patties to make the sliders and serve immediately.

Cheesy Potato Taquitos

Prep time: 5 minutes | Cook time: 6 minutes per batch | Makes 12 taquitos

2 cups mashed potatoes
½ cup shredded

Mexican cheese
12 corn tortillas
Cooking spray

1. Select AIR CRISP, set the temperature to 400ºF (204ºC), and set the time to 6 minutes. Select START/STOP to begin preheating.
2. Line a baking pan with parchment paper.
3. In a bowl, combine the potatoes and cheese until well mixed. Microwave the tortillas on high heat for 30 seconds, or until softened. Add some water to another bowl and set alongside.
4. On a clean work surface, lay the tortillas. Scoop 3 tablespoons of the potato mixture in the center of each tortilla. Roll up tightly and secure with toothpicks if necessary.
5. Arrange the filled tortillas, seam side down, in the prepared baking pan. Spritz the tortillas with cooking spray.
6. Place the pan directly in the pot. Close the hood and AIR CRISP for 6 minutes, or until crispy and golden brown, flipping once halfway through the cooking time. You may need to work in batches to avoid overcrowding.
7. Serve hot.

Eggplant Hoagies

Prep time: 15 minutes | Cook time: 12 minutes | Makes 3 hoagies

6 peeled eggplant slices (about ½ inch thick and 3 inches in diameter)
¼ cup jarred pizza sauce

6 tablespoons grated Parmesan cheese
3 Italian sub rolls, split open lengthwise, warmed
Cooking spray

1. Spritz the Crisper Basket with cooking spray.
2. Insert the Crisper Basket and close the hood. Select AIR CRISP, set the temperature to 350ºF (177ºC), and set the time to 10 minutes. Select START/STOP to begin preheating.

3. Arrange the eggplant slices in the basket and spritz with cooking spray.
4. Close the hood and AIR CRISP for 10 minutes or until lightly wilted and tender. Flip the slices halfway through.
5. Divide and spread the pizza sauce and cheese on top of the eggplant slice. Increase the temperature to 375ºF (191ºC). Close the hood and AIR CRISP for 2 more minutes or until the cheese melts.
6. Assemble each sub roll with two slices of eggplant and serve immediately.

Lamb and Feta Hamburgers

Prep time: 15 minutes | Cook time: 16 minutes | Makes 4 burgers

1½ pounds (680 g) ground lamb
¼ cup crumbled feta
1½ teaspoons tomato paste
1½ teaspoons minced garlic
1 teaspoon ground dried ginger
1 teaspoon ground

coriander
¼ teaspoon salt
¼ teaspoon cayenne pepper
4 kaiser rolls or hamburger buns, split open lengthwise, warmed
Cooking spray

1. Spritz the Crisper Basket with cooking spray.
2. Insert the Crisper Basket and close the hood. Select AIR CRISP, set the temperature to 375ºF (191ºC), and set the time to 16 minutes. Select START/STOP to begin preheating.
3. Combine all the ingredients, except for the buns, in a large bowl. Coarsely stir to mix well.
4. Shape the mixture into four balls, then pound the balls into four 5-inch diameter patties.
5. Arrange the patties in the basket and spritz with cooking spray. Close the hood and AIR CRISP for 16 minutes or until well browned. Flip the patties halfway through.
6. Assemble the buns with patties to make the burgers and serve immediately.

Cabbage and Pork Gyoza

Prep time: 10 minutes | Cook time: 10 minutes per batch | Makes 48 gyozas

1 pound (454 g) ground pork
1 small head Napa cabbage (about 1 pound / 454 g), sliced thinly and minced
½ cup minced scallions
1 teaspoon minced fresh chives
1 teaspoon soy sauce

1 teaspoon minced fresh ginger
1 tablespoon minced garlic
1 teaspoon granulated sugar
2 teaspoons kosher salt
48 to 50 wonton or dumpling wrappers
Cooking spray

1. Make the filling: Combine all the ingredients, except for the wrappers in a large bowl. Stir to mix well.
2. Unfold a wrapper on a clean work surface, then dab the edges with a little water. Scoop up 2 teaspoons of the filling mixture in the center.
3. Make the gyoza: Fold the wrapper over to filling and press the edges to seal. Pleat the edges if desired. Repeat with remaining wrappers and fillings.
4. Spritz the Crisper Basket with cooking spray.
5. Insert the Crisper Basket and close the hood. Select AIR CRISP, set the temperature to 360ºF (182ºC), and set the time to 10 minutes. Select START/STOP to begin preheating.
6. Arrange the gyozas in the basket and spritz with cooking spray. Close the hood and AIR CRISP for 10 minutes or until golden brown. Flip the gyozas halfway through. Work in batches to avoid overcrowding.
7. Serve immediately.

Montreal Steak and Seeds Burgers

Prep time: 15 minutes | Cook time: 10 minutes | Serves 4

1 teaspoon cumin seeds
1 teaspoon mustard seeds
1 teaspoon coriander seeds
1 teaspoon dried minced garlic
1 teaspoon dried red pepper flakes
1 teaspoon kosher salt

2 teaspoons ground black pepper
1 pound (454 g) 85% lean ground beef
2 tablespoons Worcestershire sauce
4 hamburger buns
Mayonnaise, for serving
Cooking spray

1. Spritz the Crisper Basket with cooking spray.
2. Insert the Crisper Basket and close the hood. Select AIR CRISP, set the temperature to 350ºF (177ºC), and set the time to 10 minutes. Select START/STOP to begin preheating.
3. Put the seeds, garlic, red pepper flakes, salt, and ground black pepper in a food processor. Pulse to coarsely ground the mixture.
4. Put the ground beef in a large bowl. Pour in the seed mixture and drizzle with Worcestershire sauce. Stir to mix well.
5. Divide the mixture into four parts and shape each part into a ball, then bash each ball into a patty.
6. Arrange the patties in the basket. Close the hood and AIR CRISP for 10 minutes or until the patties are well browned. Flip the patties with tongs halfway through.
7. Assemble the buns with the patties, then drizzle the mayo over the patties to make the burgers. Serve immediately.

Chapter 3 Vegetables

Vegan and Vegetarian

Vegetarian Meatballs

Prep time: 15 minutes | Cook time: 18 minutes | Serves 3

½ cup grated carrots
½ cup sweet onions
2 tablespoons olive oil
1 cup rolled oats
½ cup roasted cashews
2 cups cooked chickpeas

Juice of 1 lemon
2 tablespoons soy sauce
1 tablespoon flax meal
1 teaspoon garlic powder
1 teaspoon cumin
½ teaspoon turmeric

1. Select ROAST, set the temperature to 350ºF (177ºC), and set the time to 6 minutes. Select START/STOP to begin preheating.
2. Mix together the carrots, onions, and olive oil in the pot and stir to combine.
3. Close the hood and ROAST for 6 minutes.
4. Meanwhile, put the oats and cashews in a food processor or blender and pulse until coarsely ground. Transfer the mixture to a large bowl. Add the chickpeas, lemon juice, and soy sauce to the food processor and pulse until smooth. Transfer the chickpea mixture to the bowl of oat and cashew mixture.
5. Remove the carrots and onions from the pot to the bowl of chickpea mixture. Add the flax meal, garlic powder, cumin, and turmeric and stir to incorporate.
6. Scoop tablespoon-sized portions of the veggie mixture and roll them into balls with your hands. Transfer the balls to the Crisper Basket in a single layer.
7. Increase the temperature to 370ºF (188ºC) and BAKE for 12 minutes until golden through. Flip the balls halfway through the cooking time.
8. Serve warm.

Cheesy Asparagus and Potato Platter

Prep time: 5 minutes | Cook time: 26 to 30 minutes | Serves 5

4 medium potatoes, cut into wedges
Cooking spray
1 bunch asparagus, trimmed

2 tablespoons olive oil
Salt and pepper, to taste

Cheese Sauce:
¼ cup crumbled cottage cheese
¼ cup buttermilk
1 tablespoon whole-

grain mustard
Salt and black pepper, to taste

1. Insert the Crisper Basket and close the hood. Select ROAST, set the temperature to 400ºF (204ºC), and set the time to 30 minutes. Select START/STOP to begin preheating.
2. Spritz the Crisper Basket with cooking spray.
3. Put the potatoes in the Crisper Basket. Close the hood and ROAST for 20 to 22 minutes, until golden brown. Shake the basket halfway through the cooking time.
4. When ready, remove the potatoes from the basket to a platter. Cover the potatoes with foil to keep warm. Set aside.
5. Place the asparagus in the Crisper Basket and drizzle with the olive oil. Sprinkle with salt and pepper.
6. Close the hood and ROAST for 6 to 8 minutes, shaking the basket once or twice during cooking, or until the asparagus is cooked to your desired crispiness.
7. Meanwhile, make the cheese sauce by stirring together the cottage cheese, buttermilk, and mustard in a small bowl. Season with salt and pepper.
8. Transfer the asparagus to the platter of potatoes and drizzle with the cheese sauce. Serve immediately.

Corn and Potato Chowder

Prep time: 15 minutes | Cook time: 50 minutes | Serves 4

4 ears corn, shucked	unsalted butter
2 tablespoons canola oil	1 small onion, finely chopped
1½ teaspoons sea salt, plus additional to season the corn	2½ cups vegetable broth
½ teaspoon freshly ground black pepper, plus additional to season the corn	1½ cups milk
	4 cups diced potatoes
	2 cups half-and-half
3 tablespoons	1½ teaspoons chopped fresh thyme

1. Insert the Grill Grate and close the hood. Select GRILL, set the temperature to MAX, and set the time to 12 minutes. Select START/STOP to begin preheating.
2. While the unit is preheating, brush each ear of corn with ½ tablespoon of oil. Season the corn with salt and pepper to taste.
3. When the unit beeps to signify it has preheated, place the corn on the Grill Grate and close the hood. GRILL for 6 minutes.
4. After 6 minutes, flip the corn. Close the hood and continue cooking for the remaining 6 minutes.
5. When cooking is complete, remove the corn and let cool. Cut the kernels from the cobs.
6. In a food processor, purée 1 cup of corn kernels until smooth.
7. In a large pot over medium-high heat, melt the butter. Add the onion and sauté until soft, 5 to 7 minutes. Add the broth, milk, and potatoes. Bring to a simmer and cook until the potatoes are just tender, 10 to 12 minutes. Stir in the salt and pepper.
8. Stir in the puréed corn, remaining corn kernels, and half-and-half. Bring to a simmer and cook, stirring occasionally, until the potatoes are cooked through, for 15 to 20 minutes.
9. Using a potato masher or immersion blender, slightly mash some of the potatoes. Stir in the thyme, and additional salt and pepper to taste.

Honey-Glazed Roasted Veggies

Prep time: 15 minutes | Cook time: 20 minutes | Makes 3 cups

Glaze:

2 tablespoons raw honey	⅛ teaspoon dried sage
2 teaspoons minced garlic	⅛ teaspoon dried rosemary
¼ teaspoon dried marjoram	⅛ teaspoon dried thyme
¼ teaspoon dried basil	½ teaspoon salt
¼ teaspoon dried oregano	¼ teaspoon ground black pepper

Veggies:

3 to 4 medium red potatoes, cut into 1- to 2-inch pieces	1 (10.5-ounce / 298-g) package cherry tomatoes, halved
1 small zucchini, cut into 1- to 2-inch pieces	1 cup sliced mushrooms
1 small carrot, sliced into ¼-inch rounds	3 tablespoons olive oil

1. Insert the Crisper Basket and close the hood. Select ROAST, set the temperature to 380°F (193°C), and set the time to 15 minutes. Select START/STOP to begin preheating.
2. Combine the honey, garlic, marjoram, basil, oregano, sage, rosemary, thyme, salt, and pepper in a small bowl and stir to mix well. Set aside.
3. Place the red potatoes, zucchini, carrot, cherry tomatoes, and mushroom in a large bowl. Drizzle with the olive oil and toss to coat.
4. Pour the veggies into the Crisper Basket. Close the hood and ROAST for 15 minutes, shaking the basket halfway through.
5. When ready, transfer the roasted veggies to the large bowl. Pour the honey mixture over the veggies, tossing to coat.
6. Spread out the veggies in a baking pan and place in the grill.
7. Increase the temperature to 390°F (199°C) and ROAST for an additional 5 minutes, or until the veggies are tender and glazed. Serve warm.

Cauliflower Steaks with Ranch Dressing

Prep time: 10 minutes | Cook time: 15 minutes | Serves 2

1 head cauliflower, stemmed and leaves removed
¼ cup canola oil
½ teaspoon garlic powder
½ teaspoon paprika
Sea salt, to taste
Freshly ground black pepper, to taste
1 cup shredded Cheddar cheese
Ranch dressing, for garnish
4 slices bacon, cooked and crumbled
2 tablespoons chopped fresh chives

1. Cut the cauliflower from top to bottom into two 2-inch "steaks"; reserve the remaining cauliflower to cook separately.
2. Insert the Grill Grate and close the hood. Select GRILL, set the temperature to MAX, and set the time to 15 minutes. Select START/STOP to begin preheating.
3. Meanwhile, in a small bowl, whisk together the oil, garlic powder, and paprika. Season with salt and pepper. Brush each steak with the oil mixture on both sides.
4. When the unit beeps to signify it has preheated, place the steaks on the Grill Grate. Close the hood and GRILL for 10 minutes.
5. After 10 minutes, flip the steaks and top each with ½ cup of cheese. Close the hood and continue to GRILL until the cheese is melted, about 5 minutes.
6. When cooking is complete, place the cauliflower steaks on a plate and drizzle with the ranch dressing. Top with the bacon and chives.

Black Bean and Tomato Chili

Prep time: 15 minutes | Cook time: 23 minutes | Serves 6

1 tablespoon olive oil
1 medium onion, diced
3 garlic cloves, minced
1 cup vegetable broth
3 cans black beans, drained and rinsed
2 cans diced tomatoes
2 chipotle peppers, chopped
2 teaspoons cumin
2 teaspoons chili powder
1 teaspoon dried oregano
½ teaspoon salt

1. Over a medium heat, fry the garlic and onions in the olive oil for 3 minutes.
2. Add the remaining ingredients, stirring constantly and scraping the bottom to prevent sticking.
3. Select BAKE, set the temperature to 400°F (204°C), and set the time to 20 minutes. Select START/STOP to begin preheating.
4. Take a baking pan and place the mixture inside. Put a sheet of aluminum foil on top.
5. Place the pan directly in the pot. Close the hood and BAKE for 20 minutes.
6. When ready, plate up and serve immediately.

Grilled Mozzarella Eggplant Stacks

Prep time: 10 minutes | Cook time: 14 minutes | Serves 4

1 eggplant, sliced ¼-inch thick
2 tablespoons canola oil
2 beefsteak or heirloom tomatoes, sliced ¼-inch thick
12 large basil leaves
½ pound (227 g) buffalo Mozzarella, sliced ¼-inch thick
Sea salt, to taste

1. Insert the Grill Grate and close the hood. Select GRILL, set the temperature to MAX, and set the time to 14 minutes. Select START/STOP to begin preheating.
2. Meanwhile, in a large bowl, toss the eggplant and oil until evenly coated.
3. When the unit beeps to signify it has preheated, place the eggplant on the Grill Grate. Close the hood and GRILL for 8 to 12 minutes, until charred on all sides.
4. After 8 to 12 minutes, top the eggplant with one slice each of tomato and Mozzarella. Close the hood and GRILL for 2 minutes, until the cheese melts.
5. When cooking is complete, remove the eggplant stacks from the grill. Place 2 or 3 basil leaves on top of half of the stacks. Place the remaining eggplant stacks on top of those with basil so that there are four stacks total. Season with salt, garnish with the remaining basil, and serve.

Mozzarella Broccoli Calzones

Prep time: 10 minutes | Cook time: 24 minutes | Serves 4

1 head broccoli, trimmed into florets	2 cups shredded Mozzarella cheese
2 tablespoons extra-virgin olive oil	1 cup ricotta cheese
1 store-bought pizza dough (about 16 ounces / 454 g)	½ cup grated Parmesan cheese
	1 garlic clove, grated
2 to 3 tablespoons all-purpose flour, plus more for dusting	Grated zest of 1 lemon
	½ teaspoon red pepper flakes
1 egg, beaten	Cooking oil spray

1. Insert the Crisper Basket and close the hood. Select AIR CRISP, set the temperature to 390ºF (199ºC), and set the time to 12 minutes. Select START/STOP to begin preheating.
2. Meanwhile, in a large bowl, toss the broccoli and olive oil until evenly coated.
3. When the unit beeps to signify it has preheated, add the broccoli to the basket. Close the hood and AIR CRISP for 6 minutes.
4. While the broccoli is cooking, divide the pizza dough into four equal pieces. Dust a clean work surface with the flour. Place the dough on the floured surface and roll each piece into an 8-inch round of even thickness. Dust your rolling pin and work surface with additional flour, as needed, to ensure the dough does not stick. Brush a thin coating of egg wash around the edges of each round.
5. After 6 minutes, shake the basket of broccoli. Place the basket back in the unit and close the hood to resume cooking.
6. Meanwhile, in a medium bowl, combine the Mozzarella, ricotta, Parmesan cheese, garlic, lemon zest, and red pepper flakes.
7. After cooking is complete, add the broccoli to the cheese mixture. Spoon one-quarter of the mixture onto one side of each dough. Fold the other half over the filling, and press firmly to seal the edges together. Brush each calzone all over with the remaining egg wash.
8. Select AIR CRISP, set the temperature to 390ºF (199ºC), and set the time to 12 minutes. Select START/STOP to begin preheating.
9. When the unit beeps to signify it has preheated, coat the Crisper Basket with cooking spray and place the calzones in the basket. AIR CRISP for 10 to 12 minutes, until golden brown.

Grilled Vegetable Pizza

Prep time: 10 minutes | Cook time: 10 minutes | Serves 2

2 tablespoons all-purpose flour, plus more as needed	1 cup shredded Mozzarella cheese
½ store-bought pizza dough (about 8 ounces / 227 g)	½ zucchini, thinly sliced
	½ red onion, sliced
1 tablespoon canola oil, divided	½ red bell pepper, seeded and thinly sliced
½ cup pizza sauce	

1. Insert the Grill Grate and close the hood. Select GRILL, set the temperature to MAX, and set the time to 7 minutes. Select START/STOP to begin preheating.
2. While the unit is preheating, dust a clean work surface with the flour.
3. Place the dough on the floured surface and roll it into a 9-inch round of even thickness. Dust your rolling pin and work surface with additional flour, as needed, to ensure the dough does not stick.
4. Evenly brush the surface of the rolled-out dough with ½ tablespoon of oil. Flip the dough over and brush the other side with the remaining ½ tablespoon of oil. Poke the dough with a fork 5 or 6 times across its surface to prevent air pockets from forming while it cooks.
5. When the unit beeps to signify it has preheated, place the dough on the Grill Grate. Close the hood and GRILL for 4 minutes.
6. After 4 minutes, flip the dough, then spread the pizza sauce evenly over it. Sprinkle with the cheese, and top with the zucchini, onion, and pepper.
7. Close the hood and continue cooking for the remaining 2 to 3 minutes until the cheese is melted and the veggie slices begin to crisp.
8. When cooking is complete, let cool slightly before slicing.

Simple Ratatouille

Prep time: 15 minutes | Cook time: 16 minutes | Serves 2

2 Roma tomatoes, thinly sliced
1 zucchini, thinly sliced
2 yellow bell peppers, sliced
2 garlic cloves, minced

2 tablespoons olive oil
2 tablespoons herbes de Provence
1 tablespoon vinegar
Salt and black pepper, to taste

1. Select ROAST, set the temperature to 390ºF (199ºC), and set the time to 16 minutes. Select START/STOP to begin preheating.
2. Place the tomatoes, zucchini, bell peppers, garlic, olive oil, herbes de Provence, and vinegar in a large bowl and toss until the vegetables are evenly coated. Sprinkle with salt and pepper and toss again. Pour the vegetable mixture into the pot.
3. Close the hood and ROAST for 8 minutes. Stir and continue roasting for 8 minutes until tender.
4. Let the vegetable mixture stand for 5 minutes in the basket before removing and serving.

Sesame-Thyme Whole Maitake Mushrooms

Prep time: 5 minutes | Cook time: 15 minutes | Serves 2

1 tablespoon soy sauce
2 teaspoons toasted sesame oil
3 teaspoons vegetable oil, divided
1 garlic clove, minced
7 ounces (198 g) maitake (hen of the

woods) mushrooms
½ teaspoon flaky sea salt
½ teaspoon sesame seeds
½ teaspoon finely chopped fresh thyme leaves

1. Insert the Crisper Basket and close the hood. Select ROAST, set the temperature to 300ºF (149ºC), and set the time to 15 minutes. Select START/STOP to begin preheating.

2. Whisk together the soy sauce, sesame oil, 1 teaspoon of vegetable oil, and garlic in a small bowl.
3. Arrange the mushrooms in the Crisper Basket in a single layer. Drizzle the soy sauce mixture over the mushrooms. Close the hood and ROAST for 10 minutes.
4. Flip the mushrooms and sprinkle the sea salt, sesame seeds, and thyme leaves on top. Drizzle the remaining 2 teaspoons of vegetable oil all over. Roast for an additional 5 minutes.
5. Remove the mushrooms from the basket to a plate and serve hot.

Arugula and Broccoli Salad

Prep time: 10 minutes | Cook time: 12 minutes | Serves 4

2 heads broccoli, trimmed into florets
½ red onion, sliced
1 tablespoon canola oil
2 tablespoons extra-virgin olive oil
1 tablespoon freshly squeezed lemon juice
1 teaspoon honey
1 teaspoon Dijon

mustard
1 garlic clove, minced
Pinch red pepper flakes
¼ teaspoon fine sea salt
Freshly ground black pepper, to taste
4 cups arugula, torn
2 tablespoons grated Parmesan cheese

1. Insert the Grill Grate and close the hood. Select GRILL, set the temperature to MAX, and set the time to 12 minutes. Select START/STOP to begin preheating.
2. While the unit is preheating, in a large bowl, combine the broccoli, sliced onions, and canola oil and toss until coated.
3. When the unit beeps to signify it has preheated, place the vegetables on the Grill Grate. Close the hood and GRILL for 8 to 12 minutes, until charred on all sides.
4. Meanwhile, in a medium bowl, whisk together the olive oil, lemon juice, honey, mustard, garlic, red pepper flakes, salt, and pepper.
5. When cooking is complete, combine the roasted vegetables and arugula in a large serving bowl. Drizzle with the vinaigrette, and sprinkle with the Parmesan cheese.

Balsamic Mushroom Sliders with Pesto

Prep time: 10 minutes | Cook time: 8 minutes | Serves 4

8 small portobello mushrooms, trimmed with gills removed	balsamic vinegar
2 tablespoons canola oil	8 slider buns
2 tablespoons	1 tomato, sliced
	½ cup pesto
	½ cup micro greens

1. Insert the Grill Grate and close the hood. Select GRILL, set the temperature to HIGH, and set the time to 8 minutes. Select START/STOP to begin preheating.
2. While the unit is preheating, brush the mushrooms with the oil and balsamic vinegar.
3. When the unit beeps to signify it has preheated, place the mushrooms, gill-side down, on the Grill Grate. Close the hood and GRILL for 8 minutes until the mushrooms are tender.
4. When cooking is complete, remove the mushrooms from the grill, and layer on the buns with tomato, pesto, and micro greens.

Potatoes with Zucchinis

Prep time: 10 minutes | Cook time: 45 minutes | Serves 4

2 potatoes, peeled and cubed	thickly
4 carrots, cut into chunks	Salt and ground black pepper, to taste
1 head broccoli, cut into florets	¼ cup olive oil
4 zucchinis, sliced	1 tablespoon dry onion powder

1. Select BAKE, set the temperature to 400ºF (204ºC), and set the time to 45 minutes. Select START/STOP to begin preheating.
2. In a baking pan, add all the ingredients and combine well.
3. Place the pan directly in the pot. Close the hood and BAKE for 45 minutes, ensuring the vegetables are soft and the sides have browned before serving.

Rosemary Roasted Squash with Cheese

Prep time: 5 minutes | Cook time: 20 minutes | Serves 2

1 pound (454 g) butternut squash, cut into wedges	rosemary
2 tablespoons olive oil	Salt, to salt
1 tablespoon dried	1 cup crumbled goat cheese
	1 tablespoon maple syrup

1. Insert the Crisper Basket and close the hood. Select ROAST, set the temperature to 350ºF (177ºC), and set the time to 20 minutes. Select START/STOP to begin preheating.
2. Toss the squash wedges with the olive oil, rosemary, and salt in a large bowl until well coated.
3. Transfer the squash wedges to the Crisper Basket, spreading them out in as even a layer as possible.
4. Close the hood and ROAST for 10 minutes. Flip the squash and roast for another 10 minutes until golden brown.
5. Sprinkle the goat cheese on top and serve drizzled with the maple syrup.

Honey-Glazed Baby Carrots

Prep time: 5 minutes | Cook time: 12 minutes | Serves 4

1 pound (454 g) baby carrots	1 tablespoon honey
2 tablespoons olive oil	1 teaspoon dried dill
	Salt and black pepper, to taste

1. Insert the Crisper Basket and close the hood. Select ROAST, set the temperature to 350ºF (177ºC), and set the time to 12 minutes. Select START/STOP to begin preheating.
2. Place the carrots in a large bowl. Add the olive oil, honey, dill, salt, and pepper and toss to coat well.
3. Arrange the carrots in the Crisper Basket. Close the hood and ROAST for 12 minutes, until crisp-tender. Shake the basket once during cooking.
4. Serve warm.

Tofu, Carrot and Cauliflower Rice

Prep time: 10 minutes | Cook time: 22 minutes | Serves 4

½ block tofu, crumbled
1 cup diced carrot
½ cup diced onions

2 tablespoons soy sauce
1 teaspoon turmeric

Cauliflower:

3 cups cauliflower rice
½ cup chopped broccoli
½ cup frozen peas
2 tablespoons soy sauce
1 tablespoon minced

ginger
2 garlic cloves, minced
1 tablespoon rice vinegar
1½ teaspoons toasted sesame oil

1. Select ROAST, set the temperature to 370ºF (188ºC), and set the time to 22 minutes. Select START/STOP to begin preheating.
2. Mix together the tofu, carrot, onions, soy sauce, and turmeric in the pot and stir until well incorporated.
3. Place the pot in the grill. Close the hood and ROAST for 10 minutes.
4. Meanwhile, in a large bowl, combine all the ingredients for the cauliflower and toss well.
5. Remove the pot and add the cauliflower mixture to the tofu and stir to combine.
6. Return the pot to the grill and continue roasting for 12 minutes, or until the vegetables are cooked to your preference.
7. Cool for 5 minutes before serving.

Italian Baked Tofu

Prep time: 5 minutes | Cook time: 10 minutes | Serves 2

1 tablespoon soy sauce
1 tablespoon water
¹/₃ teaspoon garlic powder
¹/₃ teaspoon onion powder
¹/₃ teaspoon dried

oregano
¹/₃ teaspoon dried basil
Black pepper, to taste
6 ounces (170 g) extra firm tofu, pressed and cubed

1. In a large mixing bowl, whisk together the soy sauce, water, garlic powder, onion powder, oregano, basil, and black pepper. Add the tofu cubes, stirring to coat, and let them marinate for 10 minutes.
2. Select BAKE, set the temperature to 390ºF (199ºC), and set the time to 10 minutes. Select START/STOP to begin preheating.
3. Arrange the tofu in the baking pan. Place the pan directly in the pot. Close the hood and BAKE for 10 minutes until crisp. Flip the tofu halfway through the cooking time.
4. Remove from the basket to a plate and serve.

Asian-Inspired Broccoli

Prep time: 5 minutes | Cook time: 10 minutes | Serves 2

12 ounces (340 g) broccoli florets
2 tablespoons Asian hot chili oil
1 teaspoon ground Sichuan peppercorns (or black pepper)
2 garlic cloves, finely

chopped
1 (2-inch) piece fresh ginger, peeled and finely chopped
Kosher salt and freshly ground black pepper

1. Insert the Crisper Basket and close the hood. Select ROAST, set the temperature to 375ºF (191ºC), and set the time to 10 minutes. Select START/STOP to begin preheating.
2. Toss the broccoli florets with the chili oil, Sichuan peppercorns, garlic, ginger, salt, and pepper in a mixing bowl until thoroughly coated.
3. Transfer the broccoli florets to the Crisper Basket. Close the hood and ROAST for 10 minutes, shaking the basket halfway through, or until the broccoli florets are lightly browned and tender.
4. Remove the broccoli from the basket and serve on a plate.

Hearty Roasted Veggie Salad

Prep time: 5 minutes | Cook time: 20 minutes | Serves 2

1 potato, chopped
1 carrot, sliced diagonally
1 cup cherry tomatoes
½ small beetroot, sliced
¼ onion, sliced
½ teaspoon turmeric
½ teaspoon cumin

¼ teaspoon sea salt
2 tablespoons olive oil, divided
A handful of arugula
A handful of baby spinach
Juice of 1 lemon
3 tablespoons canned chickpeas, for serving
Parmesan shavings, for serving

1. Insert the Crisper Basket and close the hood. Select ROAST, set the temperature to 370ºF (188ºC), and set the time to 20 minutes. Select START/STOP to begin preheating.
2. Combine the potato, carrot, cherry tomatoes, beetroot, onion, turmeric, cumin, salt, and 1 tablespoon of olive oil in a large bowl and toss until well coated.
3. Arrange the veggies in the Crisper Basket. Close the hood and ROAST for 20 minutes, shaking the basket halfway through.
4. Let the veggies cool for 5 to 10 minutes in the basket.
5. Put the arugula, baby spinach, lemon juice, and remaining 1 tablespoon of olive oil in a salad bowl and stir to combine. Mix in the roasted veggies and toss well.
6. Scatter the chickpeas and Parmesan shavings on top and serve immediately.

Spicy Cauliflower Roast

Prep time: 15 minutes | Cook time: 20 minutes | Serves 4

Cauliflower:
5 cups cauliflower florets
3 tablespoons vegetable oil
½ teaspoon ground cumin

½ teaspoon ground coriander
½ teaspoon kosher salt

Sauce:
½ cup Greek yogurt or sour cream
¼ cup chopped fresh cilantro
1 jalapeño, coarsely chopped

4 cloves garlic, peeled
½ teaspoon kosher salt
2 tablespoons water

1. Insert the Crisper Basket and close the hood. Select ROAST, set the temperature to 400ºF (204ºC), and set the time to 20 minutes. Select START/STOP to begin preheating.
2. In a large bowl, combine the cauliflower, oil, cumin, coriander, and salt. Toss to coat.
3. Put the cauliflower in the Crisper Basket. Close the hood and ROAST for 20 minutes, stirring halfway through the roasting time.
4. Meanwhile, in a blender, combine the yogurt, cilantro, jalapeño, garlic, and salt. Blend, adding the water as needed to keep the blades moving and to thin the sauce.
5. At the end of roasting time, transfer the cauliflower to a large serving bowl. Pour the sauce over and toss gently to coat. Serve immediately.

Chermoula Beet Roast

Prep time: 15 minutes | Cook time: 25 minutes | Serves 4

Chermoula:

1 cup packed fresh cilantro leaves
½ cup packed fresh parsley leaves
6 cloves garlic, peeled
2 teaspoons smoked paprika
2 teaspoons ground cumin

1 teaspoon ground coriander
½ to 1 teaspoon cayenne pepper
Pinch of crushed saffron (optional)
½ cup extra-virgin olive oil
Kosher salt, to taste

Beets:

3 medium beets, trimmed, peeled, and cut
into 1-inch chunks

2 tablespoons chopped fresh cilantro
2 tablespoons chopped fresh parsley

1. In a food processor, combine the cilantro, parsley, garlic, paprika, cumin, coriander, and cayenne. Pulse until coarsely chopped. Add the saffron, if using, and process until combined. With the food processor running, slowly add the olive oil in a steady stream; process until the sauce is uniform. Season with salt.
2. Insert the Crisper Basket and close the hood. Select ROAST, set the temperature to 375ºF (191ºC), and set the time to 25 minutes. Select START/STOP to begin preheating.
3. In a large bowl, drizzle the beets with ½ cup of the chermoula to coat. Arrange the beets in the Crisper Basket. Close the hood and ROAST for 25 minutes, or until the beets are tender.
4. Transfer the beets to a serving platter. Sprinkle with the chopped cilantro and parsley and serve.

Summer Squash and Zucchini Salad

Prep time: 10 minutes | Cook time: 20 minutes | Serves 4

1 zucchini, sliced lengthwise about ¼-inch
thick
1 summer squash, sliced lengthwise about
¼-inch thick
½ red onion, sliced
4 tablespoons canola oil, divided

2 portobello mushroom caps, trimmed with
gills removed
2 ears corn, shucked
2 teaspoons freshly squeezed lemon juice
Sea salt, to taste
Freshly ground black pepper, to taste

1. Insert the Grill Grate and close the hood. Select GRILL, set the temperature to MAX, and set the time to 25 minutes. Select START/STOP to begin preheating.
2. Meanwhile, in a large bowl, toss the zucchini, squash, and onion with 2 tablespoons of oil until evenly coated.
3. When the unit beeps to signify it has preheated, arrange the zucchini, squash, and onions on the Grill Grate. Close the hood and GRILL for 6 minutes.
4. After 6 minutes, open the hood and flip the squash. Close the hood and GRILL for 6 to 9 minutes more.
5. Meanwhile, brush the mushrooms and corn with the remaining 2 tablespoons of oil.
6. When cooking is complete, remove the zucchini, squash, and onions and swap in the mushrooms and corn. Close the hood and GRILL for the remaining 10 minutes.
7. When cooking is complete, remove the mushrooms and corn, and let cool.
8. Cut the kernels from the cobs. Roughly chop all the vegetables into bite-size pieces.
9. Place the vegetables in a serving bowl and drizzle with lemon juice. Season with salt and pepper, and toss until evenly mixed.

Creamy and Cheesy Spinach

Prep time: 10 minutes | Cook time: 15 minutes | Serves 4

Vegetable oil spray
1 (10-ounce / 283-g) package frozen spinach, thawed and squeezed dry
½ cup chopped onion
2 cloves garlic, minced

4 ounces (113 g) cream cheese, diced
½ teaspoon ground nutmeg
1 teaspoon kosher salt
1 teaspoon black pepper
½ cup grated Parmesan cheese

1. Select BAKE, set the temperature to 350ºF (177ºC), and set the time to 15 minutes. Select START/STOP to begin preheating.
2. Spray a heatproof pan with vegetable oil spray.
3. In a medium bowl, combine the spinach, onion, garlic, cream cheese, nutmeg, salt, and pepper. Transfer to the prepared pan.
4. Place the pan directly in the pot. Close the hood and BAKE for 10 minutes. Open and stir to thoroughly combine the cream cheese and spinach.
5. Sprinkle the Parmesan cheese on top. Bake for 5 minutes, or until the cheese has melted and browned.
6. Serve hot.

Mascarpone Mushrooms

Prep time: 10 minutes | Cook time: 15 minutes | Serves 4

Vegetable oil spray
4 cups sliced mushrooms
1 medium yellow onion, chopped
2 cloves garlic, minced
¼ cup heavy whipping cream or half-and-half
8 ounces (227 g) mascarpone cheese

1 teaspoon dried thyme
1 teaspoon kosher salt
1 teaspoon black pepper
½ teaspoon red pepper flakes
4 cups cooked konjac noodles, for serving
½ cup grated Parmesan cheese

1. Select BAKE, set the temperature to 350ºF (177ºC), and set the time to 15 minutes. Select START/STOP to begin preheating.
2. Spray a heatproof pan with vegetable oil spray.
3. In a medium bowl, combine the mushrooms, onion, garlic, cream, mascarpone, thyme, salt, black pepper, and red pepper flakes. Stir to combine. Transfer the mixture to the prepared pan.
4. Place the pan directly in the pot. Close the hood and BAKE for 15 minutes, stirring halfway through the baking time.
5. Divide the pasta among four shallow bowls. Spoon the mushroom mixture evenly over the pasta. Sprinkle with Parmesan cheese and serve.

Vegetable Sides

Fast and Easy Asparagus

Prep time: 5 minutes | Cook time: 5 minutes | Serves 4

1 pound (454 g) fresh asparagus spears, trimmed
1 tablespoon olive oil
Salt and ground black pepper, to taste

1. Insert the Crisper Basket and close the hood. Select AIR CRISP, set the temperature to 375ºF (191ºC), and set the time to 5 minutes. Select START/STOP to begin preheating.
2. Combine all the ingredients and transfer to the Crisper Basket.
3. Close the hood and AIR CRISP for 5 minutes or until soft.
4. Serve hot.

Sriracha Golden Cauliflower

Prep time: 5 minutes | Cook time: 17 minutes | Serves 4

¼ cup vegan butter, melted
¼ cup sriracha sauce
4 cups cauliflower
florets
1 cup bread crumbs
1 teaspoon salt

1. Insert the Crisper Basket and close the hood. Select AIR CRISP, set the temperature to 375ºF (191ºC), and set the time to 17 minutes. Select START/STOP to begin preheating.
2. Mix the sriracha and vegan butter in a bowl and pour this mixture over the cauliflower, taking care to cover each floret entirely.
3. In a separate bowl, combine the bread crumbs and salt.
4. Dip the cauliflower florets in the bread crumbs, coating each one well. Transfer to the basket. Close the hood and AIR CRISP for 17 minutes.
5. Serve hot.

Roasted Lemony Broccoli

Prep time: 5 minutes | Cook time: 15 minutes | Serves 6

2 heads broccoli, cut into florets
2 teaspoons extra-virgin olive oil, plus more for coating
1 teaspoon salt
½ teaspoon black pepper
1 clove garlic, minced
½ teaspoon lemon juice

1. Cover the Crisper Basket with aluminum foil and coat with a light brushing of oil.
2. Insert the Crisper Basket and close the hood. Select ROAST, set the temperature to 375ºF (191ºC), and set the time to 15 minutes. Select START/STOP to begin preheating.
3. In a bowl, combine all ingredients, save for the lemon juice, and transfer to the Crisper Basket. Close the hood and ROAST for 15 minutes.
4. Serve with the lemon juice.

Corn Pakodas

Prep time: 10 minutes | Cook time: 8 minutes | Serves 5

1 cup flour
¼ teaspoon baking soda
¼ teaspoon salt
½ teaspoon curry powder
½ teaspoon red chili
powder
¼ teaspoon turmeric powder
¼ cup water
10 cobs baby corn, blanched
Cooking spray

1. Insert the Crisper Basket and close the hood. Select AIR CRISP, set the temperature to 425ºF (218ºC), and set the time to 8 minutes. Select START/STOP to begin preheating.
2. Cover the Crisper Basket with aluminum foil and spritz with the cooking spray.
3. In a bowl, combine all the ingredients, save for the corn. Stir with a whisk until well combined.
4. Coat the corn in the batter and put inside the basket.
5. Close the hood and AIR CRISP for 8 minutes until a golden brown color is achieved.
6. Serve hot.

Cheesy Macaroni Balls

Prep time: 10 minutes | Cook time: 10 minutes | Serves 2

2 cups leftover macaroni
1 cup shredded Cheddar cheese
½ cup flour
1 cup bread crumbs
3 large eggs
1 cup milk
½ teaspoon salt
¼ teaspoon black pepper

1. Insert the Crisper Basket and close the hood. Select AIR CRISP, set the temperature to 365ºF (185ºC), and set the time to 10 minutes. Select START/ STOP to begin preheating.
2. In a bowl, combine the leftover macaroni and shredded cheese.
3. Pour the flour in a separate bowl. Put the bread crumbs in a third bowl. Finally, in a fourth bowl, mix the eggs and milk with a whisk.
4. With an ice-cream scoop, create balls from the macaroni mixture. Coat them the flour, then in the egg mixture, and lastly in the bread crumbs.
5. Arrange the balls in the basket. Close the hood and AIR CRISP for 10 minutes, giving them an occasional stir. Ensure they crisp up nicely.
6. Serve hot.

Charred Green Beans with Sesame Seeds

Prep time: 5 minutes | Cook time: 8 minutes | Serves 4

1 tablespoon reduced-sodium soy sauce or tamari
½ tablespoon Sriracha sauce
4 teaspoons toasted
sesame oil, divided
12 ounces (340 g) trimmed green beans
½ tablespoon toasted sesame seeds

1. Insert the Crisper Basket and close the hood. Select AIR CRISP, set the temperature to 375ºF (191ºC), and set the time to 8 minutes. Select START/ STOP to begin preheating.
2. Whisk together the soy sauce, Sriracha sauce, and 1 teaspoon of sesame oil in a small bowl until smooth.

3. Toss the green beans with the remaining sesame oil in a large bowl until evenly coated.
4. Place the green beans in the Crisper Basket in a single layer. You may need to work in batches to avoid overcrowding.
5. Close the hood and AIR CRISP for 8 minutes until the green beans are lightly charred and tender. Shake the basket halfway through the cooking time.
6. Remove from the basket to a platter. Repeat with the remaining green beans.
7. Pour the prepared sauce over the top of green beans and toss well. Serve sprinkled with the toasted sesame seeds.

Cheesy Broccoli Gratin

Prep time: 5 minutes | Cook time: 12 to 14 minutes | Serves 2

$^{1}/_{3}$ cup fat-free milk
1 tablespoon all-purpose or gluten-free flour
½ tablespoon olive oil
½ teaspoon ground sage
¼ teaspoon kosher salt
⅛ teaspoon freshly ground black pepper
2 cups roughly chopped broccoli florets
6 tablespoons shredded Cheddar cheese
2 tablespoons panko bread crumbs
1 tablespoon grated Parmesan cheese
Olive oil spray

1. Select BAKE, set the temperature to 330ºF (166ºC), and set the time to 14 minutes. Select START/STOP to begin preheating.
2. Spritz a baking pan with olive oil spray.
3. Mix the milk, flour, olive oil, sage, salt, and pepper in a medium bowl and whisk to combine. Stir in the broccoli florets, Cheddar cheese, bread crumbs, and Parmesan cheese and toss to coat.
4. Pour the broccoli mixture into the prepared baking pan. Place the pan directly in the pot.
5. Close the hood and BAKE for 12 to 14 minutes until the top is golden brown and the broccoli is tender.
6. Serve immediately.

Rosemary Roasted Potatoes

Prep time: 5 minutes | Cook time: 20 to 22 minutes | Serves 4

1½ pounds (680 g) small red potatoes, cut into 1-inch cubes
2 tablespoons olive oil
2 tablespoons minced fresh rosemary
1 tablespoon minced garlic
1 teaspoon salt, plus additional as needed
½ teaspoon freshly ground black pepper, plus additional as needed

1. Insert the Crisper Basket and close the hood. Select ROAST, set the temperature to 400°F (204°C), and set the time to 22 minutes. Select START/STOP to begin preheating.
2. Toss the potato cubes with the olive oil, rosemary, garlic, salt, and pepper in a large bowl until thoroughly coated.
3. Arrange the potato cubes in the Crisper Basket in a single layer. Close the hood and ROAST for 20 to 22 minutes until the potatoes are tender. Shake the basket a few times during cooking for even cooking.
4. Remove from the basket to a plate. Taste and add additional salt and pepper as needed.

Creamy Corn Casserole

Prep time: 5 minutes | Cook time: 15 minutes | Serves 4

2 cups frozen yellow corn
1 egg, beaten
3 tablespoons flour
½ cup grated Swiss or Havarti cheese
½ cup light cream
¼ cup milk
Pinch salt
Freshly ground black pepper, to taste
2 tablespoons butter, cut into cubes
Nonstick cooking spray

1. Select BAKE, set the temperature to 320°F (160°C), and set the time to 15 minutes. Select START/STOP to begin preheating.
2. Spritz a baking pan with nonstick cooking spray.
3. Stir together the remaining ingredients except the butter in a medium bowl until well incorporated.
4. Transfer the mixture to the prepared baking pan and scatter with the butter cubes.
5. Place the pan directly in the pot. Close the hood and BAKE for 15 minutes, or until the top is golden brown and a toothpick inserted in the center comes out clean.
6. Let the casserole cool for 5 minutes before slicing into wedges and serving.

Parmesan Asparagus Fries

Prep time: 15 minutes | Cook time: 5 to 7 minutes | Serves 4

2 egg whites
¼ cup water
¼ cup plus 2 tablespoons grated Parmesan cheese, divided
¾ cup panko bread crumbs
¼ teaspoon salt
12 ounces (340 g) fresh asparagus spears, woody ends trimmed
Cooking spray

1. Insert the Crisper Basket and close the hood. Select AIR CRISP, set the temperature to 390°F (199°C), and set the time to 7 minutes. Select START/STOP to begin preheating.
2. In a shallow dish, whisk together the egg whites and water until slightly foamy. In a separate shallow dish, thoroughly combine ¼ cup of Parmesan cheese, bread crumbs, and salt.
3. Dip the asparagus in the egg white, then roll in the cheese mixture to coat well.
4. Place the asparagus in the Crisper Basket in a single layer, leaving space between each spear. You may need to work in batches to avoid overcrowding.
5. Spritz the asparagus with cooking spray. Close the hood and AIR CRISP for 5 to 7 minutes until golden brown and crisp.
6. Repeat with the remaining asparagus spears.
7. Sprinkle with the remaining 2 tablespoons of cheese and serve hot.

Garlic Roasted Asparagus

Prep time: 5 minutes | Cook time: 10 minutes | Serves 4

1 pound (454 g) asparagus, woody ends trimmed	balsamic vinegar
	2 teaspoons minced garlic
2 tablespoons olive oil	Salt and freshly ground black pepper, to taste
1 tablespoon	

1. Insert the Crisper Basket and close the hood. Select ROAST, set the temperature to 400ºF (204ºC), and set the time to 10 minutes. Select START/STOP to begin preheating.
2. In a large shallow bowl, toss the asparagus with the olive oil, balsamic vinegar, garlic, salt, and pepper until thoroughly coated.
3. Arrange the asparagus in the Crisper Basket. Close the hood and ROAST for 10 minutes until crispy. Flip the asparagus with tongs halfway through the cooking time.
4. Serve warm.

Spicy Cabbage

Prep time: 5 minutes | Cook time: 7 minutes | Serves 4

1 head cabbage, sliced into 1-inch-thick ribbons	1 teaspoon red pepper flakes
	1 teaspoon salt
1 tablespoon olive oil	1 teaspoon freshly ground black pepper
1 teaspoon garlic powder	

1. Insert the Crisper Basket and close the hood. Select ROAST, set the temperature to 350ºF (177ºC), and set the time to 7 minutes. Select START/STOP to begin preheating.
2. Toss the cabbage with the olive oil, garlic powder, red pepper flakes, salt, and pepper in a large mixing bowl until well coated.
3. Arrange the cabbage in the Crisper Basket. Close the hood and ROAST for 7 minutes until crisp. Flip the cabbage with tongs halfway through the cooking time.
4. Remove from the basket to a plate and serve warm.

Simple Pesto Gnocchi

Prep time: 10 minutes | Cook time: 15 minutes | Serves 4

1 (1-pound / 454-g) package gnocchi	1 tablespoon extra-virgin olive oil
1 medium onion, chopped	1 (8-ounce / 227-g) jar pesto
3 cloves garlic, minced	1/3 cup grated Parmesan cheese

1. Insert the Crisper Basket and close the hood. Select AIR CRISP, set the temperature to 340ºF (171ºC), and set the time to 15 minutes. Select START/STOP to begin preheating.
2. In a large bowl combine the onion, garlic, and gnocchi, and drizzle with the olive oil. Mix thoroughly.
3. Transfer the mixture to the basket. Close the hood and AIR CRISP for 15 minutes, stirring occasionally, making sure the gnocchi become light brown and crispy.
4. Add the pesto and Parmesan cheese, and give everything a good stir before serving.

Buttered Broccoli with Parmesan

Prep time: 5 minutes | Cook time: 4 minutes | Serves 4

1 pound (454 g) broccoli florets	unsalted butter, melted
1 medium shallot, minced	2 teaspoons minced garlic
2 tablespoons olive oil	1/4 cup grated Parmesan cheese
2 tablespoons	

1. Insert the Crisper Basket and close the hood. Select ROAST, set the temperature to 360ºF (182ºC), and set the time to 4 minutes. Select START/STOP to begin preheating.
2. Combine the broccoli florets with the shallot, olive oil, butter, garlic, and Parmesan cheese in a medium bowl and toss until the broccoli florets are thoroughly coated.
3. Arrange the broccoli florets in the Crisper Basket in a single layer. Close the hood and ROAST for 4 minutes until crisp-tender.
4. Serve warm.

Crusted Brussels Sprouts with Sage

Prep time: 5 minutes | Cook time: 15 minutes | Serves 4

1 pound (454 g) Brussels sprouts, halved
1 cup bread crumbs
2 tablespoons grated Grana Padano cheese
1 tablespoon paprika
2 tablespoons canola oil
1 tablespoon chopped sage

1. Line the Crisper Basket with parchment paper.
2. Insert the Crisper Basket and close the hood. Select ROAST, set the temperature to 400ºF (204ºC), and set the time to 15 minutes. Select START/STOP to begin preheating.
3. In a small bowl, thoroughly mix the bread crumbs, cheese, and paprika. In a large bowl, place the Brussels sprouts and drizzle the canola oil over the top. Sprinkle with the bread crumb mixture and toss to coat.
4. Place the Brussels sprouts in the Crisper Basket. Close the hood and ROAST for 15 minutes, or until the Brussels sprouts are lightly browned and crisp. Shake the basket a few times during cooking to ensure even cooking.
5. Transfer the Brussels sprouts to a plate and sprinkle the sage on top before serving.

Cinnamon-Spiced Acorn Squash

Prep time: 5 minutes | Cook time: 15 minutes | Serves 2

1 medium acorn squash, halved crosswise and deseeded
1 teaspoon coconut oil
1 teaspoon light brown sugar
Few dashes of ground cinnamon
Few dashes of ground nutmeg

1. Insert the Crisper Basket and close the hood. Select AIR CRISP, set the temperature to 325ºF (163ºC), and set the time to 15 minutes. Select START/STOP to begin preheating.
2. On a clean work surface, rub the cut sides of the acorn squash with coconut oil. Scatter with the brown sugar, cinnamon, and nutmeg.
3. Put the squash halves in the Crisper Basket, cut-side up. Close the hood and AIR CRISP for 15 minutes until just tender when pierced in the center with a paring knife.
4. Rest for 5 to 10 minutes and serve warm.

Baked Potatoes with Yogurt and Chives

Prep time: 5 minutes | Cook time: 35 minutes | Serves 4

4 (7-ounce / 198-g) russet potatoes, rinsed
Olive oil spray
½ teaspoon kosher salt, divided
½ cup 2% plain Greek yogurt
¼ cup minced fresh chives
Freshly ground black pepper, to taste

1. Insert the Crisper Basket and close the hood. Select BAKE, set the temperature to 400ºF (204ºC), and set the time to 35 minutes. Select START/STOP to begin preheating.
2. Pat the potatoes dry and pierce them all over with a fork. Spritz the potatoes with olive oil spray. Sprinkle with ¼ teaspoon of the salt.
3. Put the potatoes in the Crisper Basket. Close the hood and BAKE for 35 minutes, or until a knife can be inserted into the center of the potatoes easily.
4. Remove from the basket and split open the potatoes. Top with the yogurt, chives, the remaining ¼ teaspoon of salt, and finish with the black pepper. Serve immediately.

Stuffed Vegetables

Beef Stuffed Bell Peppers

Prep time: 10 minutes | Cook time: 30 minutes | Serves 4

1 pound (454 g) ground beef
1 tablespoon taco seasoning mix
1 can diced tomatoes and green chilis
4 green bell peppers
1 cup shredded Monterey jack cheese, divided

1. Insert the Crisper Basket and close the hood. Select AIR CRISP, set the temperature to 350ºF (177ºC), and set the time to 15 minutes. Select START/STOP to begin preheating.
2. Set a skillet over a high heat and cook the ground beef for 8 minutes. Make sure it is cooked through and browned all over. Drain the fat.
3. Stir in the taco seasoning mix, and the diced tomatoes and green chilis. Allow the mixture to cook for a further 4 minutes.
4. In the meantime, slice the tops off the green peppers and remove the seeds and membranes.
5. When the meat mixture is fully cooked, spoon equal amounts of it into the peppers and top with the Monterey jack cheese. Then place the peppers into the basket. Close the hood and AIR CRISP for 15 minutes.
6. The peppers are ready when they are soft, and the cheese is bubbling and brown. Serve warm.

Cashew Stuffed Mushrooms

Prep time: 10 minutes | Cook time: 15 minutes | Serves 6

1 cup basil
½ cup cashew, soaked overnight
½ cup nutritional yeast
1 tablespoon lemon juice
2 cloves garlic
1 tablespoon olive oil
Salt, to taste
1 pound (454 g) baby bella mushroom, stems removed

1. Insert the Crisper Basket and close the hood. Select AIR CRISP, set the temperature to 400ºF (204ºC), and set the time to 15 minutes. Select START/STOP to begin preheating.
2. Prepare the pesto. In a food processor, blend the basil, cashew nuts, nutritional yeast, lemon juice, garlic and olive oil to combine well. Sprinkle with salt, as desired.
3. Turn the mushrooms cap-side down and spread the pesto on the underside of each cap.
4. Transfer to the basket. Close the hood and AIR CRISP for 15 minutes.
5. Serve warm.

Kidney Beans Oatmeal in Peppers

Prep time: 15 minutes | Cook time: 6 minutes | Serves 2 to 4

2 large bell peppers, halved lengthwise, deseeded
2 tablespoons cooked kidney beans
2 tablespoons cooked chick peas
2 cups cooked oatmeal
1 teaspoon ground cumin
½ teaspoon paprika
½ teaspoon salt or to taste
¼ teaspoon black pepper powder
¼ cup yogurt

1. Insert the Crisper Basket and close the hood. Select AIR CRISP, set the temperature to 355ºF (179ºC), and set the time to 6 minutes. Select START/STOP to begin preheating.
2. Put the bell peppers, cut-side down, in the Crisper Basket. Close the hood and AIR CRISP for 2 minutes.
3. Take the peppers out of the grill and let cool.
4. In a bowl, combine the rest of the ingredients.
5. Divide the mixture evenly and use each portion to stuff a pepper.
6. Return the stuffed peppers to the basket. Close the hood and AIR CRISP for 4 minutes.
7. Serve hot.

Prosciutto Mini Mushroom Pizza

Prep time: 10 minutes | Cook time: 5 minutes | Serves 3

3 portobello mushroom caps, cleaned and scooped
3 tablespoons olive oil
Pinch of salt

Pinch of dried Italian seasonings
3 tablespoons tomato sauce
3 tablespoons shredded Mozzarella cheese
12 slices prosciutto

1. Insert the Crisper Basket and close the hood. Select AIR CRISP, set the temperature to 330ºF (166ºC), and set the time to 5 minutes. Select START/STOP to begin preheating.
2. Season both sides of the portobello mushrooms with a drizzle of olive oil, then sprinkle salt and the Italian seasonings on the insides.
3. With a knife, spread the tomato sauce evenly over the mushroom, before adding the Mozzarella on top.
4. Put the portobello in the Crisper Basket. Close the hood and AIR CRISP for 1 minutes, before taking the Crisper Basket out of the grill and putting the prosciutto slices on top. AIR CRISP for another 4 minutes.
5. Serve warm.

Cheesy Rice and Olives Stuffed Peppers

Prep time: 5 minutes | Cook time: 16 to 17 minutes | Serves 4

4 red bell peppers, tops sliced off
2 cups cooked rice
1 cup crumbled feta cheese
1 onion, chopped
¼ cup sliced kalamata olives

¾ cup tomato sauce
1 tablespoon Greek seasoning
Salt and black pepper, to taste
2 tablespoons chopped fresh dill, for serving

1. Select BAKE, set the temperature to 360ºF (182ºC), and set the time to 15 minutes. Select START/STOP to begin preheating.
2. Microwave the red bell peppers for 1 to 2 minutes until tender.
3. When ready, transfer the red bell peppers to a plate to cool.
4. Mix together the cooked rice, feta cheese, onion, kalamata olives, tomato sauce, Greek seasoning, salt, and pepper in a medium bowl and stir until well combined.
5. Divide the rice mixture among the red bell peppers and transfer to a greased baking pan.
6. Place the pan directly in the pot. Close the hood and BAKE for 15 minutes, or until the rice is heated through and the vegetables are soft.
7. Remove from the basket and serve with the dill sprinkled on top.

Vegetable and Cheese Stuffed Tomatoes

Prep time: 10 minutes | Cook time: 16 to 20 minutes | Serves 4

4 medium beefsteak tomatoes, rinsed
½ cup grated carrot
1 medium onion, chopped
1 garlic clove, minced

2 teaspoons olive oil
2 cups fresh baby spinach
¼ cup crumbled low-sodium feta cheese
½ teaspoon dried basil

1. Select BAKE, set the temperature to 350°F (177°C), and set the time to 20 minutes. Select START/STOP to begin preheating.
2. On your cutting board, cut a thin slice off the top of each tomato. Scoop out a ¼- to ½-inch-thick tomato pulp and place the tomatoes upside down on paper towels to drain. Set aside.
3. Stir together the carrot, onion, garlic, and olive oil in a baking pan. Place the pan directly in the pot. Close the hood and BAKE for 4 to 6 minutes, or until the carrot is crisp-tender.
4. Remove the pan from the grill and stir in the spinach, feta cheese, and basil.
5. Spoon ¼ of the vegetable mixture into each tomato and transfer the stuffed tomatoes to the pan.
6. Place the pan directly in the pot. Close the hood and BAKE for 12 to 14 minutes, or until the filling is hot and the tomatoes are lightly caramelized.
7. Let the tomatoes cool for 5 minutes and serve.

Stuffed Squash with Tomatoes and Poblano

Prep time: 5 minutes | Cook time: 30 minutes | Serves 4

1 pound (454 g) butternut squash, ends trimmed
2 teaspoons olive oil, divided
6 grape tomatoes, halved

1 poblano pepper, cut into strips
Salt and black pepper, to taste
¼ cup grated Mozzarella cheese

1. Insert the Crisper Basket and close the hood. Select ROAST, set the temperature to 350°F (177°C), and set the time to 30 minutes. Select START/STOP to begin preheating.
2. Using a large knife, cut the squash in half lengthwise on a flat work surface. This recipe just needs half of the squash. Scoop out the flesh to make room for the stuffing. Coat the squash half with 1 teaspoon of olive oil.
3. Put the squash half in the Crisper Basket. Close the hood and ROAST for 15 minutes.
4. Meanwhile, thoroughly combine the tomatoes, poblano pepper, remaining 1 teaspoon of olive oil, salt, and pepper in a bowl.
5. Remove the basket and spoon the tomato mixture into the squash. Return to the grill and roast for 12 minutes until the tomatoes are soft.
6. Scatter the Mozzarella cheese on top and continue roasting for about 3 minutes, or until the cheese is melted.
7. Cool for 5 minutes before serving.

Chapter 4 Appetizers and Snacks

Crispy Prosciutto-Wrapped Asparagus

Prep time: 5 minutes | Cook time: 16 to 24 minutes | Serves 6

12 asparagus spears, woody ends trimmed

24 pieces thinly sliced prosciutto

Cooking spray

1. Insert the Crisper Basket and close the hood. Select AIR CRISP, set the temperature to 360ºF (182ºC), and set the time to 4 minutes. Select START/STOP to begin preheating.
2. Wrap each asparagus spear with 2 slices of prosciutto, then repeat this process with the remaining asparagus and prosciutto.
3. Spray the Crisper Basket with cooking spray, then place 2 to 3 bundles in the basket. Close the hood and AIR CRISP for 4 minutes. Repeat this process with the remaining asparagus bundles.
4. Remove the bundles and allow to cool on a wire rack for 5 minutes before serving.

Bacon-Wrapped Dates

Prep time: 10 minutes | Cook time: 10 to 14 minutes | Serves 6

12 dates, pitted

6 slices high-quality bacon, cut in half

Cooking spray

1. Insert the Crisper Basket and close the hood. Select BAKE, set the temperature to 360ºF (182ºC), and set the time to 7 minutes. Select START/STOP to begin preheating.
2. Wrap each date with half a bacon slice and secure with a toothpick.
3. Spray the Crisper Basket with cooking spray, then place 6 bacon-wrapped dates in the basket. Place the pan directly in the pot. Close the hood and BAKE for 5 to 7 minutes or until the bacon is crispy. Repeat this process with the remaining dates.
4. Remove the dates and allow to cool on a wire rack for 5 minutes before serving.

Buttermilk Marinated Chicken Wings

Prep time: 1 hour 20 minutes | Cook time: 17 to 19 minutes | Serves 4

2 pounds (907 g) chicken wings

Marinade:
1 cup buttermilk

½ teaspoon salt

½ teaspoon black pepper

Coating:
1 cup flour

1 cup panko bread crumbs

2 tablespoons poultry seasoning

2 teaspoons salt

Cooking spray

1. Whisk together all the ingredients for the marinade in a large bowl.
2. Add the chicken wings to the marinade and toss well. Transfer to the refrigerator to marinate for at least an hour.
3. Spritz the Crisper Basket with cooking spray.
4. Insert the Crisper Basket and close the hood. Select AIR CRISP, set the temperature to 360ºF (182ºC), and set the time to 19 minutes. Select START/STOP to begin preheating.
5. Thoroughly combine all the ingredients for the coating in a shallow bowl.
6. Remove the chicken wings from the marinade and shake off any excess. Roll them in the coating mixture.
7. Place the chicken wings in the Crisper Basket in a single layer. Mist the wings with cooking spray. You'll need to work in batches to avoid overcrowding.
8. Close the hood and AIR CRISP for 17 to 19 minutes, or until the wings are crisp and golden brown on the outside. Flip the wings halfway through the cooking time.
9. Remove from the basket to a plate and repeat with the remaining wings.
10. Serve hot.

Dill Pickles

Prep time: 10 minutes | Cook time: 10 minutes | Serves 4

20 dill pickle slices
¼ cup all-purpose flour
⅛ teaspoon baking powder
3 tablespoons beer or seltzer water
⅛ teaspoon sea salt
2 tablespoons water, plus more if needed
2 tablespoons

cornstarch
1½ cups panko bread crumbs
1 teaspoon paprika
1 teaspoon garlic powder
¼ teaspoon cayenne pepper
2 tablespoons canola oil, divided

1. Pat the pickle slices dry, and place them on a dry plate in the freezer.
2. In a medium bowl, stir together the flour, baking powder, beer, salt, and water. The batter should be the consistency of cake batter. If it is too thick, add more water, 1 teaspoon at a time.
3. Place the cornstarch in a small shallow bowl.
4. In a separate large shallow bowl, combine the bread crumbs, paprika, garlic powder, and cayenne pepper.
5. Remove the pickles from the freezer. Dredge each one in cornstarch. Tap off any excess, then coat in the batter. Lastly, coat evenly with the bread crumb mixture.
6. Insert the Crisper Basket and close the hood. Select AIR CRISP, set the temperature to 360°F (182°C), and set the time to 10 minutes. Select START/STOP to begin preheating.
7. When the unit beeps to signify it has preheated, place the breaded pickles in the basket, stacking them if necessary, and gently brush them with 1 tablespoon of oil. Close the hood and AIR CRISP for 5 minutes.
8. After 5 minutes, shake the basket and gently brush the pickles with the remaining 1 tablespoon of oil. Place the basket back in the unit and close the hood to resume cooking.
9. When cooking is complete, serve immediately.

Grilled Shishito Peppers

Prep time: 5 minutes | Cook time: 10 minutes | Serves 4

3 cups whole shishito peppers
2 tablespoons

vegetable oil
Flaky sea salt, for garnish

1. Insert the Grill Grate and close the hood. Select GRILL, set the temperature to MAX, and set the time to 10 minutes. Select START/STOP to begin preheating.
2. While the unit is preheating, in a medium bowl, toss the peppers in the oil until evenly coated.
3. When the unit beeps to signify it has preheated, place the peppers on the Grill Grate. Gently press the peppers down to maximize grill marks. Close the hood and GRILL for 8 to 10 minutes, until they are blistered on all sides.
4. When cooking is complete, place the peppers in a serving dish and top with the flaky sea salt. Serve immediately.

Garlicky and Lemony Artichokes

Prep time: 10 minutes | Cook time: 10 minutes | Serves 4

Juice of ½ lemon
½ cup canola oil
3 garlic cloves, chopped
Sea salt, to taste

Freshly ground black pepper, to taste
2 large artichokes, trimmed and halved

1. Insert the Grill Grate and close the hood. Select GRILL, set the temperature to MAX, and set the time to 10 minutes. Select START/STOP to begin preheating.
2. While the unit is preheating, in a medium bowl, combine the lemon juice, oil, and garlic. Season with salt and pepper, then brush the artichoke halves with the lemon-garlic mixture.
3. When the unit beeps to signify it has preheated, place the artichokes on the Grill Grate, cut side down. Gently press them down to maximize grill marks. Close the hood and GRILL for 8 to 10 minutes, occasionally basting generously with the lemon-garlic mixture throughout cooking, until blistered on all sides.

Blistered Lemony Green Beans

Prep time: 5 minutes | Cook time: 10 minutes | Serves 4

1 pound (454 g) haricots verts or green beans, trimmed	Pinch red pepper flakes
2 tablespoons vegetable oil	Flaky sea salt, to taste
Juice of 1 lemon	Freshly ground black pepper, to taste

1. Insert the Grill Grate and close the hood. Select GRILL, set the temperature to MAX, and set the time to 10 minutes. Select START/STOP to begin preheating.
2. While the unit is preheating, in a medium bowl, toss the green beans in oil until evenly coated.
3. When the unit beeps to signify it has preheated, place the green beans on the Grill Grate. Close the hood and GRILL for 8 to 10 minutes, tossing frequently until blistered on all sides.
4. When cooking is complete, place the green beans on a large serving platter. Squeeze lemon juice over the green beans, top with red pepper flakes, and season with sea salt and black pepper.

Brussels Sprouts and Bacon

Prep time: 10 minutes | Cook time: 12 minutes | Serves 4

1 pound (454 g) Brussels sprouts, trimmed and halved	1 teaspoon sea salt
2 tablespoons extra-virgin olive oil	½ teaspoon freshly ground black pepper
	6 slices bacon, chopped

1. Insert the Crisper Basket and close the hood. Select AIR CRISP, set the temperature to 390ºF (199ºC), and set the time to 12 minutes. Select START/STOP to begin preheating.
2. Meanwhile, in a large bowl, toss the Brussels sprouts with the olive oil, salt, pepper, and bacon.
3. When the unit beeps to signify it has preheated, add the Brussels sprouts to the basket. Close the hood and AIR CRISP for 10 minutes.

4. After 6 minutes, shake the basket of Brussels sprouts. Place the basket back in the unit and close the hood to resume cooking.
5. After 6 minutes, check for desired crispness. Continue cooking up to 2 more minutes, if necessary.

Cheese and Ham Stuffed Baby Bella

Prep time: 15 minutes | Cook time: 12 minutes | Serves 8

4 ounces (113 g) Mozzarella cheese, cut into pieces	¼ teaspoon ground oregano
½ cup diced ham	¼ teaspoon ground black pepper
2 green onions, chopped	1 to 2 teaspoons olive oil
2 tablespoons bread crumbs	16 fresh Baby Bella mushrooms, stemmed removed
½ teaspoon garlic powder	

1. Process the cheese, ham, green onions, bread crumbs, garlic powder, oregano, and pepper in a food processor until finely chopped.
2. With the food processor running, slowly drizzle in 1 to 2 teaspoons olive oil until a thick paste has formed. Transfer the mixture to a bowl.
3. Evenly divide the mixture into the mushroom caps and lightly press down the mixture.
4. Insert the Crisper Basket and close the hood. Select ROAST, set the temperature to 390ºF (199ºC), and set the time to 12 minutes. Select START/STOP to begin preheating.
5. Lay the mushrooms in the Crisper Basket in a single layer. You'll need to work in batches to avoid overcrowding.
6. Close the hood and ROAST for 12 minutes until the mushrooms are lightly browned and tender.
7. Remove from the basket to a plate and repeat with the remaining mushrooms.
8. Let the mushrooms cool for 5 minutes and serve warm.

Balsamic Broccoli

Prep time: 10 minutes | Cook time: 10 minutes | Serves 4

4 tablespoons soy sauce	syrup
4 tablespoons balsamic vinegar	2 heads broccoli, trimmed into florets
2 tablespoons canola oil	Red pepper flakes, for garnish
2 teaspoons maple	Sesame seeds, for garnish

1. Insert the Grill Grate and close the hood. Select GRILL, set the temperature to MAX, and set the time to 10 minutes. Select START/STOP to begin preheating.
2. While the unit is preheating, in a large bowl, whisk together the soy sauce, balsamic vinegar, oil, and maple syrup. Add the broccoli and toss to coat evenly.
3. When the unit beeps to signify it has preheated, place the broccoli on the Grill Grate. Close the hood and GRILL for 8 to 10 minutes, until charred on all sides.
4. When cooking is complete, place the broccoli on a large serving platter. Garnish with red pepper flakes and sesame seeds. Serve immediately.

Cheesy Summer Squash with Red Onion

Prep time: 15 minutes | Cook time: 15 minutes | Serves 4

½ cup vegetable oil, plus 3 tablespoons	and cut into wedges
¼ cup white wine vinegar	Sea salt, to taste
1 garlic clove, grated	Freshly ground black pepper, to taste
2 summer squash, sliced lengthwise about ¼-inch thick	1 (8-ounce / 227-g) package crumbled feta cheese
1 red onion, peeled	Red pepper flakes, as needed

1. Insert the Grill Grate and close the hood. Select GRILL, set the temperature to MAX, and set the time to 15 minutes. Select START/STOP to begin preheating.
2. Meanwhile, in a small bowl, whisk together ½ cup oil, vinegar, and garlic, and set aside.

3. In a large bowl, toss the squash and onion with remaining 3 tablespoons of oil until evenly coated. Season with the salt and pepper.
4. When the unit beeps to signify it has preheated, arrange the squash and onions on the Grill Grate. Close the hood and GRILL for 6 minutes.
5. After 6 minutes, open the hood and flip the squash. Close the hood and GRILL for 6 to 9 minutes more.
6. When vegetables are cooked to desired doneness, remove them from the grill. Arrange the vegetables on a large platter and top with the feta cheese. Drizzle the dressing over the top, and sprinkle with the red pepper flakes. Let stand for 15 minutes before serving.

Grilled Carrots with Honey Glazed

Prep time: 10 minutes | Cook time: 10 minutes | Serves 4

6 medium carrots, peeled and cut lengthwise	unsalted butter, melted
1 tablespoon canola oil	¼ cup brown sugar, melted
2 tablespoons	¼ cup honey
	⅛ teaspoon sea salt

1. Insert the Grill Grate and close the hood. Select GRILL, set the temperature to MAX, and set the time to 10 minutes. Select START/STOP to begin preheating.
2. In a large bowl, toss the carrots and oil until well coated.
3. When the unit beeps to signify it has preheated, place carrots on the center of the Grill Grate. Close the hood and GRILL for 5 minutes.
4. Meanwhile, in a small bowl, whisk together the butter, brown sugar, honey, and salt.
5. After 5 minutes, open the hood and baste the carrots with the glaze. Using tongs, turn the carrots and baste the other side. Close the hood and GRILL for another 5 minutes.
6. When cooking is complete, serve immediately.

Crispy Spiced Potatoes

Prep time: 10 minutes | Cook time: 20 minutes | Serves 4

2 pounds (907 g) baby red potatoes, quartered
2 tablespoons extra-virgin olive oil
¼ cup dried onion flakes
1 teaspoon dried rosemary
½ teaspoon onion powder
½ teaspoon garlic powder
¼ teaspoon celery powder
¼ teaspoon freshly ground black pepper
½ teaspoon dried parsley
½ teaspoon sea salt

1. Insert the Crisper Basket and close the hood. Select AIR CRISP, set the temperature to 390ºF (199ºC), and set the time to 20 minutes. Select START/STOP to begin preheating.
2. Meanwhile, place all the ingredients in a large bowl and toss until evenly coated.
3. When the unit beeps to signify it has preheated, add the potatoes to the basket. Close the hood and AIR CRISP for 10 minutes.
4. After 10 minutes, shake the basket well. Place the basket back in the unit and close the hood to resume cooking.
5. After 10 minutes, check for desired crispness. Continue cooking up to 5 minutes more, if necessary.

BLT with Grilled Heirloom Tomato

Prep time: 10 minutes | Cook time: 10 minutes | Serves 4

8 slices white bread
8 tablespoons mayonnaise
2 heirloom tomatoes, sliced ¼-inch thick
2 tablespoons canola oil
Sea salt, to taste
Freshly ground black pepper, to taste
8 slices bacon, cooked
8 leaves iceberg lettuce

1. Insert the Grill Grate, and close the hood. Select GRILL, set the temperature to MAX, and set the time to 10 minutes. Select START/STOP to begin preheating.
2. While the unit is preheating, spread a thin layer of mayonnaise on one side of each piece of bread.
3. When the unit beeps to signify it has preheated, place the bread, mayonnaise-side down, on the Grill Grate. Close the hood and GRILL for 2 to 3 minutes, until crisp.
4. Meanwhile, remove the watery pulp and seeds from the tomato slices. Brush both sides of the tomatoes with the oil and season with salt and pepper.
5. After 2 to 3 minutes, remove the bread and place the tomatoes on the grill. Close the hood and continue grilling for the remaining 6 to 8 minutes.
6. To assemble, spread a thin layer of mayonnaise on the non-grilled sides of the bread. Layer the tomatoes, bacon, and lettuce on the bread, and top with the remaining slices of bread. Slice each sandwich in half and serve.

French Fries

Prep time: 15 minutes | Cook time: 25 minutes | Serves 4

1 pound (454 g) russet or Idaho potatoes, cut in
2-inch strips
3 tablespoons canola oil

1. Place the potatoes in a large bowl and cover them with cold water. Let soak for 30 minutes. Drain well, then pat with a paper towel until very dry.
2. Insert the Crisper Basket and close the hood. Select AIR CRISP, set the temperature to 390ºF (199ºC), and set the time to 25 minutes. Select START/STOP to begin preheating.
3. Meanwhile, in a large bowl, toss the potatoes with the oil.
4. When the unit beeps to signify it has preheated, add the potatoes to the basket. Close the hood and AIR CRISP for 10 minutes.
5. After 10 minutes, shake the basket well. Place the basket back in the unit and close the hood to resume cooking.
6. After 10 minutes, check for desired crispness. Continue cooking up to 5 minutes more, if necessary.
7. When cooking is complete, serve immediately with your favorite dipping sauce.

Sweet Potato Chips

Prep time: 10 minutes | Cook time: 8 to 10 hours | Makes 1 cup

1 sweet potato, peeled
½ tablespoon

avocado oil
½ teaspoon sea salt

1. Using a mandoline, thinly slice (⅛ inch or less) the sweet potato.
2. In a large bowl, toss the sweet potato slices with the oil until evenly coated. Season with the salt.
3. Place the sweet potato slices flat on the Crisper Basket. Arrange them in a single layer, without any slices touching each another.
4. Place the basket in the pot and close the hood.
5. Select DEHYDRATE, set the temperature to 120ºF (49ºC), and set the time to 10 hours. Select START/STOP.
6. After 8 hours, check for desired doneness. Continue dehydrating for 2 more hours, if necessary.
7. When cooking is complete, remove the basket from the pot. Transfer the sweet potato chips to an airtight container and store at room temperature.

Cheesy Steak Fries

Prep time: 5 minutes | Cook time: 20 minutes | Serves 5

1 (28-ounce / 794-g) bag frozen steak fries
Cooking spray
Salt and pepper, to taste

½ cup beef gravy
1 cup shredded Mozzarella cheese
2 scallions, green parts only, chopped

1. Insert the Crisper Basket and close the hood. Select AIR CRISP, set the temperature to 400ºF (204ºC), and set the time to 20 minutes. Select START/STOP to begin preheating.
2. Place the frozen steak fries in the basket. Close the hood and AIR CRISP for 10 minutes. Shake the basket and spritz the fries with cooking spray. Sprinkle with salt and pepper. AIR CRISP for an additional 8 minutes.
3. Pour the beef gravy into a medium, microwave-safe bowl. Microwave for 30 seconds, or until the gravy is warm.
4. Sprinkle the fries with the cheese. Close the hood and AIR CRISP for an additional 2 minutes, until the cheese is melted.
5. Transfer the fries to a serving dish. Drizzle the fries with gravy and sprinkle the scallions on top for a green garnish. Serve.

Sausage and Mushroom Empanadas

Prep time: 5 minutes | Cook time: 12 minutes | Serves 4

½ pound (227 g) Kielbasa smoked sausage, chopped
4 chopped canned mushrooms
2 tablespoons chopped onion
½ teaspoon ground cumin

¼ teaspoon paprika
Salt and black pepper, to taste
½ package puff pastry dough, at room temperature
1 egg, beaten
Cooking spray

1. Spritz the Crisper Basket with cooking spray.
2. Insert the Crisper Basket and close the hood. Select AIR CRISP, set the temperature to 360ºF (182ºC), and set the time to 12 minutes. Select START/STOP to begin preheating.
3. Combine the sausage, mushrooms, onion, cumin, paprika, salt, and pepper in a bowl and stir to mix well.
4. Make the empanadas: Place the puff pastry dough on a lightly floured surface. Cut circles into the dough with a glass. Place 1 tablespoon of the sausage mixture into the center of each pastry circle. Fold each in half and pinch the edges to seal. Using a fork, crimp the edges. Brush them with the beaten egg and mist with cooking spray.
5. Place the empanadas in the Crisper Basket. Close the hood and AIR CRISP for 12 minutes until golden brown. Flip the empanadas halfway through the cooking time.
6. Allow them to cool for 5 minutes and serve hot.

Breaded Green Olives

Prep time: 5 minutes | Cook time: 8 minutes | Serves 4

1 (5½-ounce / 156-g) jar pitted green olives
½ cup all-purpose flour
Salt and pepper, to taste
½ cup bread crumbs
1 egg
Cooking spray

1. Insert the Crisper Basket and close the hood. Select AIR CRISP, set the temperature to 400ºF (204ºC), and set the time to 8 minutes. Select START/ STOP to begin preheating.
2. Remove the olives from the jar and dry thoroughly with paper towels.
3. In a small bowl, combine the flour with salt and pepper to taste. Place the bread crumbs in another small bowl. In a third small bowl, beat the egg.
4. Spritz the Crisper Basket with cooking spray.
5. Dip the olives in the flour, then the egg, and then the bread crumbs.
6. Place the breaded olives in the basket. It is okay to stack them. Spray the olives with cooking spray. Close the hood and AIR CRISP for 6 minutes. Flip the olives and AIR CRISP for an additional 2 minutes, or until brown and crisp.
7. Cool before serving.

Cheesy Apple Roll-Ups

Prep time: 5 minutes | Cook time: 4 to 5 minutes | Makes 8 roll-ups

8 slices whole wheat sandwich bread
4 ounces (113 g) Colby Jack cheese, grated
½ small apple, chopped
2 tablespoons butter, melted

1. Insert the Crisper Basket and close the hood. Select AIR CRISP, set the temperature to 390ºF (199ºC), and set the time to 5 minutes. Select START/ STOP to begin preheating.
2. Remove the crusts from the bread and flatten the slices with a rolling pin. Don't be gentle. Press hard so that bread will be very thin.
3. Top bread slices with cheese and chopped apple, dividing the ingredients evenly.
4. Roll up each slice tightly and secure each with one or two toothpicks.
5. Brush outside of rolls with melted butter.
6. Place in the Crisper Basket. Close the hood and AIR CRISP for 4 to 5 minutes, or until outside is crisp and nicely browned.
7. Serve hot.

Easy Muffuletta Sliders with Olives

Prep time: 10 minutes | Cook time: 5 to 7 minutes | Makes 8 sliders

¼ pound (113 g) thinly sliced deli ham
¼ pound (113 g) thinly sliced pastrami
4 ounces (113 g) low-fat Mozzarella
cheese, grated
8 slider buns, split in half
Cooking spray
1 tablespoon sesame seeds

Olive Mix:
½ cup sliced green olives with pimentos
¼ cup sliced black olives
¼ cup chopped kalamata olives
1 teaspoon red wine vinegar
¼ teaspoon basil
⅛ teaspoon garlic powder

1. Insert the Crisper Basket and close the hood. Select BAKE, set the temperature to 360ºF (182ºC), and set the time to 7 minutes. Select START/STOP to begin preheating.
2. Combine all the ingredients for the olive mix in a small bowl and stir well.
3. Stir together the ham, pastrami, and cheese in a medium bowl and divide the mixture into 8 equal portions.
4. Assemble the sliders: Top each bottom bun with 1 portion of meat and cheese, 2 tablespoons of olive mix, finished by the remaining buns. Lightly spritz the tops with cooking spray. Scatter the sesame seeds on top.
5. Working in batches, arrange the sliders in the Crisper Basket. Close the hood and BAKE for 5 t0 7 minutes until the cheese melts.
6. Transfer to a large plate and repeat with the remaining sliders.
7. Serve immediately.

Herbed Pita Chips

Prep time: 5 minutes | Cook time: 5 to 6 minutes | Serves 4

¼ teaspoon dried basil
¼ teaspoon marjoram
¼ teaspoon ground oregano
¼ teaspoon garlic powder
¼ teaspoon ground thyme
¼ teaspoon salt
2 whole 6-inch pitas, whole grain or white
Cooking spray

1. Insert the Crisper Basket and close the hood. Select BAKE, set the temperature to 330ºF (166ºC), and set the time to 6 minutes. Select START/STOP to begin preheating.
2. Mix all the seasonings together.
3. Cut each pita half into 4 wedges. Break apart wedges at the fold.
4. Mist one side of pita wedges with oil. Sprinkle with half of seasoning mix.
5. Turn pita wedges over, mist the other side with oil, and sprinkle with remaining seasonings.
6. Place pita wedges in Crisper Basket. Close the hood and BAKE for 2 minutes.
7. Shake the basket and bake for 2 minutes longer. Shake again, and if needed, bake for 1 or 2 more minutes, or until crisp. Watch carefully because at this point they will cook very quickly.
8. Serve hot.

Cayenne Sesame Nut Mix

Prep time: 10 minutes | Cook time: 2 minutes | Makes 4 cups

1 tablespoon buttery spread, melted
2 teaspoons honey
¼ teaspoon cayenne pepper
2 teaspoons sesame seeds
¼ teaspoon kosher salt
¼ teaspoon freshly ground black pepper
1 cup cashews
1 cup almonds
1 cup mini pretzels
1 cup rice squares cereal
Cooking spray

1. Select BAKE, set the temperature to 360ºF (182ºC), and set the time to 2 minutes. Select START/STOP to begin preheating.

2. In a large bowl, combine the buttery spread, honey, cayenne pepper, sesame seeds, kosher salt, and black pepper, then add the cashews, almonds, pretzels, and rice squares, tossing to coat.
3. Spray a baking pan with cooking spray, then pour the mixture into the pan. Place the pan directly in the pot. Close the hood and BAKE for 2 minutes.
4. Remove the sesame mix from the grill and allow to cool in the pan on a wire rack for 5 minutes before serving.

Breaded Artichoke Hearts

Prep time: 5 minutes | Cook time: 8 minutes | Serves 14

14 whole artichoke hearts, packed in water
1 egg
½ cup all-purpose flour
$1/_3$ cup panko bread crumbs
1 teaspoon Italian seasoning
Cooking spray

1. Insert the Crisper Basket and close the hood. Select AIR CRISP, set the temperature to 380ºF (193ºC), and set the time to 8 minutes. Select START/STOP to begin preheating.
2. Squeeze excess water from the artichoke hearts and place them on paper towels to dry.
3. In a small bowl, beat the egg. In another small bowl, place the flour. In a third small bowl, combine the bread crumbs and Italian seasoning, and stir.
4. Spritz the Crisper Basket with cooking spray.
5. Dip the artichoke hearts in the flour, then the egg, and then the bread crumb mixture.
6. Place the breaded artichoke hearts in the Crisper Basket. Spray them with cooking spray.
7. Close the hood and AIR CRISP for 8 minutes, or until the artichoke hearts have browned and are crisp, flipping once halfway through.
8. Let cool for 5 minutes before serving.

Turkey Bacon-Wrapped Dates

Prep time: 10 minutes | Cook time: 5 to 7 minutes | Makes 16 appetizers

16 whole dates, pitted
16 whole almonds

6 to 8 strips turkey bacon, cut in half

Special Equipment:
16 toothpicks, soaked in water for at least 30 minutes

1. Insert the Crisper Basket and close the hood. Select AIR CRISP, set the temperature to 390°F (199°C), and set the time to 7 minutes. Select START/STOP to begin preheating.
2. On a flat work surface, stuff each pitted date with a whole almond.
3. Wrap half slice of bacon around each date and secure it with a toothpick.
4. Place the bacon-wrapped dates in the Crisper Basket. Close the hood and AIR CRISP for 5 to 7 minutes, or until the bacon is cooked to your desired crispiness.
5. Transfer the dates to a paper towel-lined plate to drain. Serve hot.

Cheesy Crab Toasts

Prep time: 10 minutes | Cook time: 5 minutes | Makes 15 to 18 toasts

1 (6-ounce / 170-g) can flaked crab meat, well drained
3 tablespoons light mayonnaise
¼ cup shredded Parmesan cheese
¼ cup shredded Cheddar cheese

1 teaspoon Worcestershire sauce
½ teaspoon lemon juice
1 loaf artisan bread, French bread, or baguette, cut into ⅜-inch-thick slices

1. Insert the Crisper Basket and close the hood. Select BAKE, set the temperature to 360°F (182°C), and set the time to 5 minutes. Select START/STOP to begin preheating.
2. In a large bowl, stir together all the ingredients except the bread slices.

3. On a clean work surface, lay the bread slices. Spread ½ tablespoon of crab mixture onto each slice of bread.
4. Arrange the bread slices in the Crisper Basket in a single layer. You'll need to work in batches to avoid overcrowding.
5. Close the hood and BAKE for 5 minutes until the tops are lightly browned.
6. Transfer to a plate and repeat with the remaining bread slices.
7. Serve warm.

Bruschetta with Tomato and Basil

Prep time: 5 minutes | Cook time: 6 minutes | Serves 6

4 tomatoes, diced
⅓ cup shredded fresh basil
¼ cup shredded Parmesan cheese
1 tablespoon balsamic vinegar
1 tablespoon minced garlic

1 teaspoon olive oil
1 teaspoon salt
1 teaspoon freshly ground black pepper
1 loaf French bread, cut into 1-inch-thick slices
Cooking spray

1. Insert the Crisper Basket and close the hood. Select BAKE, set the temperature to 250°F (121°C), and set the time to 3 minutes. Select START/STOP to begin preheating.
2. Mix together the tomatoes and basil in a medium bowl. Add the cheese, vinegar, garlic, olive oil, salt, and pepper and stir until well incorporated. Set aside.
3. Spritz the Crisper Basket with cooking spray. Working in batches, lay the bread slices in the basket in a single layer. Spray the slices with cooking spray.
4. Close the hood and BAKE for 3 minutes until golden brown.
5. Remove from the basket to a plate. Repeat with the remaining bread slices.
6. Top each slice with a generous spoonful of the tomato mixture and serve.

Zucchini and Potato Tots

Prep time: 5 minutes | Cook time: 20 minutes | Serves 4

1 large zucchini, grated
1 medium baked potato, skin removed and mashed
¼ cup shredded

Cheddar cheese
1 large egg, beaten
½ teaspoon kosher salt
Cooking spray

1. Select AIR CRISP, set the temperature to 390ºF (199ºC), and set the time to 10 minutes. Select START/STOP to begin preheating.
2. Wrap the grated zucchini in a paper towel and squeeze out any excess liquid, then combine the zucchini, baked potato, shredded Cheddar cheese, egg, and kosher salt in a large bowl.
3. Spray a baking pan with cooking spray, then place individual tablespoons of the zucchini mixture in the pan. Place the pan directly in the pot. Close the hood and AIR CRISP for 10 minutes. Repeat this process with the remaining mixture.
4. Remove the tots and allow to cool on a wire rack for 5 minutes before serving.

Cuban Sandwiches

Prep time: 20 minutes | Cook time: 8 minutes | Makes 4 sandwiches

8 slices ciabatta bread, about ¼-inch thick

Cooking spray
1 tablespoon brown mustard

Toppings:
6 to 8 ounces (170 to 227 g) thinly sliced leftover roast pork
4 ounces (113 g) thinly sliced deli turkey

⅓ cup bread and butter pickle slices
2 to 3 ounces (57 to 85 g) Pepper Jack cheese slices

1. Insert the Crisper Basket and close the hood. Select AIR CRISP, set the temperature to 390ºF (199ºC), and set the time to 8 minutes. Select START/STOP to begin preheating.
2. On a clean work surface, spray one side of each slice of bread with cooking spray. Spread the other side of each slice of bread evenly with brown mustard.
3. Top 4 of the bread slices with the roast pork, turkey, pickle slices, cheese, and finish with remaining bread slices. Transfer to the Crisper Basket.
4. Close the hood and AIR CRISP for 8 minutes until golden brown.
5. Cool for 5 minutes and serve warm.

Crispy Cod Fingers

Prep time: 5 minutes | Cook time: 12 minutes | Serves 4

2 eggs
2 tablespoons milk
2 cups flour
1 cup cornmeal
1 teaspoon seafood seasoning

Salt and black pepper, to taste
1 cup bread crumbs
1 pound (454 g) cod fillets, cut into 1-inch strips

1. Insert the Crisper Basket and close the hood. Select AIR CRISP, set the temperature to 400ºF (204ºC), and set the time to 12 minutes. Select START/STOP to begin preheating.
2. Beat the eggs with the milk in a shallow bowl. In another shallow bowl, combine the flour, cornmeal, seafood seasoning, salt, and pepper. On a plate, place the bread crumbs.
3. Dredge the cod strips, one at a time, in the flour mixture, then in the egg mixture, finally in the bread crumb to coat evenly.
4. Arrange the cod strips in the Crisper Basket. Close the hood and AIR CRISP for 12 minutes until crispy.
5. Transfer the cod strips to a paper towel-lined plate and serve warm.

Spicy Kale Chips

Prep time: 5 minutes | Cook time: 8 to 12 minutes | Serves 4

5 cups kale, large stems removed and chopped
2 teaspoons canola oil

¼ teaspoon smoked paprika
¼ teaspoon kosher salt
Cooking spray

1. Insert the Crisper Basket and close the hood. Select AIR CRISP, set the temperature to 390ºF (199ºC), and set the time to 6 minutes. Select START/STOP to begin preheating.
2. In a large bowl, toss the kale, canola oil, smoked paprika, and kosher salt.
3. Spray the Crisper Basket with cooking spray, then place half the kale in the basket. Close the hood and AIR CRISP for 2 to 3 minutes.
4. Shake the basket and AIR CRISP for 2 to 3 more minutes, or until crispy. Repeat this process with the remaining kale.
5. Remove the kale and allow to cool on a wire rack for 3 to 5 minutes before serving.

Rosemary Baked Cashews

Prep time: 5 minutes | Cook time: 3 minutes | Makes 2 cups

2 sprigs of fresh rosemary (1 chopped and 1 whole)
1 teaspoon olive oil
1 teaspoon kosher salt

½ teaspoon honey
2 cups roasted and unsalted whole cashews
Cooking spray

1. Insert the Crisper Basket and close the hood. Select BAKE, set the temperature to 300ºF (149ºC), and set the time to 3 minutes. Select START/STOP to begin preheating.
2. In a medium bowl, whisk together the chopped rosemary, olive oil, kosher salt, and honey. Set aside.
3. Spray the Crisper Basket with cooking spray, then place the cashews and the whole rosemary sprig in the basket. Close the hood and BAKE for 3 minutes.
4. Remove the cashews and rosemary from the grill, then discard the rosemary and add the cashews to the olive oil mixture, tossing to coat.
5. Allow to cool for 15 minutes before serving.

Roasted Mixed Nuts

Prep time: 5 minutes | Cook time: 20 minutes | Serves 6

2 cups mixed nuts (walnuts, pecans, and almonds)
2 tablespoons egg white
2 tablespoons sugar

1 teaspoon paprika
1 teaspoon ground cinnamon
Cooking spray

1. Spray the Crisper Basket with cooking spray.
2. Insert the Crisper Basket and close the hood. Select ROAST, set the temperature to 300ºF (149ºC), and set the time to 20 minutes. Select START/STOP to begin preheating.
3. Stir together the mixed nuts, egg white, sugar, paprika, and cinnamon in a small bowl until the nuts are fully coated.
4. Put the nuts in the Crisper Basket. Close the hood and ROAST for 20 minutes. Shake the basket halfway through the cooking time for even cooking.
5. Transfer the nuts to a bowl and serve warm.

Deluxe Cheese Sandwiches

Prep time: 10 minutes | Cook time: 5 to 6 minutes | Serves 4 to 8

8 ounces (227 g) Brie
8 slices oat nut bread
1 large ripe pear, cored and cut into ½-inch-

thick slices
2 tablespoons butter, melted

1. Select BAKE, set the temperature to 360ºF (182ºC), and set the time to 6 minutes. Select START/STOP to begin preheating. .
2. Make the sandwiches: Spread each of 4 slices of bread with ¼ of the Brie. Top the Brie with the pear slices and remaining 4 bread slices.
3. Brush the melted butter lightly on both sides of each sandwich.
4. Arrange the sandwiches in a baking pan. You may need to work in batches to avoid overcrowding.
5. Place the pan directly in the pot. Close the hood and BAKE for 5 to 6 minutes until the cheese is melted. Repeat with the remaining sandwiches.
6. Serve warm.

Homemade BBQ Chicken Pizza

Prep time: 5 minutes | Cook time: 8 minutes | Serves 1

1 piece naan bread
¼ cup Barbecue sauce
¼ cup shredded Monterrey Jack cheese
¼ cup shredded Mozzarella cheese

½ chicken herby sausage, sliced
2 tablespoons red onion, thinly sliced
Chopped cilantro or parsley, for garnish
Cooking spray

1. Insert the Crisper Basket and close the hood. Select AIR CRISP, set the temperature to 400ºF (204ºC), and set the time to 8 minutes. Select START/STOP to begin preheating.
2. Spritz the bottom of naan bread with cooking spray, then transfer to the Crisper Basket.
3. Brush with the Barbecue sauce. Top with the cheeses, sausage, and finish with the red onion.
4. Close the hood and AIR CRISP for 8 minutes until the cheese is melted.
5. Garnish with the chopped cilantro or parsley before slicing to serve.

Cajun Zucchini Chips

Prep time: 5 minutes | Cook time: 15 to 16 minutes | Serves 4

2 large zucchini, cut into ⅛-inch-thick slices
2 teaspoons Cajun seasoning

Cooking spray

1. Spray the Crisper Basket lightly with cooking spray.
2. Insert the Crisper Basket and close the hood. Select AIR CRISP, set the temperature to 370ºF (188ºC), and set the time to 16 minutes. Select START/STOP to begin preheating.
3. Put the zucchini slices in a medium bowl and spray them generously with cooking spray.
4. Sprinkle the Cajun seasoning over the zucchini and stir to make sure they are evenly coated with oil and seasoning.
5. Place the slices in a single layer in the Crisper Basket, making sure not to overcrowd. You will need to cook these in several batches.
6. Close the hood and AIR CRISP for 8 minutes. Flip the slices over and AIR CRISP for an additional 7 to 8 minutes, or until they are as crisp and brown as you prefer.
7. Serve immediately.

Caramelized Peaches

Prep time: 10 minutes | Cook time: 10 to 13 minutes | Serves 4

2 tablespoons sugar
¼ teaspoon ground cinnamon

4 peaches, cut into wedges
Cooking spray

1. Lightly spray the Crisper Basket with cooking spray.
2. Insert the Crisper Basket and close the hood. Select AIR CRISP, set the temperature to 350ºF (177ºC), and set the time to 13 minutes. Select START/STOP to begin preheating.
3. Toss the peaches with the sugar and cinnamon in a medium bowl until evenly coated.
4. Arrange the peaches in the Crisper Basket in a single layer. Lightly mist the peaches with cooking spray. You may need to work in batches to avoid overcrowding.
5. Close the hood and AIR CRISP for 5 minutes. Flip the peaches and AIR CRISP for another 5 to 8 minutes, or until the peaches are caramelized.
6. Repeat with the remaining peaches.
7. Let the peaches cool for 5 minutes and serve warm.

Mushroom and Spinach Calzones

Prep time: 15 minutes | Cook time: 26 to 27 minutes | Serves 4

2 tablespoons olive oil
1 onion, chopped
2 garlic cloves, minced
¼ cup chopped mushrooms
1 pound (454 g) spinach, chopped
1 tablespoon Italian seasoning

½ teaspoon oregano
Salt and black pepper, to taste
1½ cups marinara sauce
1 cup ricotta cheese, crumbled
1 (13-ounce / 369-g) pizza crust
Cooking spray

Make the Filling:
1. Heat the olive oil in a pan over medium heat until shimmering.
2. Add the onion, garlic, and mushrooms and sauté for 4 minutes, or until softened.
3. Stir in the spinach and sauté for 2 to 3 minutes, or until the spinach is wilted. Sprinkle with the Italian seasoning, oregano, salt, and pepper and mix well.
4. Add the marinara sauce and cook for about 5 minutes, stirring occasionally, or until the sauce is thickened.
5. Remove the pan from the heat and stir in the ricotta cheese. Set aside.

Make the Calzones:
1. Spritz the Crisper Basket with cooking spray.
2. Insert the Crisper Basket and close the hood. Select AIR CRISP, set the temperature to 375ºF (191ºC), and set the time to 15 minutes. Select START/STOP to begin preheating.
3. Roll the pizza crust out with a rolling pin on a lightly floured work surface, then cut it into 4 rectangles.
4. Spoon ¼ of the filling into each rectangle and fold in half. Crimp the edges with a fork to seal. Mist them with cooking spray.
5. Place the calzones in the Crisper Basket. Close the hood and AIR CRISP for 15 minutes, flipping once, or until the calzones are golden brown and crisp.
6. Transfer the calzones to a paper towel-lined plate and serve.

Chapter 5 Poultry

Lemony Chicken and Veggie Kebabs

Prep time: 15 minutes | Cook time: 14 minutes | Serves 4

2 tablespoons plain Greek yogurt
¼ cup extra-virgin olive oil
Juice of 4 lemons
Grated zest of 1 lemon
4 garlic cloves, minced
2 tablespoons dried oregano
1 teaspoon sea salt
½ teaspoon freshly ground black pepper
1 pound (454 g) boneless, skinless chicken breasts, cut into 2-inch cubes
1 red onion, quartered
1 zucchini, sliced

1. In a large bowl, whisk together the Greek yogurt, oil, lemon juice, zest, garlic, oregano, salt, and pepper until well combined.
2. Place the chicken and half of the marinade into a large resealable plastic bag or container. Move the chicken around to coat evenly. Refrigerate for at least 30 minutes.
3. Insert the Grill Grate and close the hood. Select GRILL, set the temperature to MEDIUM, and set the time to 14 minutes. Select START/STOP to begin preheating.
4. While the unit is preheating, assemble the kebabs by threading the chicken on the wood skewers, alternating with the red onion and zucchini. Ensure the ingredients are pushed almost completely down to the end of the skewers.
5. When the unit beeps to signify it has preheated, place the skewers on the Grill Grate. Close hood and GRILL for 10 to 14 minutes, occasionally basting the kebabs with the remaining marinade while cooking.
6. Cooking is complete when the internal temperature of the chicken reaches 165ºF (74ºC) on a food thermometer.

Spicy Chicken Kebabs

Prep time: 15 minutes | Cook time: 14 minutes | Serves 4

1 tablespoon ground cumin
1 tablespoon garlic powder
1 tablespoon chili powder
2 teaspoons paprika
¼ teaspoon sea salt
¼ teaspoon freshly ground black pepper
1 pound (454 g) boneless, skinless
chicken breasts, cut in 2-inch cubes
2 tablespoons extra-virgin olive oil, divided
2 red bell peppers, seeded and cut into 1-inch cubes
1 red onion, quartered
Juice of 1 lime

1. In a small mixing bowl, combine the cumin, garlic powder, chili powder, paprika, salt, and pepper, and mix well.
2. Place the chicken, 1 tablespoon oil, and half of the spice mixture into a large resealable plastic bag or container. Toss to coat evenly.
3. Place the bell pepper, onion, remaining 1 tablespoon of oil, and remaining spice mixture into a large resealable plastic bag or container. Toss to coat evenly. Refrigerate the chicken and vegetables for at least 30 minutes.
4. Insert the Grill Grate and close the hood. Select GRILL, set the temperature to HIGH, and set the time to 14 minutes. Select START/STOP to begin preheating.
5. While the unit is preheating, assemble the kebabs by threading the chicken onto the wood skewers, alternating with the peppers and onion. Ensure the ingredients are pushed almost completely down to the end of the skewers.
6. When the unit beeps to signify it has preheated, place the skewers on the Grill Grate. Close the hood and GRILL for 10 to 14 minutes.
7. Cooking is complete when the internal temperature of the chicken reaches 165ºF (74ºC). When cooking is complete, remove from the heat, and drizzle with lime juice.

Herbed Grilled Chicken Thighs

Prep time: 10 minutes | Cook time: 13 minutes | Serves 4

Grated zest of 2 lemons
Juice of 2 lemons
3 sprigs fresh rosemary, leaves finely chopped
3 sprigs fresh sage, leaves finely chopped
2 garlic cloves, minced
¼ teaspoon red pepper flakes
¼ cup canola oil
Sea salt
4 (4- to 7-ounce / 113- to 198-g) boneless chicken thighs

1. In a small bowl, whisk together the lemon zest and juice, rosemary, sage, garlic, red pepper flakes, and oil. Season with salt.
2. Place the chicken and lemon-herb mixture in a large resealable plastic bag or container. Toss to coat evenly. Refrigerate the chicken for at least 30 minutes.
3. Insert the Grill Grate and close the hood. Select GRILL, set the temperature to HIGH, and set the time to 13 minutes. Select START/STOP to begin preheating.
4. When the unit beeps to signify it has preheated, place the chicken on the Grill Grate. Close the hood and GRILL for 10 to 13 minutes.
5. Cooking is complete when the internal temperature of the chicken reaches at least 165ºF (74ºC) on a food thermometer.

Teriyaki Chicken and Bell Pepper Kebabs

Prep time: 15 minutes | Cook time: 14 minutes | Serves 4

1 pound (454 g) boneless, skinless chicken breasts, cut into 2-inch cubes
1 cup teriyaki sauce, divided
2 green bell peppers, seeded and cut into 1-inch cubes
2 cups fresh pineapple, cut into 1-inch cubes

1. Place the chicken and ½ cup of teriyaki sauce in a large resealable plastic bag or container. Toss to coat evenly. Refrigerate for at least 30 minutes.
2. Insert the Grill Grate and close the hood. Select GRILL, set the temperature to MEDIUM, and set the time to 14 minutes. Select START/STOP to begin preheating.
3. While the unit is preheating, assemble the kebabs by threading the chicken onto the wood skewers, alternating with the peppers and pineapple. Ensure the ingredients are pushed almost completely down to the end of the skewers.
4. When the unit beeps to signify it has preheated, place the skewers on the Grill Grate. Close the hood and GRILL for 10 to 14 minutes, occasionally basting the kebabs with the remaining ½ cup of teriyaki sauce while cooking.
5. Cooking is complete when the internal temperature of the chicken reaches 165ºF (74ºC) on a food thermometer.

Mayonnaise-Mustard Chicken

Prep time: 10 minutes | Cook time: 15 minutes | Serves 4

6 tablespoons mayonnaise
2 tablespoons coarse-ground mustard
2 teaspoons honey (optional)
2 teaspoons curry powder
1 teaspoon kosher salt
1 teaspoon cayenne pepper
1 pound (454 g) chicken tenders

1. Insert the Crisper Basket and close the hood. Select BAKE, set the temperature to 350ºF (177ºC), and set the time to 15 minutes. Select START/STOP to begin preheating.
2. In a large bowl, whisk together the mayonnaise, mustard, honey (if using), curry powder, salt, and cayenne. Transfer half of the mixture to a serving bowl to serve as a dipping sauce. Add the chicken tenders to the large bowl and toss until well coated.
3. Place the tenders in the Crisper Basket. Close the hood and BAKE for 15 minutes. Use a meat thermometer to ensure the chicken has reached an internal temperature of 165ºF (74ºC).
4. Serve the chicken with the dipping sauce.

Maple-Teriyaki Chicken Wings

Prep time: 5 minutes | Cook time: 14 minutes | Serves 4

1 cup maple syrup
1/3 cup soy sauce
1/4 cup teriyaki sauce
3 garlic cloves, minced
2 teaspoons garlic powder
2 teaspoons onion

powder
1 teaspoon freshly ground black pepper
2 pounds (907 g) bone-in chicken wings (drumettes and flats)

1. Insert the Grill Grate and close the hood. Select GRILL, set the temperature to MEDIUM, and set the time to 14 minutes. Select START/STOP to begin preheating.
2. Meanwhile, in a large bowl, whisk together the maple syrup, soy sauce, teriyaki sauce, garlic, garlic powder, onion powder, and black pepper. Add the wings, and use tongs to toss and coat.
3. When the unit has beeped to signify it has preheated, place the chicken wings on the Grill Grate. Close the hood and GRILL for 5 minutes. After 5 minutes, flip the wings, close the hood, and GRILL for an additional 5 minutes.
4. Check the wings for doneness. Cooking is complete when the internal temperature of the meat reaches at least 165ºF (74ºC) on a food thermometer. If needed, GRILL for up to 4 minutes more.
5. Remove from the grill and serve.

Spicy BBQ Chicken Drumsticks

Prep time: 10 minutes | Cook time: 20 minutes | Serves 4

2 cups barbecue sauce
Juice of 1 lime
2 tablespoons honey
1 tablespoon hot sauce

Sea salt, to taste
Freshly ground black pepper, to taste
1 pound (454 g) chicken drumsticks

1. In a large bowl, combine the barbecue sauce, lime juice, honey, and hot sauce. Season with salt and pepper. Set aside 1/2 cup of the sauce. Add the drumsticks to the bowl, and toss until evenly coated.

2. Insert the Grill Grate and close the hood. Select GRILL, set the temperature to MEDIUM, and set the time to 20 minutes. Select START/STOP to begin preheating.
3. When the unit beeps to signify it has preheated, place the drumsticks on the Grill Grate. Close the hood and GRILL for 18 minutes, basting often during cooking.
4. Cooking is complete when the internal temperature of the meat reaches at least 165ºF (74ºC) on a food thermometer. If necessary, close the hood and continue grilling for 2 minutes more.

Lime-Garlic Grilled Chicken

Prep time: 5 minutes | Cook time: 18 minutes | Serves 4

1½ tablespoons extra-virgin olive oil
3 garlic cloves, minced
1/4 teaspoon ground cumin
Sea salt, to taste

Freshly ground black pepper, to taste
Grated zest of 1 lime
Juice of 1 lime
4 boneless, skinless chicken breasts

1. In a large shallow bowl, stir together the oil, garlic, cumin, salt, pepper, zest, and lime juice. Add the chicken breasts and coat well. Cover and marinate in the refrigerator for 30 minutes.
2. Insert the Grill Grate and close the hood. Select GRILL, set the temperature to MEDIUM, and set the time to 18 minutes. Select START/STOP to begin preheating.
3. When the unit has beeped to signify it has preheated, place the chicken breasts on the Grill Grate. Close the hood and GRILL for 7 minutes. After 7 minutes, flip the chicken, close the hood, and GRILL for an additional 7 minutes.
4. Check the chicken for doneness. If needed, GRILL up to 4 minutes more. Cooking is complete when the internal temperature of the chicken reaches at least 165ºF (74ºC) on a food thermometer.
5. Remove from the grill, and place on a cutting board or platter to rest for 5inutes. Serve.

Lemon Parmesan Chicken

Prep time: 10 minutes | Cook time: 20 minutes | Serves 4

1 egg
2 tablespoons lemon juice
2 teaspoons minced garlic
½ teaspoon salt
½ teaspoon freshly ground black pepper
4 boneless, skinless chicken breasts, thin cut
Olive oil spray
½ cup whole-wheat bread crumbs
¼ cup grated Parmesan cheese

1. In a medium bowl, whisk together the egg, lemon juice, garlic, salt, and pepper. Add the chicken breasts, cover, and refrigerate for up to 1 hour.
2. In a shallow bowl, combine the bread crumbs and Parmesan cheese.
3. Spray the Crisper Basket lightly with olive oil spray.
4. Insert the Crisper Basket and close the hood. Select AIR CRISP, set the temperature to 360ºF (182ºC), and set the time to 20 minutes. Select START/STOP to begin preheating.
5. Remove the chicken breasts from the egg mixture, then dredge them in the bread crumb mixture, and place in the Crisper Basket in a single layer. Lightly spray the chicken breasts with olive oil spray. You may need to cook the chicken in batches.
6. Close the hood and AIR CRISP for 8 minutes. Flip the chicken over, lightly spray with olive oil spray, and AIR CRISP for an additional 7 to 12 minutes, until the chicken reaches an internal temperature of 165ºF (74ºC).
7. Serve warm.

Spiced Breaded Chicken Cutlets

Prep time: 5 minutes | Cook time: 11 minutes | Serves 2

½ pound (227 g) boneless, skinless chicken breasts, horizontally sliced in half, into cutlets
½ tablespoon extra-virgin olive oil
⅛ cup bread crumbs
¼ teaspoon sea salt
¼ teaspoon freshly ground black pepper
¼ teaspoon paprika
¼ teaspoon garlic powder
⅛ teaspoon onion powder

1. Insert the Crisper Basket and close the hood. Select AIR CRISP, set the temperature to 375ºF (191ºC), and set the time to 11 minutes. Select START/STOP to begin preheating.
2. Brush each side of the chicken cutlets with the oil.
3. Combine the bread crumbs, salt, pepper, paprika, garlic powder, and onion powder in a medium shallow bowl. Dredge the chicken cutlets in the bread crumb mixture, turning several times, to ensure the chicken is fully coated.
4. When the unit beeps to signify it has preheated, place the chicken in the basket. Close the hood and AIR CRISP for 9 minutes. Cooking is complete when the internal temperature of the meat reaches at least 165ºF (74ºC) on a food thermometer. If needed, AIR CRISP for up to 2 minutes more.
5. Remove the chicken cutlets and serve immediately.

Simple Whole Chicken Bake

Prep time: 10 minutes | Cook time: 1 hour | Serves 2 to 4

½ cup melted butter
3 tablespoons garlic, minced
Salt, to taste
1 teaspoon ground black pepper
1 (1-pound / 454-g) whole chicken

1. Select BAKE, set the temperature to 350ºF (177ºC), and set the time to 1 hour. Select START/STOP to begin preheating.
2. Combine the butter with garlic, salt, and ground black pepper in a small bowl.
3. Brush the butter mixture over the whole chicken, then place the chicken in a baking pan, skin side down.
4. Place the pan directly in the pot. Close the hood and BAKE for 1 hour, or until an instant-read thermometer inserted in the thickest part of the chicken registers at least 165ºF (74ºC). Flip the chicken halfway through.
5. Remove the chicken from the grill and allow to cool for 15 minutes before serving.

Sweet-and-Sour Drumsticks

Prep time: 5 minutes | Cook time: 23 to 25 minutes | Serves 4

6 chicken drumsticks	3 tablespoons honey
3 tablespoons lemon juice, divided	3 tablespoons brown sugar
3 tablespoons low-sodium soy sauce, divided	2 tablespoons ketchup
1 tablespoon peanut oil	¼ cup pineapple juice

1. Insert the Crisper Basket and close the hood. Select BAKE, set the temperature to 350ºF (177ºC), and set the time to 18 minutes. Select START/STOP to begin preheating.
2. Sprinkle the drumsticks with 1 tablespoon of lemon juice and 1 tablespoon of soy sauce. Place in the Crisper Basket and drizzle with the peanut oil. Toss to coat. Close the hood and BAKE for 18 minutes, or until the chicken is almost done.
3. Meanwhile, in a metal bowl, combine the remaining 2 tablespoons of lemon juice, the remaining 2 tablespoons of soy sauce, honey, brown sugar, ketchup, and pineapple juice.
4. Add the cooked chicken to the bowl and stir to coat the chicken well with the sauce.
5. Place the metal bowl in the basket. Bake for 5 to 7 minutes or until the chicken is glazed and registers 165ºF (74ºC) on a meat thermometer. Serve warm.

Dill Chicken Strips

Prep time: 15 minutes | Cook time: 10 minutes | Serves 4

2 whole boneless, skinless chicken breasts, halved lengthwise	1 tablespoon dried dill weed
1 cup Italian dressing	1 tablespoon garlic powder
3 cups finely crushed potato chips	1 large egg, beaten
	Cooking spray

1. In a large resealable bag, combine the chicken and Italian dressing. Seal the bag and refrigerate to marinate at least 1 hour.
2. In a shallow dish, stir together the potato chips, dill, and garlic powder. Place the beaten egg in a second shallow dish.
3. Remove the chicken from the marinade. Roll the chicken pieces in the egg and the potato chip mixture, coating thoroughly.
4. Select BAKE, set the temperature to 325ºF (163ºC), and set the time to 10 minutes. Select START/STOP to begin preheating.
5. Place the coated chicken in a baking pan and spritz with cooking spray.
6. Place the pan directly in the pot. Close the hood and BAKE for 5 minutes. Flip the chicken, spritz it with cooking spray, and bake for 5 minutes more until the outsides are crispy and the insides are no longer pink. Serve immediately.

Roasted Chicken Tenders with Veggies

Prep time: 10 minutes | Cook time: 18 to 20 minutes | Serves 4

1 pound (454 g) chicken tenders	bread crumbs
1 tablespoon honey	½ teaspoon dried thyme
Pinch salt	1 tablespoon olive oil
Freshly ground black pepper, to taste	2 carrots, sliced
½ cup soft fresh	12 small red potatoes

1. Insert the Crisper Basket and close the hood. Select ROAST, set the temperature to 380ºF (193ºC), and set the time to 20 minutes. Select START/STOP to begin preheating.
2. In a medium bowl, toss the chicken tenders with the honey, salt, and pepper.
3. In a shallow bowl, combine the bread crumbs, thyme, and olive oil, and mix.
4. Coat the tenders in the bread crumbs, pressing firmly onto the meat.
5. Place the carrots and potatoes in the Crisper Basket and top with the chicken tenders.
6. Close the hood and ROAST for 18 to 20 minutes, or until the chicken is cooked to 165ºF (74ºC) and the vegetables are tender, shaking the basket halfway during the cooking time.
7. Serve warm.

Potato Cheese Crusted Chicken

Prep time: 15 minutes | Cook time: 22 to 25 minutes | Serves 4

¼ cup buttermilk
1 large egg, beaten
1 cup instant potato flakes
¼ cup grated Parmesan cheese
1 teaspoon salt
½ teaspoon freshly

ground black pepper
2 whole boneless, skinless chicken breasts (about 1 pound / 454 g each), halved
Cooking spray

1. Insert the Crisper Basket and close the hood. Select BAKE, set the temperature to 325ºF (163ºC), and set the time to 25 minutes. Select START/STOP to begin preheating.
2. Line the Crisper Basket with parchment paper.
3. In a shallow bowl, whisk the buttermilk and egg until blended. In another shallow bowl, stir together the potato flakes, cheese, salt, and pepper.
4. One at a time, dip the chicken pieces in the buttermilk mixture and the potato flake mixture, coating thoroughly.
5. Place the coated chicken on the parchment and spritz with cooking spray.
6. Close the hood and BAKE for 15 minutes. Flip the chicken, spritz it with cooking spray, and bake for 7 to 10 minutes more until the outside is crispy and the inside is no longer pink. Serve immediately.

Blackened Chicken Breasts

Prep time: 10 minutes | Cook time: 20 minutes | Serves 4

1 large egg, beaten
¾ cup Blackened seasoning
2 whole boneless, skinless chicken

breasts (about 1 pound / 454 g each), halved
Cooking spray

1. Line the Crisper Basket with parchment paper.
2. Insert the Crisper Basket and close the hood. Select AIR CRISP, set the temperature to 360ºF (182ºC), and set the time to 20 minutes. Select START/STOP to begin preheating.
3. Place the beaten egg in one shallow bowl and the Blackened seasoning in another shallow bowl.
4. One at a time, dip the chicken pieces in the beaten egg and the Blackened seasoning, coating thoroughly.
5. Place the chicken pieces on the parchment and spritz with cooking spray.
6. Close the hood and AIR CRISP for 10 minutes. Flip the chicken, spritz it with cooking spray, and AIR CRISP for 10 minutes more until the internal temperature reaches 165ºF (74ºC) and the chicken is no longer pink inside.
7. Let sit for 5 minutes before serving.

Honey Rosemary Chicken

Prep time: 10 minutes | Cook time: 20 minutes | Serves 4

¼ cup balsamic vinegar
¼ cup honey
2 tablespoons olive oil
1 tablespoon dried rosemary leaves
1 teaspoon salt

½ teaspoon freshly ground black pepper
2 whole boneless, skinless chicken breasts (about 1 pound / 454 g each), halved
Cooking spray

1. In a large resealable bag, combine the vinegar, honey, olive oil, rosemary, salt, and pepper. Add the chicken pieces, seal the bag, and refrigerate to marinate for at least 2 hours.
2. Insert the Crisper Basket and close the hood. Select BAKE, set the temperature to 325ºF (163ºC), and set the time to 20 minutes. Select START/STOP to begin preheating.
3. Line the Crisper Basket with parchment paper.
4. Remove the chicken from the marinade and place it on the parchment. Spritz with cooking spray.
5. Close the hood and BAKE for 10 minutes. Flip the chicken, spritz it with cooking spray, and bake for 10 minutes more until the internal temperature reaches 165ºF (74ºC) and the chicken is no longer pink inside. Let sit for 5 minutes before serving.

Sriracha-Honey Glazed Chicken Thighs

Prep time: 5 minutes | Cook time: 17 minutes | Serves 4

1 cup sriracha
Juice of 2 lemons
¼ cup honey

4 bone-in chicken thighs

1. Place the sriracha, lemon juice, and honey in a large resealable plastic bag or container. Add the chicken thighs and toss to coat evenly. Refrigerate for 30 minutes.
2. Insert the Grill Grate and close the hood. Select GRILL, set the temperature to MEDIUM, and set the time to 14 minutes. Select START/STOP to begin preheating.
3. When the unit beeps to signify it has preheated, place the chicken thighs onto the Grill Grate, gently pressing them down to maximize grill marks. Close the hood and GRILL for 7 minutes.
4. After 7 minutes, flip the chicken thighs using tongs. Close the hood and GRILL for 7 minutes more.
5. Cooking is complete when the internal temperature of the meat reaches at least 165ºF (74ºC) on a food thermometer. If necessary, close the hood and continue grilling for 2 to 3 minutes more.
6. When cooking is complete, remove the chicken from the grill, and let it rest for 5 minutes before serving.

Roasted Cajun Turkey

Prep time: 10 minutes | Cook time: 30 minutes | Serves 4

2 pounds (907 g) turkey thighs, skinless and boneless
1 red onion, sliced
2 bell peppers, sliced
1 habanero pepper, minced
1 carrot, sliced

1 tablespoon Cajun seasoning mix
1 tablespoon fish sauce
2 cups chicken broth
Nonstick cooking spray

1. Select ROAST, set the temperature to 360ºF (182ºC), and set the time to 30 minutes. Select START/STOP to begin preheating.
2. Spritz the bottom and sides of the pot with nonstick cooking spray.
3. Arrange the turkey thighs in the pot. Add the onion, peppers, and carrot. Sprinkle with Cajun seasoning. Add the fish sauce and chicken broth.
4. Close the hood and ROAST for 30 minutes until cooked through. Serve warm.

Sweet and Spicy Turkey Meatballs

Prep time: 15 minutes | Cook time: 15 minutes | Serves 6

1 pound (454 g) lean ground turkey
½ cup whole-wheat panko bread crumbs
1 egg, beaten
1 tablespoon soy sauce
¼ cup plus 1 tablespoon hoisin

sauce, divided
2 teaspoons minced garlic
⅛ teaspoon salt
⅛ teaspoon freshly ground black pepper
1 teaspoon sriracha
Olive oil spray

1. Spray the Crisper Basket lightly with olive oil spray.
2. Insert the Crisper Basket and close the hood. Select AIR CRISP, set the temperature to 350ºF (177ºC), and set the time to 15 minutes. Select START/STOP to begin preheating.
3. In a large bowl, mix together the turkey, panko bread crumbs, egg, soy sauce, 1 tablespoon of hoisin sauce, garlic, salt, and black pepper.
4. Using a tablespoon, form the mixture into 24 meatballs.
5. In a small bowl, combine the remaining ¼ cup of hoisin sauce and sriracha to make a glaze and set aside.
6. Place the meatballs in the Crisper Basket in a single layer. You may need to cook them in batches.
7. Close the hood and AIR CRISP for 8 minutes. Brush the meatballs generously with the glaze and AIR CRISP until cooked through, an additional 4 to 7 minutes.
8. Serve warm.

Nutty Chicken Tenders

Prep time: 5 minutes | Cook time: 12 minutes | Serves 4

1 pound (454 g) chicken tenders	paprika
1 teaspoon kosher salt	¼ cup coarse mustard
1 teaspoon black pepper	2 tablespoons honey
½ teaspoon smoked	1 cup finely crushed pecans

1. Insert the Crisper Basket and close the hood. Select BAKE, set the temperature to 350ºF (177ºC), and set the time to 12 minutes. Select START/STOP to begin preheating.
2. Place the chicken in a large bowl. Sprinkle with the salt, pepper, and paprika. Toss until the chicken is coated with the spices. Add the mustard and honey and toss until the chicken is coated.
3. Place the pecans on a plate. Working with one piece of chicken at a time, roll the chicken in the pecans until both sides are coated. Lightly brush off any loose pecans. Place the chicken in the Crisper Basket.
4. Close the hood and BAKE for 12 minutes, or until the chicken is cooked through and the pecans are golden brown.
5. Serve warm.

Crispy Chicken Strips

Prep time: 15 minutes | Cook time: 20 minutes | Serves 4

1 tablespoon olive oil	½ teaspoon garlic powder
1 pound (454 g) boneless, skinless chicken tenderloins	½ cup whole-wheat seasoned bread crumbs
1 teaspoon salt	
½ teaspoon freshly ground black pepper	1 teaspoon dried parsley
½ teaspoon paprika	Cooking spray

1. Spray the Crisper Basket lightly with cooking spray.
2. Insert the Crisper Basket and close the hood. Select AIR CRISP, set the temperature to 370ºF (188ºC), and set

the time to 20 minutes. Select START/ STOP to begin preheating.
3. In a medium bowl, toss the chicken with the salt, pepper, paprika, and garlic powder until evenly coated.
4. Add the olive oil and toss to coat the chicken evenly.
5. In a separate, shallow bowl, mix together the bread crumbs and parsley.
6. Coat each piece of chicken evenly in the bread crumb mixture.
7. Place the chicken in the Crisper Basket in a single layer and spray it lightly with cooking spray. You may need to cook them in batches.
8. Close the hood and AIR CRISP for 10 minutes. Flip the chicken over, lightly spray it with cooking spray, and AIR CRISP for an additional 8 to 10 minutes, until golden brown. Serve.

Fried Buffalo Chicken Taquitos

Prep time: 15 minutes | Cook time: 5 to 10 minutes | Serves 6

8 ounces (227 g) fat-free cream cheese, softened	cooked chicken
	12 (7-inch) low-carb flour tortillas
⅛ cup Buffalo sauce	Olive oil spray
2 cups shredded	

1. Spray the Crisper Basket lightly with olive oil spray.
2. Insert the Crisper Basket and close the hood. Select AIR CRISP, set the temperature to 360ºF (182ºC), and set the time to 10 minutes. Select START/ STOP to begin preheating.
3. In a large bowl, mix together the cream cheese and Buffalo sauce until well combined. Add the chicken and stir until combined.
4. Place the tortillas on a clean workspace. Spoon 2 to 3 tablespoons of the chicken mixture in a thin line down the center of each tortilla. Roll up the tortillas.
5. Place the tortillas in the Crisper Basket, seam-side down. Spray each tortilla lightly with olive oil spray. You may need to cook the taquitos in batches.
6. Close the hood and AIR CRISP for 5 to 10 minutes until golden brown.
7. Serve hot.

Easy Asian Turkey Meatballs

Prep time: 10 minutes | Cook time: 11 to 14 minutes | Serves 4

2 tablespoons peanut oil, divided
1 small onion, minced
¼ cup water chestnuts, finely chopped
½ teaspoon ground ginger
2 tablespoons low-sodium soy sauce
¼ cup panko bread crumbs
1 egg, beaten
1 pound (454 g) ground turkey

1. Select AIR CRISP, set the temperature to 400ºF (204ºC), and set the time to 2 minutes. Select START/STOP to begin preheating.
2. In a round metal pan, combine 1 tablespoon of peanut oil and onion. Place the pan directly in the pot. Close the hood and AIR CRISP for 1 to 2 minutes or until crisp and tender. Transfer the onion to a medium bowl.
3. Add the water chestnuts, ground ginger, soy sauce, and bread crumbs to the onion and mix well. Add egg and stir well. Mix in the ground turkey until combined.
4. Form the mixture into 1-inch meatballs. Drizzle the remaining 1 tablespoon of oil over the meatballs. Arrange the meatballs in the pan.
5. Place the pan directly in the pot. Close the hood and BAKE for 10 to 12 minutes, or until they are 165ºF (74ºC) on a meat thermometer. Rest for 5 minutes before serving.

Spiced Turkey Tenderloin

Prep time: 20 minutes | Cook time: 30 minutes | Serves 4

½ teaspoon paprika
½ teaspoon garlic powder
½ teaspoon salt
½ teaspoon freshly ground black pepper
Pinch cayenne pepper
1½ pounds (680 g) turkey breast tenderloin
Olive oil spray

1. Spray the Crisper Basket lightly with olive oil spray.

2. Insert the Crisper Basket and close the hood. Select AIR CRISP, set the temperature to 370ºF (188ºC), and set the time to 30 minutes. Select START/STOP to begin preheating.
3. In a small bowl, combine the paprika, garlic powder, salt, black pepper, and cayenne pepper. Rub the mixture all over the turkey.
4. Place the turkey in the Crisper Basket and lightly spray with olive oil spray.
5. Close the hood and AIR CRISP for 15 minutes. Flip the turkey over and lightly spray with olive oil spray. AIR CRISP until the internal temperature reaches at least 170ºF (77ºC) for an additional 10 to 15 minutes.
6. Let the turkey rest for 10 minutes before slicing and serving.

Mini Turkey Meatloaves with Carrot

Prep time: 6 minutes | Cook time: 20 to 24 minutes | Serves 4

1/3 cup minced onion
¼ cup grated carrot
2 garlic cloves, minced
2 tablespoons ground almonds
2 teaspoons olive oil
1 teaspoon dried marjoram
1 egg white
¾ pound (340 g) ground turkey breast

1. Select BAKE, set the temperature to 400ºF (204ºC), and set the time to 24 minutes. Select START/STOP to begin preheating.
2. In a medium bowl, stir together the onion, carrot, garlic, almonds, olive oil, marjoram, and egg white.
3. Add the ground turkey. With your hands, gently but thoroughly mix until combined.
4. Double 16 foil muffin cup liners to make 8 cups. Divide the turkey mixture evenly among the liners. Transfer to the pot.
5. Close the hood and BAKE for 20 to 24 minutes, or until the meatloaves reach an internal temperature of 165ºF (74ºC) on a meat thermometer. Serve immediately.

Rosemary Turkey Scotch Eggs

Prep time: 15 minutes | Cook time: 12 minutes | Serves 4

1 egg
1 cup panko breadcrumbs
½ teaspoon rosemary
1 pound (454 g) ground turkey

4 hard-boiled eggs, peeled
Salt and ground black pepper, to taste
Cooking spray

1. Spritz the Crisper Basket with cooking spray.
2. Insert the Crisper Basket and close the hood. Select AIR CRISP, set the temperature to 400ºF (204ºC), and set the time to 12 minutes. Select START/STOP to begin preheating.
3. Whisk the egg with salt in a bowl. Combine the breadcrumbs with rosemary in a shallow dish.
4. Stir the ground turkey with salt and ground black pepper in a separate large bowl, then divide the ground turkey into four portions.
5. Wrap each hard-boiled egg with a portion of ground turkey. Dredge in the whisked egg, then roll over the breadcrumb mixture.
6. Place the wrapped eggs in the basket and spritz with cooking spray. Close the hood and AIR CRISP for 12 minutes or until golden brown and crunchy. Flip the eggs halfway through.
7. Serve immediately.

Turkey and Cauliflower Meatloaf

Prep time: 15 minutes | Cook time: 50 minutes | Serves 6

2 pounds (907 g) lean ground turkey
1⅓ cups riced cauliflower
2 large eggs, lightly beaten
¼ cup almond flour
⅔ cup chopped yellow or white onion
1 teaspoon ground dried turmeric

1 teaspoon ground cumin
1 teaspoon ground coriander
1 tablespoon minced garlic
1 teaspoon salt
1 teaspoon ground black pepper
Cooking spray

1. Select BAKE, set the temperature to 350ºF (177ºC), and set the time to 25 minutes. Select START/STOP to begin preheating.
2. Spritz a loaf pan with cooking spray.
3. Combine all the ingredients in a large bowl. Stir to mix well. Pour half of the mixture in the prepared loaf pan and press with a spatula to coat the bottom evenly. Spritz the mixture with cooking spray.
4. Place the pan directly in the pot. Close the hood and BAKE for 25 minutes, or until the meat is well browned and the internal temperature reaches at least 165ºF (74ºC). Repeat with remaining mixture.
5. Remove the loaf pan from the grill and serve immediately.

Strawberry-Glazed Turkey

Prep time: 15 minutes | Cook time: 37 minutes | Serves 2

2 pounds (907 g) turkey breast
1 tablespoon olive oil
Salt and ground black

pepper, to taste
1 cup fresh strawberries

1. Insert the Crisper Basket and close the hood. Select AIR CRISP, set the temperature to 375ºF (191ºC), and set the time to 37 minutes. Select START/STOP to begin preheating.
2. Rub the turkey bread with olive oil on a clean work surface, then sprinkle with salt and ground black pepper.
3. Transfer the turkey in the basket. Close the hood and AIR CRISP for 30 minutes or until the internal temperature of the turkey reaches at least 165ºF (74ºC). flip the turkey breast halfway through.
4. Meanwhile, put the strawberries in a food processor and pulse until smooth.
5. When the cooking of the turkey is complete, spread the puréed strawberries over the turkey. Close the hood and AIR CRISP for 7 more minutes.
6. Serve immediately.

Deep Fried Duck Leg Quarters

Prep time: 5 minutes | Cook time: 45 minutes | Serves 4

4 (½-pound / 227-g) skin-on duck leg quarters
2 medium garlic

cloves, minced
½ teaspoon salt
½ teaspoon ground black pepper

1. Spritz the Crisper Basket with cooking spray.
2. Insert the Crisper Basket and close the hood. Select AIR CRISP, set the temperature to 300ºF (149ºC), and set the time to 45 minutes. Select START/ STOP to begin preheating.
3. On a clean work surface, rub the duck leg quarters with garlic, salt, and black pepper.
4. Arrange the leg quarters in the basket and spritz with cooking spray.
5. Close the hood and AIR CRISP for 30 minutes, then flip the leg quarters and increase the temperature to 375ºF (191ºC). AIR CRISP for 15 more minutes or until well browned and crispy.
6. Remove the duck leg quarters from the grill and allow to cool for 10 minutes before serving.

Fried Chicken Piccata

Prep time: 5 minutes | Cook time: 22 minutes | Serves 2

2 large eggs
½ cup all-purpose flour
½ teaspoon freshly ground black pepper
2 boneless, skinless

chicken breasts
4 tablespoons unsalted butter
Juice of 1 lemon
1 tablespoon capers, drained

1. Insert the Crisper Basket and close the hood. Select AIR CRISP, set the temperature to 375ºF (191ºC), and set the time to 22 minutes. Select START/ STOP to begin preheating.
2. Meanwhile, in a medium shallow bowl, whisk the eggs until they are fully beaten.
3. In a separate medium shallow bowl, combine the flour and black pepper, using a fork to distribute the pepper evenly throughout.

4. Dredge the chicken in the flour to coat it completely, then dip it into the egg, then back in the flour.
5. When the unit beeps to signify it has preheated, place the chicken in the basket. Close the hood and AIR CRISP for 18 minutes.
6. While the chicken is cooking, melt the butter in a skillet over medium heat. Add the lemon juice and capers, and bring to a simmer. Reduce the heat to low, and simmer for 4 minutes.
7. After 18 minutes, check the chicken. Cooking is complete when the internal temperature of the meat reaches at least 165ºF (74ºC) on a food thermometer. If necessary, close the hood and continue cooking for up to 3 minutes more.
8. Plate the chicken, and drizzle the butter sauce over each serving.

Duck Breasts with Marmalade Balsamic Glaze

Prep time: 5 minutes | Cook time: 13 minutes | Serves 4

4 (6-ounce / 170-g) skin-on duck breasts
1 teaspoon salt
¼ cup orange marmalade

1 tablespoon white balsamic vinegar
¾ teaspoon ground black pepper

1. Insert the Crisper Basket and close the hood. Select AIR CRISP, set the temperature to 400ºF (204ºC), and set the time to 10 minutes. Select START/ STOP to begin preheating.
2. Cut 10 slits into the skin of the duck breasts, then sprinkle with salt on both sides.
3. Place the breasts in the basket, skin side up. Close the hood and AIR CRISP for 10 minutes.
4. Meanwhile, combine the remaining ingredients in a small bowl. Stir to mix well.
5. When the frying is complete, brush the duck skin with the marmalade mixture. Flip the breast and AIR CRISP for 3 more minutes or until the skin is crispy and the breast is well browned.
6. Serve immediately.

Hearty Turkey Burger

Prep time: 5 minutes | Cook time: 13 minutes | Serves 4

1 pound (454 g) ground turkey
½ red onion, minced
1 jalapeño pepper, seeded, stemmed, and minced
3 tablespoons bread crumbs
1½ teaspoons ground cumin
1 teaspoon paprika

½ teaspoon cayenne pepper
½ teaspoon sea salt
½ teaspoon freshly ground black pepper
4 burger buns, for serving
Lettuce, tomato, and cheese, if desired, for serving
Ketchup and mustard, if desired, for serving

1. Insert the Grill Grate and close the hood. Select GRILL, set the temperature to HIGH, and set the time to 13 minutes. Select START/STOP to begin preheating.
2. Meanwhile, in a large bowl, use your hands to combine the ground turkey, red onion, jalapeño pepper, bread crumbs, cumin, paprika, cayenne pepper, salt, and black pepper. Mix until just combined; be careful not to overwork the burger mixture.
3. Dampen your hands with cool water and form the turkey mixture into four patties.
4. When the unit beeps to signify it has preheated, place the burgers on the Grill Grate. Close the hood and GRILL for 11 minutes.
5. After 11 minutes, check the burgers for doneness. Cooking is complete when the internal temperature reaches at least 165ºF (74ºC) on a food thermometer. If necessary, close the hood and continue grilling for up to 2 minutes more.
6. Once the burgers are done cooking, place each patty on a bun. Top with your preferred fixings, such as lettuce, tomato, cheese, ketchup, and/or mustard.

Ginger Chicken Thighs

Prep time: 10 minutes | Cook time: 10 minutes | Serves 4

¼ cup julienned peeled fresh ginger
2 tablespoons vegetable oil
1 tablespoon honey
1 tablespoon soy sauce
1 tablespoon ketchup
1 teaspoon garam masala
1 teaspoon ground turmeric

¼ teaspoon kosher salt
½ teaspoon cayenne pepper
Vegetable oil spray
1 pound (454 g) boneless, skinless chicken thighs, cut crosswise into thirds
¼ cup chopped fresh cilantro, for garnish

1. In a small bowl, combine the ginger, oil, honey, soy sauce, ketchup, garam masala, turmeric, salt, and cayenne. Whisk until well combined. Place the chicken in a resealable plastic bag and pour the marinade over. Seal the bag and massage to cover all of the chicken with the marinade. Marinate at room temperature for 30 minutes or in the refrigerator for up to 24 hours.
2. Insert the Crisper Basket and close the hood. Select BAKE, set the temperature to 350ºF (177ºC), and set the time to 10 minutes. Select START/STOP to begin preheating.
3. Spray the Crisper Basket with vegetable oil spray and add the chicken and as much of the marinade and julienned ginger as possible.
4. Close the hood and BAKE for 10 minutes. Use a meat thermometer to ensure the chicken has reached an internal temperature of 165ºF (74ºC).
5. To serve, garnish with cilantro.

Orange and Honey Glazed Duck with Apples

Prep time: 5 minutes | Cook time: 15 minutes | Serves 2 to 3

1 pound (454 g) duck breasts (2 to 3 breasts)
Kosher salt and pepper, to taste
Juice and zest of 1 orange

¼ cup honey
2 sprigs thyme, plus more for garnish
2 firm tart apples, such as Fuji

1. Insert the Crisper Basket and close the hood. Select ROAST, set the temperature to 400ºF (204ºC), and set the time to 13 minutes. Select START/STOP to begin preheating.
2. Pat the duck breasts dry and, using a sharp knife, make 3 to 4 shallow, diagonal slashes in the skin. Turn the breasts and score the skin on the diagonal in the opposite direction to create a cross-hatch pattern. Season well with salt and pepper.
3. Place the duck breasts skin-side up in the Crisper Basket. Close the hood and ROAST for 8 minutes. Flip and roast for 4 more minutes on the second side.
4. While the duck is roasting, prepare the sauce. Combine the orange juice and zest, honey, and thyme in a small saucepan. Bring to a boil, stirring to dissolve the honey, then reduce the heat and simmer until thickened. Core the apples and cut into quarters. Cut each quarter into 3 or 4 slices depending on the size.
5. After the duck has cooked on both sides, turn it and brush the skin with the orange-honey glaze. Roast for 1 more minute. Remove the duck breasts to a cutting board and allow to rest.
6. Toss the apple slices with the remaining orange-honey sauce in a medium bowl. Arrange the apples in a single layer in the Crisper Basket. AIR CRISP for 10 minutes while the duck breast rests. Slice the duck breasts on the bias and divide them and the apples among 2 or 3 plates.
7. Serve warm, garnished with additional thyme.

Turkey Hoisin Burgers

Prep time: 10 minutes | Cook time: 20 minutes | Serves 4

1 pound (454 g) lean ground turkey
¼ cup whole-wheat bread crumbs
¼ cup hoisin sauce

2 tablespoons soy sauce
4 whole-wheat buns
Olive oil spray

1. In a large bowl, mix together the turkey, bread crumbs, hoisin sauce, and soy sauce.
2. Form the mixture into 4 equal patties. Cover with plastic wrap and refrigerate the patties for 30 minutes.
3. Spray the Crisper Basket lightly with olive oil spray.
4. Insert the Crisper Basket and close the hood. Select AIR CRISP, set the temperature to 370ºF (188ºC), and set the time to 20 minutes. Select START/STOP to begin preheating.
5. Place the patties in the Crisper Basket in a single layer. Spray the patties lightly with olive oil spray.
6. Close the hood and AIR CRISP for 10 minutes. Flip the patties over, lightly spray with olive oil spray, and AIR CRISP for an additional 5 to 10 minutes, until golden brown.
7. Place the patties on buns and top with your choice of low-calorie burger toppings like sliced tomatoes, onions, and cabbage slaw. Serve immediately.

Pecan-Crusted Turkey Cutlets

Prep time: 10 minutes | Cook time: 10 to 12 minutes | Serves 4

¾ cup panko bread crumbs
¼ teaspoon salt
¼ teaspoon pepper
¼ teaspoon dry mustard
¼ teaspoon poultry seasoning
½ cup pecans

¼ cup cornstarch
1 egg, beaten
1 pound (454 g) turkey cutlets, ½-inch thick
Salt and pepper, to taste
Cooking spray

1. Insert the Crisper Basket and close the hood. Select AIR CRISP, set the temperature to 360ºF (182ºC), and set the time to 12 minutes. Select START/STOP to begin preheating.
2. Place the panko crumbs, salt, pepper, mustard, and poultry seasoning in a food processor. Process until crumbs are finely crushed. Add pecans and process just until nuts are finely chopped.
3. Place cornstarch in a shallow dish and beaten egg in another. Transfer coating mixture from food processor into a third shallow dish.
4. Sprinkle turkey cutlets with salt and pepper to taste.
5. Dip cutlets in cornstarch and shake off excess, then dip in beaten egg and finally roll in crumbs, pressing to coat well. Spray both sides with cooking spray.
6. Place 2 cutlets in Crisper Basket in a single layer. Close the hood and AIR CRISP for 10 to 12 minutes. Repeat with the remaining cutlets.
7. Serve warm.

Crispy Dill Pickle Chicken Wings

Prep time: 5 minutes | Cook time: 26 minutes | Serves 4

2 pounds (907 g) bone-in chicken wings
(drumettes and flats)
1½ cups dill pickle juice
1½ tablespoons vegetable oil

½ tablespoon dried dill
¾ teaspoon garlic powder
Sea salt, to taste
Freshly ground black pepper, to taste

1. Place the chicken wings in a large shallow bowl. Pour the pickle juice over the top, ensuring all of the wings are coated and as submerged as possible. Cover and refrigerate for 2 hours.
2. Insert the Crisper Basket and close the hood. Select AIR CRISP, set the temperature to 390ºF (199ºC), and set the time to 26 minutes. Select START/STOP to begin preheating.
3. While the unit is preheating, rinse the brined chicken wings under cool water, then pat them dry with a paper towel. Place in a large bowl.
4. In a small bowl, whisk together the oil, dill, garlic powder, salt, and pepper. Drizzle over the wings and toss to fully coat them.
5. When the unit beeps to signify it has preheated, place the wings in the basket, spreading them out evenly. Close the hood and AIR CRISP for 11 minutes.
6. After 11 minutes, flip the wings with tongs. Close the hood and AIR CRISP for 11 minutes more.
7. Check the wings for doneness. Cooking is complete when the internal temperature of the chicken reaches at least 165ºF (74ºC) on a food thermometer. If needed, AIR CRISP for up to 4 more minutes.
8. Remove the wings from the basket and serve immediately.

Turkey Stuffed Bell Peppers

Prep time: 20 minutes | Cook time: 15 minutes | Serves 4

½ pound (227 g) lean ground turkey
4 medium bell peppers
1 (15-ounce / 425-g) can black beans, drained and rinsed
1 cup shredded reduced-fat Cheddar cheese
1 cup cooked long-grain brown rice
1 cup mild salsa

1¼ teaspoons chili powder
1 teaspoon salt
½ teaspoon ground cumin
½ teaspoon freshly ground black pepper
Olive oil spray
Chopped fresh cilantro, for garnish

1. Insert the Crisper Basket and close the hood. Select AIR CRISP, set the temperature to 360ºF (182ºC), and set the time to 15 minutes. Select START/STOP to begin preheating.
2. In a large skillet over medium-high heat, cook the turkey, breaking it up with a spoon, until browned, about 5 minutes. Drain off any excess fat.
3. Cut about ½ inch off the tops of the peppers and then cut in half lengthwise. Remove and discard the seeds and set the peppers aside.
4. In a large bowl, combine the browned turkey, black beans, Cheddar cheese, rice, salsa, chili powder, salt, cumin, and black pepper. Spoon the mixture into the bell peppers.
5. Lightly spray the Crisper Basket with olive oil spray.
6. Place the stuffed peppers in the Crisper Basket. Close the hood and AIR CRISP for 10 to 15 minutes until heated through.
7. Garnish with cilantro and serve.

Lettuce Chicken Tacos with Peanut Sauce

Prep time: 10 minutes | Cook time: 6 minutes | Serves 4

1 pound (454 g) ground chicken
2 cloves garlic, minced
¼ cup diced onions

¼ teaspoon sea salt
Cooking spray

Peanut Sauce:
¼ cup creamy peanut butter, at room temperature
2 tablespoons tamari
1½ teaspoons hot sauce

2 tablespoons lime juice
2 tablespoons grated fresh ginger
2 tablespoons chicken broth
2 teaspoons sugar

For Serving:
2 small heads butter lettuce, leaves separated

Lime slices (optional)

1. Select BAKE, set the temperature to 350ºF (177ºC), and set the time to 5 minutes. Select START/STOP to begin preheating.
2. Spritz a baking pan with cooking spray.
3. Combine the ground chicken, garlic, and onions in the baking pan, then sprinkle with salt. Use a fork to break the ground chicken and combine them well.
4. Place the pan directly in the pot. Close the hood and BAKE for 5 minutes, or until the chicken is lightly browned. Stir them halfway through the cooking time.
5. Meanwhile, combine the ingredients for the sauce in a small bowl. Stir to mix well.
6. Pour the sauce in the pan of chicken, then cook for 1 more minute or until heated through.
7. Unfold the lettuce leaves on a large serving plate, then divide the chicken mixture on the lettuce leaves. Drizzle with lime juice and serve immediately.

Lime Chicken with Cilantro

Prep time: 35 minutes | Cook time: 20 minutes | Serves 4

4 (4-ounce / 113-g) boneless, skinless chicken breasts
½ cup chopped fresh cilantro
Juice of 1 lime

Chicken seasoning or rub, to taste
Salt and ground black pepper, to taste
Cooking spray

1. Put the chicken breasts in the large bowl, then add the cilantro, lime juice, chicken seasoning, salt, and black pepper. Toss to coat well.
2. Wrap the bowl in plastic and refrigerate to marinate for at least 30 minutes.
3. Spritz the Crisper Basket with cooking spray.
4. Insert the Crisper Basket and close the hood. Select AIR CRISP, set the temperature to 400ºF (204ºC), and set the time to 10 minutes. Select START/STOP to begin preheating.
5. Remove the marinated chicken breasts from the bowl and place in the preheated grill. Spritz with cooking spray. You may need to work in batches to avoid overcrowding.
6. Close the hood and AIR CRISP for 10 minutes or until the internal temperature of the chicken reaches at least 165ºF (74ºC). Flip the breasts halfway through.
7. Serve immediately.

Glazed Duck with Cherry Sauce

Prep time: 20 minutes | Cook time: 32 minutes | Serves 12

1 whole duck (about 5 pounds / 2.3 kg in total), split in half, back and rib bones removed, fat trimmed

1 teaspoon olive oil
Salt and freshly ground black pepper, to taste

Cherry Sauce:
1 tablespoon butter
1 shallot, minced
½ cup sherry
1 cup chicken stock

1 teaspoon white wine vinegar
¾ cup cherry preserves
1 teaspoon fresh thyme leaves
Salt and freshly ground black pepper, to taste

1.
2. Insert the Crisper Basket and close the hood. Select AIR CRISP, set the temperature to 400ºF (204ºC), and set the time to 25 minutes. Select START/STOP to begin preheating.
3. On a clean work surface, rub the duck with olive oil, then sprinkle with salt and ground black pepper to season.
4. Place the duck in the basket, breast side up. Close the hood and AIR CRISP for 25 minutes or until well browned. Flip the duck during the last 10 minutes.
5. Meanwhile, make the cherry sauce: Heat the butter in a nonstick skillet over medium-high heat or until melted.
6. Add the shallot and sauté for 5 minutes or until lightly browned.
7. Add the sherry and simmer for 6 minutes or until it reduces in half.
8. Add the chicken stick, white wine vinegar, and cherry preserves. Stir to combine well. Simmer for 6 more minutes or until thickened.
9. Fold in the thyme leaves and sprinkle with salt and ground black pepper. Stir to mix well.
10. When cooking of the duck is complete, glaze the duck with a quarter of the cherry sauce, then AIR CRISP for another 4 minutes.
11. Flip the duck and glaze with another quarter of the cherry sauce. AIR CRISP for an additional 3 minutes.
12. Transfer the duck on a large plate and serve with remaining cherry sauce.

China Spicy Turkey Thighs

Prep time: 10 minutes | Cook time: 25 minutes | Serves 6

2 pounds (907 g) turkey thighs
1 teaspoon Chinese five-spice powder
¼ teaspoon Sichuan pepper
1 teaspoon pink Himalayan salt
1 tablespoon Chinese rice vinegar

1 tablespoon mustard
1 tablespoon chili sauce
2 tablespoons soy sauce
Cooking spray

1. Spritz the Crisper Basket with cooking spray.
2. Insert the Crisper Basket and close the hood. Select AIR CRISP, set the temperature to 360ºF (182ºC), and set the time to 22 minutes. Select START/STOP to begin preheating.
3. Rub the turkey thighs with five-spice powder, Sichuan pepper, and salt on a clean work surface.
4. Put the turkey thighs in the basket and spritz with cooking spray. You may need to work in batches to avoid overcrowding.
5. Close the hood and AIR CRISP for 22 minutes or until well browned. Flip the thighs at least three times during the cooking.
6. Meanwhile, heat the remaining ingredients in a saucepan over medium-high heat. Cook for 3 minutes or until the sauce is thickened and reduces to two thirds.
7. Transfer the thighs onto a plate and baste with sauce before serving.

Rosemary Turkey Breast

Prep time: 2 hours 20 minutes | Cook time: 30 minutes | Serves 6

½ teaspoon dried rosemary
2 minced garlic cloves
2 teaspoons salt
1 teaspoon ground black pepper
¼ cup olive oil

2½ pounds (1.1 kg) turkey breast
¼ cup pure maple syrup
1 tablespoon stone-ground brown mustard
1 tablespoon melted vegan butter

1. Combine the rosemary, garlic, salt, ground black pepper, and olive oil in a large bowl. Stir to mix well.
2. Dunk the turkey breast in the mixture and wrap the bowl in plastic. Refrigerate for 2 hours to marinate.
3. Remove the bowl from the refrigerator and let sit for half an hour before cooking.
4. Spritz the Crisper Basket with cooking spray.
5. Insert the Crisper Basket and close the hood. Select AIR CRISP, set the temperature to 400ºF (204ºC), and set the time to 30 minutes. Select START/STOP to begin preheating.
6. Remove the turkey from the marinade and place in the basket. Close the hood and AIR CRISP for 20 minutes or until well browned. Flip the breast halfway through.
7. Meanwhile, combine the remaining ingredients in a small bowl. Stir to mix well.
8. Pour half of the butter mixture over the turkey breast in the basket. Close the hood and AIR CRISP for 10 more minutes. Flip the breast and pour the remaining half of butter mixture over halfway through.
9. Transfer the turkey on a plate and slice to serve.

Chapter 6 Meats

Grilled Filet Mignon with Pineapple Salsa

Prep time: 15 minutes | Cook time: 8 minutes | Serves 4

4 (6- to 8-ounce / 170- to 227-g) filet mignon steaks
1 tablespoon canola oil, divided
Sea salt, to taste
Freshly ground black pepper, to taste
½ medium pineapple, cored and diced
1 medium red onion, diced
1 jalapeño pepper, seeded, stemmed, and diced
1 tablespoon freshly squeezed lime juice
¼ cup chopped fresh cilantro leaves
Chili powder
Ground coriander

1. Rub each filet on all sides with ½ tablespoon of the oil, then season with the salt and pepper.
2. Insert the Grill Grate and close the hood. Select GRILL, set temperature to HIGH, and set time to 8 minutes. Select START/STOP to begin preheating.
3. When the unit beeps to signify it has preheated, add the filets to the Grill Grate. Gently press the filets down to maximize grill marks, then close the hood.
4. After 4 minutes, open the hood and flip the filets. Close the hood and continue grilling for an additional 4 minutes, or until the filets' internal temperature reads 125ºF (52ºC) on a food thermometer. Remove the filets from the grill; they will continue to cook (called carry-over cooking) to a food-safe temperature even after you've removed them from the grill.
5. Let the filets rest for a total of 10 minutes; this allows the natural juices to redistribute into the steak.
6. While the filets rest, in a medium bowl, combine the pineapple, onion, and jalapeño. Stir in the lime juice and cilantro, then season to taste with the chili powder and coriander.
7. Plate the filets, and pile the salsa on top of each before serving.

Cheesy Jalapeño Popper Burgers

Prep time: 5 minutes | Cook time: 9 minutes | Serves 4

2 jalapeño peppers, seeded, stemmed, and minced
½ cup shredded Cheddar cheese
4 ounces (113 g) cream cheese, at room temperature
4 slices bacon, cooked and crumbled
2 pounds (907 g) ground beef
½ teaspoon chili powder
¼ teaspoon paprika
¼ teaspoon freshly ground black pepper
4 hamburger buns
4 slices pepper Jack cheese
Lettuce, sliced tomato, and sliced red onion, for topping (optional)

1. Insert the Grill Grate and close the hood. Select GRILL, set the temperature to HIGH, and set the time to 9 minutes. Select START/STOP to begin preheating.
2. In a medium bowl, combine the peppers, Cheddar cheese, cream cheese, and bacon until well combined.
3. Form the ground beef into 8¼-inch-thick patties. Spoon some of the filling mixture onto four of the patties, then place a second patty on top of each to make four burgers. Use your fingers to pinch the edges of the patties together to seal in the filling. Reshape the patties with your hands as needed.
4. Combine the chili powder, paprika, and pepper in a small bowl. Sprinkle the mixture onto both sides of the burgers.
5. When the units beeps to signify it has preheated, place the burgers on the Grill Grate. Close the hood and GRILL for 4 minutes without flipping. Cooking is complete when the internal temperature of the beef reaches at least 145ºF (63ºC) on a food thermometer. If needed, GRILL for up to 5 more minutes.
6. Place the burgers on the hamburger buns and top with pepper Jack cheese. Add lettuce, tomato, and red onion, if desired.

Korean BBQ Beef

Prep time: 5 minutes | Cook time: 5 minutes | Serves 4

⅓ cup soy sauce
2 tablespoons sesame oil
2½ tablespoons brown sugar
3 garlic cloves, minced
½ teaspoon freshly

ground black pepper
1 pound (454 g) rib eye steak, thinly sliced
2 scallions, thinly sliced, for garnish
Toasted sesame seeds, for garnish

1. In a small bowl, whisk together the soy sauce, sesame oil, brown sugar, garlic, and black pepper until fully combined.
2. Place the beef into a large shallow bowl, and pour the sauce over the slices. Cover and refrigerate for 1 hour.
3. Insert the Grill Grate and close the hood. Select GRILL, set the temperature to MEDIUM, and set the time to 5 minutes. Select START/STOP to begin preheating.
4. When the unit beeps to signify it has preheated, place the beef onto the Grill Grate. Close the hood and GRILL for 4 minutes without flipping.
5. After 4 minutes, check the steak for desired doneness, grilling for up to 1 minute more, if desired.
6. When cooking is complete, top with scallions and sesame seeds and serve immediately.

Spiced Flank Steak

Prep time: 10 minutes | Cook time: 8 minutes | Serves 2

1 tablespoon chili powder
1 teaspoon dried oregano
2 teaspoons ground cumin

1 teaspoon sea salt
¼ teaspoon freshly ground black pepper
2 (8-ounce / 227-g) flank steaks

1. Insert the Grill Grate and close the hood. Select GRILL, set the temperature to HIGH, and set the time to 8 minutes. Select START/STOP to begin preheating.
2. In a small bowl, mix together the chili powder, oregano, cumin, salt, and pepper. Use your hands to rub the spice mixture on all sides of the steaks.

3. When the unit beeps to signify it has preheated, place the steaks on the Grill Grate. Gently press the steaks down to maximize grill marks. Close the hood and GRILL for 4 minutes. After 4 minutes, flip the steaks, close the hood, and GRILL for 4 minutes more.
4. Remove the steaks from the grill, and transfer them to a cutting board. Let rest for 5 minutes before slicing and serving.

Asian-Flavored Steak Kebabs

Prep time: 5 minutes | Cook time: 12 minutes | Serves 4

¾ cup soy sauce
5 garlic cloves, minced
3 tablespoons sesame oil
½ cup canola oil
⅓ cup sugar
¼ teaspoon dried ground ginger
2 (10- to 12-ounce /

284- to 340-g) New York strip steaks, cut in 2-inch cubes
1 cup whole white mushrooms
1 red bell pepper, seeded, and cut into 2-inch cubes
1 red onion, cut into 2-inch wedges

1. In a medium bowl, whisk together the soy sauce, garlic, sesame oil, canola oil, sugar, and ginger until well combined. Add the steak and toss to coat. Cover and refrigerate for at least 30 minutes.
2. Insert the Grill Grate and close the hood. Select GRILL, set the temperature to MEDIUM, and set the time to 12 minutes. Select START/STOP to begin preheating.
3. While the unit is preheating, assemble the skewers in the following order: steak, mushroom, bell pepper, onion. Ensure the ingredients are pushed almost completely down to the end of the wood skewers.
4. When the unit beeps to signify it has preheated, place the skewers on the Grill Grate. Close the hood and GRILL for 8 minutes without flipping.
5. After 8 minutes, check the steak for desired doneness, grilling up to 4 minutes more if desired.
6. When cooking is complete, serve immediately.

Honey-Caramelized Pork Tenderloin

Prep time: 5 minutes | Cook time: 15 to 20 minutes | Serves 4

2 tablespoons honey
1 tablespoon soy sauce
½ teaspoon garlic powder
½ teaspoon sea salt
1 (1½-pound / 680-g) pork tenderloin

1. Insert the Grill Grate and close the hood. Select GRILL, set the temperature to MEDIUM, and set the time to 20 minutes. Select START/STOP to begin preheating.
2. Meanwhile, in a small bowl, combine the honey, soy sauce, garlic powder, and salt.
3. When the unit beeps to signify it has preheated, place the pork tenderloin on the Grill Grate. Baste all sides with the honey glaze. Close the hood and GRILL for 8 minutes. After 8 minutes, flip the pork tenderloin and baste with any remaining glaze. Close the hood and GRILL for 7 minutes more.
4. Cooking is complete when the internal temperature of the pork reaches 145ºF (63ºC) on a food thermometer. If needed, GRILL for up to 5 minutes more.
5. Remove the pork, and set it on a cutting board to rest for 5 minutes. Slice and serve.

Mozzarella Meatball Sandwiches with Basil

Prep time: 5 minutes | Cook time: 10 minutes | Serves 4

12 frozen meatballs
8 slices Mozzarella cheese
4 sub rolls, halved lengthwise
½ cup marinara sauce, warmed
12 fresh basil leaves

1. Insert the Crisper Basket and close the hood. Select AIR CRISP, set the temperature to 350ºF (177ºC), and set the time to 10 minutes. Select START/STOP to begin preheating.
2. When the unit beeps to signify it has preheated, place the meatballs in the basket. Close the hood and AIR CRISP for 5 minutes.

3. After 5 minutes, shake the basket of meatballs. Place the basket back in the unit and close the hood to resume cooking.
4. While the meatballs are cooking, place two slices of Mozzarella cheese on each sub roll. Use a spoon to spread the marinara sauce on top of the cheese slices. Press three leaves of basil into the sauce on each roll.
5. When cooking is complete, place three meatballs on each sub roll. Serve immediately.

Baby Back Ribs in Gochujang Marinade

Prep time: 10 minutes | Cook time: 22 minutes | Serves 4

¼ cup gochujang paste
¼ cup soy sauce
¼ cup freshly squeezed orange juice
2 tablespoons apple cider vinegar
2 tablespoons sesame oil
6 garlic cloves, minced
1½ tablespoons brown sugar
1 tablespoon grated fresh ginger
1 teaspoon salt
4 (8- to 10-ounce / 227- to 284-g) baby back ribs

1. In a medium bowl, add the gochujang paste, soy sauce, orange juice, vinegar, oil, garlic, sugar, ginger, and salt, and stir to combine.
2. Place the baby back ribs on a baking sheet and coat all sides with the sauce. Cover with aluminum foil and refrigerate for 6 hours.
3. Insert the Grill Grate and close the hood. Select GRILL, set the temperature to MEDIUM, and set the time to 22 minutes. Select START/STOP to begin preheating.
4. When the unit beeps to signify it has preheated, place the ribs on the Grill Grate. Close the hood and GRILL for 11 minutes. After 11 minutes, flip the ribs, close the hood, and GRILL for an additional 11 minutes.
5. When cooking is complete, serve immediately.

Classic Walliser Schnitzel

Prep time: 5 minutes | Cook time: 14 minutes | Serves 2

½ cup pork rinds
½ tablespoon fresh parsley
½ teaspoon fennel seed
½ teaspoon mustard
$\frac{1}{3}$ tablespoon cider vinegar

1 teaspoon garlic salt
$\frac{1}{3}$ teaspoon ground black pepper
2 eggs
2 pork schnitzel, halved
Cooking spray

1. Spritz the Crisper Basket with cooking spray.
2. Insert the Crisper Basket and close the hood. Select AIR CRISP, set the temperature to 350ºF (177ºC), and set the time to 14 minutes. Select START/ STOP to begin preheating.
3. Put the pork rinds, parsley, fennel seeds, and mustard in a food processor. Pour in the vinegar and sprinkle with salt and ground black pepper. Pulse until well combined and smooth.
4. Pour the pork rind mixture in a large bowl. Whisk the eggs in a separate bowl.
5. Dunk the pork schnitzel in the whisked eggs, then dunk in the pork rind mixture to coat well. Shake the excess off.
6. Arrange the schnitzel in the basket and spritz with cooking spray. Close the hood and AIR CRISP for 14 minutes or until golden and crispy. Flip the schnitzel halfway through.
7. Serve immediately.

Golden Wasabi Spam

Prep time: 5 minutes | Cook time: 12 minutes | Serves 3

$\frac{2}{3}$ cup all-purpose flour
2 large eggs
1½ tablespoons wasabi paste

2 cups panko breadcrumbs
6 ½-inch-thick spam slices
Cooking spray

1. Spritz the Crisper Basket with cooking spray.
2. Insert the Crisper Basket and close the hood. Select AIR CRISP, set the temperature to 400ºF (204ºC), and set

the time to 12 minutes. Select START/ STOP to begin preheating.
3. Pour the flour in a shallow plate. Whisk the eggs with wasabi in a large bowl. Pour the panko in a separate shallow plate.
4. Dredge the spam slices in the flour first, then dunk in the egg mixture, and then roll the spam over the panko to coat well. Shake the excess off.
5. Arrange the spam slices in a single layer in the basket and spritz with cooking spray.
6. Close the hood and AIR CRISP for 12 minutes or until the spam slices are golden and crispy. Flip the spam slices halfway through.
7. Serve immediately.

Crispy Pork Tenderloin

Prep time: 5 minutes | Cook time: 10 minutes | Serves 6

2 large egg whites
1½ tablespoons Dijon mustard
2 cups crushed pretzel crumbs

1½ pounds (680 g) pork tenderloin, cut into ¼-pound (113-g) sections
Cooking spray

1. Spritz the Crisper Basket with cooking spray.
2. Insert the Crisper Basket and close the hood. Select AIR CRISP, set the temperature to 350ºF (177ºC), and set the time to 10 minutes. Select START/ STOP to begin preheating.
3. Whisk the egg whites with Dijon mustard in a bowl until bubbly. Pour the pretzel crumbs in a separate bowl.
4. Dredge the pork tenderloin in the egg white mixture and press to coat. Shake the excess off and roll the tenderloin over the pretzel crumbs.
5. Arrange the well-coated pork tenderloin in batches in a single layer in the Crisper Basket and spritz with cooking spray.
6. Close the hood and AIR CRISP for 10 minutes or until the pork is golden brown and crispy. Flip the pork halfway through. Repeat with remaining pork sections.
7. Serve immediately.

Homemade Teriyaki Pork Ribs

Prep time: 5 minutes | Cook time: 30 minutes | Serves 4

¼ cup soy sauce
¼ cup honey
1 teaspoon garlic powder
1 teaspoon ground

dried ginger
4 (8-ounce / 227-g) boneless country-style pork ribs
Cooking spray

1. Spritz the Crisper Basket with cooking spray.
2. Insert the Crisper Basket and close the hood. Select AIR CRISP, set the temperature to 350ºF (177ºC), and set the time to 30 minutes. Select START/STOP to begin preheating.
3. Make the teriyaki sauce: combine the soy sauce, honey, garlic powder, and ginger in a bowl. Stir to mix well.
4. Brush the ribs with half of the teriyaki sauce, then arrange the ribs in the basket. Spritz with cooking spray. You may need to work in batches to avoid overcrowding.
5. Close the hood and AIR CRISP for 30 minutes or until the internal temperature of the ribs reaches at least 145ºF (63ºC). Brush the ribs with remaining teriyaki sauce and flip halfway through.
6. Serve immediately.

Lechon Kawali

Prep time: 10 minutes | Cook time: 30 minutes | Serves 4

1 pound (454 g) pork belly, cut into three thick chunks
6 garlic cloves
2 bay leaves
2 tablespoons soy sauce

1 teaspoon kosher salt
1 teaspoon ground black pepper
3 cups water
Cooking spray

1. Put all the ingredients in a pressure cooker, then put the lid on and cook on high for 15 minutes.
2. Natural release the pressure and release any remaining pressure, transfer the tender pork belly on a clean work surface. Allow to cool under room temperature until you can handle.

3. Generously spritz the Crisper Basket with cooking spray.
4. Insert the Crisper Basket and close the hood. Select AIR CRISP, set the temperature to 400ºF (204ºC), and set the time to 15 minutes. Select START/STOP to begin preheating.
5. Cut each chunk into two slices, then put the pork slices in the basket.
6. Close the hood and AIR CRISP for 15 minutes or until the pork fat is crispy. Spritz the pork with more cooking spray, if necessary.
7. Serve immediately.

Spicy Pork with Candy Onions

Prep time: 10 minutes | Cook time: 52 minutes | Serves 4

2 teaspoons sesame oil
1 teaspoon dried sage, crushed
1 teaspoon cayenne pepper
1 rosemary sprig, chopped
1 thyme sprig, chopped

Sea salt and ground black pepper, to taste
2 pounds (907 g) pork leg roast, scored
½ pound (227 g) candy onions, sliced
4 cloves garlic, finely chopped
2 chili peppers, minced

1. Select AIR CRISP, set the temperature to 400ºF (204ºC), and set the time to 52 minutes. Select START/STOP to begin preheating.
2. In a mixing bowl, combine the sesame oil, sage, cayenne pepper, rosemary, thyme, salt and black pepper until well mixed. In another bowl, place the pork leg and brush with the seasoning mixture.
3. Place the seasoned pork leg in a baking pan. Place the pan directly in the pot. Close the hood and AIR CRISP for 40 minutes, or until lightly browned, flipping halfway through. Add the candy onions, garlic and chili peppers to the pan and AIR CRISP for another 12 minutes.
4. Transfer the pork leg to a plate. Let cool for 5 minutes and slice. Spread the juices left in the pan over the pork and serve warm with the candy onions.

Citrus Carnitas

Prep time: 1 hour 10 minutes | Cook time: 25 minutes | Serves 6

2½ pounds (1.1 kg) boneless country-style pork ribs, cut into 2-inch pieces
3 tablespoons olive brine
1 tablespoon minced fresh oregano leaves
⅓ cup orange juice
1 teaspoon ground cumin
1 tablespoon minced garlic
1 teaspoon salt
1 teaspoon ground black pepper
Cooking spray

1. Combine all the ingredients in a large bowl. Toss to coat the pork ribs well. Wrap the bowl in plastic and refrigerate for at least an hour to marinate.
2. Spritz the Crisper Basket with cooking spray.
3. Insert the Crisper Basket and close the hood. Select AIR CRISP, set the temperature to 400°F (204°C), and set the time to 25 minutes. Select START/ STOP to begin preheating.
4. Arrange the marinated pork ribs in a single layer in the basket and spritz with cooking spray.
5. Close the hood and AIR CRISP for 25 minutes or until well browned. Flip the ribs halfway through.
6. Serve immediately.

Sausage Ratatouille

Prep time: 10 minutes | Cook time: 25 minutes | Serves 4

4 pork sausages

Ratatouille:

2 zucchinis, sliced
1 eggplant, sliced
15 ounces (425 g) tomatoes, sliced
1 red bell pepper, sliced
1 medium red onion, sliced
1 cup canned butter beans, drained
1 tablespoon balsamic vinegar
2 garlic cloves, minced
1 red chili, chopped
2 tablespoons fresh thyme, chopped
2 tablespoons olive oil

1. Insert the Crisper Basket and close the hood. Select AIR CRISP, set the temperature to 390°F (199°C), and set the time to 10 minutes. Select START/ STOP to begin preheating.
2. Place the sausages in the basket. Close the hood and AIR CRISP for 10 minutes or until the sausage is lightly browned. Flip the sausages halfway through.
3. Meanwhile, make the ratatouille: arrange the vegetable slices on the a baking pan alternatively, then add the remaining ingredients on top.
4. Transfer the sausage to a plate. Place the pan directly in the pot. Close the hood and BAKE for 15 minutes or until the vegetables are tender.
5. Serve the ratatouille with the sausage on top.

Pork Sausage with Cauliflower Mash

Prep time: 5 minutes | Cook time: 27 minutes | Serves 6

1 pound (454 g) cauliflower, chopped
6 pork sausages, chopped
½ onion, sliced
3 eggs, beaten
⅓ cup Colby cheese
1 teaspoon cumin powder
½ teaspoon tarragon
½ teaspoon sea salt
½ teaspoon ground black pepper
Cooking spray

1. Select BAKE, set the temperature to 365°F (185°C), and set the time to 27 minutes. Select START/STOP to begin preheating.
2. Spritz a baking pan with cooking spray.
3. In a saucepan over medium heat, boil the cauliflower until tender. Place the boiled cauliflower in a food processor and pulse until puréed. Transfer to a large bowl and combine with remaining ingredients until well blended.
4. Pour the cauliflower and sausage mixture into the baking pan. Place the pan directly in the pot. Close the hood and BAKE for 27 minutes, or until lightly browned.
5. Divide the mixture among six serving dishes and serve warm.

Lamb Ribs with Fresh Mint

Prep time: 5 minutes | Cook time: 18 minutes | Serves 4

2 tablespoons mustard
1 pound (454 g) lamb ribs
1 teaspoon rosemary, chopped
Salt and ground black pepper, to taste
¼ cup mint leaves, chopped
1 cup Greek yogurt

1. Insert the Crisper Basket and close the hood. Select AIR CRISP, set the temperature to 350ºF (177ºC), and set the time to 18 minutes. Select START/STOP to begin preheating.
2. Use a brush to apply the mustard to the lamb ribs, and season with rosemary, salt, and pepper. Transfer to the basket.
3. Close the hood and AIR CRISP for 18 minutes.
4. Meanwhile, combine the mint leaves and yogurt in a bowl.
5. Remove the lamb ribs from the grill when cooked and serve with the mint yogurt.

Fast Lamb Satay

Prep time: 5 minutes | Cook time: 8 minutes | Serves 2

¼ teaspoon cumin
1 teaspoon ginger
½ teaspoons nutmeg
Salt and ground black
pepper, to taste
2 boneless lamb steaks
Cooking spray

1. Combine the cumin, ginger, nutmeg, salt and pepper in a bowl.
2. Cube the lamb steaks and massage the spice mixture into each one.
3. Leave to marinate for 10 minutes, then transfer onto metal skewers.
4. Insert the Crisper Basket and close the hood. Select AIR CRISP, set the temperature to 400ºF (204ºC), and set the time to 8 minutes. Select START/STOP to begin preheating.
5. Place the skewers in the basket and spritz with cooking spray. Close the hood and AIR CRISP for 8 minutes.
6. Take care when removing them from the grill and serve.

Mushroom and Beef Meatloaf

Prep time: 10 minutes | Cook time: 25 minutes | Serves 4

1 pound (454 g) ground beef
1 egg, beaten
1 mushrooms, sliced
1 tablespoon thyme
1 small onion,
chopped
3 tablespoons bread crumbs
Ground black pepper, to taste

1. Select BAKE, set the temperature to 400ºF (204ºC), and set the time to 25 minutes. Select START/STOP to begin preheating.
2. Put all the ingredients into a large bowl and combine entirely.
3. Transfer the meatloaf mixture into the loaf pan. Place the pan directly in the pot.
4. Close the hood and BAKE for 25 minutes.
5. Slice up before serving.

Pepperoni and Bell Pepper Pockets

Prep time: 5 minutes | Cook time: 8 minutes | Serves 4

4 bread slices, 1-inch thick
Olive oil, for misting
24 slices pepperoni
1 ounce (28 g) roasted red peppers,
drained and patted dry
1 ounce (28 g) Pepper Jack cheese, cut into 4 slices

1. Insert the Crisper Basket and close the hood. Select AIR CRISP, set the temperature to 360ºF (182ºC), and set the time to 8 minutes. Select START/STOP to begin preheating.
2. Spray both sides of bread slices with olive oil.
3. Stand slices upright and cut a deep slit in the top to create a pocket (almost to the bottom crust, but not all the way through).
4. Stuff each bread pocket with 6 slices of pepperoni, a large strip of roasted red pepper, and a slice of cheese.
5. Put bread pockets in Crisper Basket, standing up. Close the hood and AIR CRISP for 8 minutes, until filling is heated through and bread is lightly browned.
6. Serve hot.

Spaghetti Squash Lasagna

Prep time: 5 minutes | Cook time: 1 hour 15 minutes | Serves 6

2 large spaghetti squash, cooked (about 2¾ pounds / 1.2 kg)
4 pounds (1.8 kg) ground beef
1 (2½-pound / 1.1-

kg) large jar Marinara sauce
25 slices Mozzarella cheese
30 ounces whole-milk ricotta cheese

1. Select BAKE, set the temperature to 375ºF (191ºC), and set the time to 45 minutes. Select START/STOP to begin preheating.
2. Slice the spaghetti squash and place it face down inside a baking pan. Fill with water until covered.
3. Place the pan directly in the pot. Close the hood and BAKE for 45 minutes until skin is soft.
4. Sear the ground beef in a skillet over medium-high heat for 5 minutes or until browned, then add the marinara sauce and heat until warm. Set aside.
5. Scrape the flesh off the cooked squash to resemble strands of spaghetti.
6. Layer the lasagna in a large greased pan in alternating layers of spaghetti squash, beef sauce, Mozzarella, ricotta. Repeat until all the ingredients have been used.
7. Place the pan directly in the pot. Close the hood and BAKE for 30 minutes.
8. Serve.

Rack of Lamb Chops with Rosemary

Prep time: 5 minutes | Cook time: 14 minutes | Serves 2

3 tablespoons extra-virgin olive oil
1 garlic clove, minced
1 tablespoon fresh rosemary, chopped

½ rack lamb (4 bones)
Sea salt, to taste
Freshly ground black pepper, to taste

1. Combine the oil, garlic, and rosemary in a large bowl. Season the rack of lamb with the salt and pepper, then place the lamb in the bowl, using tongs to turn and coat fully in the oil mixture. Cover and refrigerate for 2 hours.

2. Insert the Grill Grate and close the hood. Select GRILL, set the temperature to HIGH, and set the time to 14 minutes. Select START/STOP to begin preheating.
3. When the unit beeps to signify it has preheated, place the lamb on the Grill Grate. Close the hood and GRILL for 6 minutes. After 6 minutes, flip the lamb and continue grilling for 6 minutes more.
4. Cooking is complete when the internal temperature of the lamb reaches 145ºF (63ºC) on a food thermometer. If needed, GRILL for up to 2 minutes more.

Korean-Style Steak Tips

Prep time: 5 minutes | Cook time: 13 minutes | Serves 4

4 garlic cloves, minced
½ apple, peeled and grated
3 tablespoons sesame oil
3 tablespoons brown

sugar
⅓ cup soy sauce
1 teaspoon freshly ground black pepper
Sea salt
1½ pounds (680 g) beef tips

1. In a medium bowl, combine the garlic, apple, sesame oil, sugar, soy sauce, pepper, and salt until well mixed.
2. Place the beef tips in a large shallow bowl and pour the marinade over them. Cover and refrigerate for 30 minutes.
3. Insert the Grill Grate and close the hood. Select GRILL, set the temperature to MEDIUM, and set the time to 13 minutes. Select START/STOP to begin preheating.
4. When the unit beeps to signify it has preheated, place the steak tips on the Grill Grate. Close the hood and GRILL for 11 minutes.
5. Cooking is complete to medium doneness when the internal temperature of the meat reaches 145ºF (63ºC) on a food thermometer. If desired, GRILL for up to 2 minutes more.
6. Remove the steak, and set it on a cutting board to rest for 5 minutes. Serve.

Balsamic London Broil

Prep time: 15 minutes | Cook time: 25 minutes | Serves 8

2 pounds (907 g) London broil
3 large garlic cloves, minced
3 tablespoons balsamic vinegar
3 tablespoons whole-grain mustard
2 tablespoons olive oil
Sea salt and ground black pepper, to taste
½ teaspoons dried hot red pepper flakes

1. Wash and dry the London broil. Score its sides with a knife.
2. Mix the remaining ingredients. Rub this mixture into the broil, coating it well. Allow to marinate for a minimum of 3 hours.
3. Insert the Crisper Basket and close the hood. Select AIR CRISP, set the temperature to 400ºF (204ºC), and set the time to 25 minutes. Select START/ STOP to begin preheating.
4. Place the meat in the basket. Close the hood and AIR CRISP for 15 minutes. Turn it over and AIR CRISP for an additional 10 minutes before serving.

Pork Chops in Bourbon

Prep time: 5 minutes | Cook time: 35 minutes | Serves 4

2 cups ketchup
¾ cup bourbon
¼ cup apple cider vinegar
¼ cup soy sauce
1 cup packed brown sugar
3 tablespoons
Worcestershire sauce
½ tablespoon dry mustard powder
4 boneless pork chops
Sea salt, to taste
Freshly ground black pepper, to taste

1. In a medium saucepan over high heat, combine the ketchup, bourbon, vinegar, soy sauce, sugar, Worcestershire sauce, and mustard powder. Stir to combine and bring to a boil.
2. Reduce the heat to low and simmer, uncovered and stirring occasionally, for 20 minutes. The barbecue sauce will thicken while cooking. Once thickened, remove the pan from the heat and set aside.
3. While the barbecue sauce is cooking, insert the Grill Grate into the unit and close the hood. Select GRILL, set the temperature to MEDIUM, and set the time to 15 minutes. Select START/STOP to begin preheating.
4. When the unit beeps to signify it has preheated, place the pork chops on the Grill Grate. Close the hood, and GRILL for 8 minutes. After 8 minutes, flip the pork chops and baste the cooked side with the barbecue sauce. Close the hood, and GRILL for 5 minutes more.
5. Open the hood, and flip the pork chops again, basting both sides with the barbecue sauce. Close the hood, and GRILL for the final 2 minutes.
6. When cooking is complete, season with salt and pepper and serve immediately.

Swedish Beef Meatballs

Prep time: 10 minutes | Cook time: 12 minutes | Serves 8

1 pound (454 g) ground beef
1 egg, beaten
2 carrots, shredded
2 bread slices, crumbled
1 small onion, minced
½ teaspoons garlic salt
Pepper and salt, to taste
1 cup tomato sauce
2 cups pasta sauce

1. Insert the Crisper Basket and close the hood. Select AIR CRISP, set the temperature to 400ºF (204ºC), and set the time to 7 minutes. Select START/ STOP to begin preheating.
2. In a bowl, combine the ground beef, egg, carrots, crumbled bread, onion, garlic salt, pepper and salt.
3. Divide the mixture into equal amounts and shape each one into a small meatball.
4. Put them in the Crisper Basket. Close the hood and AIR CRISP for 7 minutes.
5. Transfer the meatballs to an oven-safe dish and top with the tomato sauce and pasta sauce.
6. Set the dish into the pot and allow to AIR CRISP at 320ºF (160ºC) for 5 more minutes. Serve hot.

Miso Marinated Steak

Prep time: 5 minutes | Cook time: 12 minutes | Serves 4

¾ pound (340 g) flank steak
1½ tablespoons sake
1 tablespoon brown miso paste
1 teaspoon honey
2 cloves garlic, pressed
1 tablespoon olive oil

1. Put all the ingredients in a Ziploc bag. Shake to cover the steak well with the seasonings and refrigerate for at least 1 hour.
2. Insert the Crisper Basket and close the hood. Select AIR CRISP, set the temperature to 400ºF (204ºC), and set the time to 12 minutes. Select START/STOP to begin preheating.
3. Coat all sides of the steak with cooking spray. Put the steak in the basket.
4. Close the hood and AIR CRISP for 12 minutes, turning the steak twice during the cooking time, then serve immediately.

Steak and Lettuce Salad

Prep time: 5 minutes | Cook time: 16 minutes | Serves 4 to 6

4 (8-ounce / 227-g) skirt steaks
Sea salt, to taste
Freshly ground black pepper, to taste
6 cups chopped romaine lettuce
¾ cup cherry
tomatoes, halved
¼ cup blue cheese, crumbled
1 cup croutons
2 avocados, peeled and sliced
1 cup blue cheese dressing

1. Insert the Grill Grate and close the hood. Select GRILL, set the temperature to HIGH, and set the time to 8 minutes. Select START/STOP to begin preheating.
2. Season the steaks on both sides with the salt and pepper.
3. When the unit beeps to signify it has preheated, place 2 steaks on the Grill Grate. Gently press the steaks down to maximize grill marks. Close the hood and GRILL for 4 minutes. After 4 minutes, flip the steaks, close the hood, and GRILL for an additional 4 minutes.

4. Remove the steaks from the grill and transfer to them a cutting board. Tent with aluminum foil.
5. Repeat step 3 with the remaining 2 steaks.
6. While the second set of steaks is cooking, assemble the salad by tossing together the lettuce, tomatoes, blue cheese crumbles, and croutons. Top with the avocado slices.
7. Once the second set of steaks has finished cooking, slice all four of the steaks into thin strips, and place on top of the salad. Drizzle with the blue cheese dressing and serve.

Vietnamese Pork Chops

Prep time: 15 minutes | Cook time: 12 minutes | Serves 2

1 tablespoon chopped shallot
1 tablespoon chopped garlic
1 tablespoon fish sauce
3 tablespoons lemongrass
1 teaspoon soy sauce
1 tablespoon brown sugar
1 tablespoon olive oil
1 teaspoon ground black pepper
2 pork chops

1. Combine shallot, garlic, fish sauce, lemongrass, soy sauce, brown sugar, olive oil, and pepper in a bowl. Stir to mix well.
2. Put the pork chops in the bowl. Toss to coat well. Place the bowl in the refrigerator to marinate for 2 hours.
3. Insert the Crisper Basket and close the hood. Select AIR CRISP, set the temperature to 400ºF (204ºC), and set the time to 12 minutes. Select START/STOP to begin preheating.
4. Remove the pork chops from the bowl and discard the marinade. Transfer the chops into the basket.
5. Close the hood and AIR CRISP for 12 minutes or until lightly browned. Flip the pork chops halfway through the cooking time.
6. Remove the pork chops from the basket and serve hot.

Cheesy Beef Meatballs

Prep time: 5 minutes | Cook time: 18 minutes | Serves 6

1 pound (454 g) ground beef	garlic
½ cup grated Parmesan cheese	½ cup Mozzarella cheese
1 tablespoon minced	1 teaspoon freshly ground pepper

1. Insert the Crisper Basket and close the hood. Select AIR CRISP, set the temperature to 400ºF (204ºC), and set the time to 18 minutes. Select START/STOP to begin preheating.
2. In a bowl, mix all the ingredients together.
3. Roll the meat mixture into 5 generous meatballs. Transfer to the basket.
4. Close the hood and AIR CRISP for 18 minutes.
5. Serve immediately.

Smoked Beef

Prep time: 10 minutes | Cook time: 45 minutes | Serves 8

2 pounds (907 g) roast beef, at room temperature	black pepper
	1 teaspoon smoked paprika
2 tablespoons extra-virgin olive oil	Few dashes of liquid smoke
1 teaspoon sea salt flakes	2 jalapeño peppers, thinly sliced
1 teaspoon ground	

1. Select ROAST, set the temperature to 330ºF (166ºC), and set the time to 45 minutes. Select START/STOP to begin preheating.
2. With kitchen towels, pat the beef dry.
3. Massage the extra-virgin olive oil, salt, black pepper, and paprika into the meat. Cover with liquid smoke.
4. Put the beef in the pot. Close the hood and ROAST for 30 minutes. Flip the roast over and allow to roast for another 15 minutes.
5. When cooked through, serve topped with sliced jalapeños.

Barbecue Pork Ribs

Prep time: 5 minutes | Cook time: 30 minutes | Serves 4

1 tablespoon barbecue dry rub	1 teaspoon sesame oil
1 teaspoon mustard	1 pound (454 g) pork ribs, chopped
1 tablespoon apple cider vinegar	

1. Combine the dry rub, mustard, apple cider vinegar, and sesame oil, then coat the ribs with this mixture. Refrigerate the ribs for 20 minutes.
2. Insert the Crisper Basket and close the hood. Select AIR CRISP, set the temperature to 360ºF (182ºC), and set the time to 30 minutes. Select START/STOP to begin preheating.
3. When the ribs are ready, place them in the basket. Close the hood and AIR CRISP for 15 minutes. Flip them and AIR CRISP on the other side for a further 15 minutes.
4. Serve immediately.

Easy Beef Schnitzel

Prep time: 5 minutes | Cook time: 12 minutes | Serves 1

½ cup friendly bread crumbs	Pepper and salt, to taste
2 tablespoons olive oil	1 egg, beaten
	1 thin beef schnitzel

1. Insert the Crisper Basket and close the hood. Select AIR CRISP, set the temperature to 350ºF (177ºC), and set the time to 12 minutes. Select START/STOP to begin preheating.
2. In a shallow dish, combine the bread crumbs, oil, pepper, and salt.
3. In a second shallow dish, place the beaten egg.
4. Dredge the schnitzel in the egg before rolling it in the bread crumbs.
5. Put the coated schnitzel in the Crisper Basket. Close the hood and AIR CRISP for 12 minutes. Flip the schnitzel halfway through.
6. Serve immediately.

Char Siew

Prep time: 10 minutes | Cook time: 20 minutes | Serves 4 to 6

1 strip of pork shoulder butt with a good amount of fat	marbling Olive oil, for brushing the pan

Marinade:

1 teaspoon sesame oil	1 teaspoon light soy sauce
4 tablespoons raw honey	1 tablespoon rose wine
1 teaspoon low-sodium dark soy sauce	2 tablespoons Hoisin sauce

1. Combine all the marinade ingredients together in a Ziploc bag. Put pork in bag, making sure all sections of pork strip are engulfed in the marinade. Chill for 3 to 24 hours.
2. Take out the strip 30 minutes before planning to roast.
3. Select ROAST, set the temperature to 350ºF (177ºC), and set the time to 20 minutes. Select START/STOP to begin preheating.
4. Put foil on the pot and brush with olive oil. Put marinated pork strip onto prepared pot.
5. Close the hood and ROAST for 20 minutes.
6. Glaze with marinade every 5 to 10 minutes.
7. Remove strip and leave to cool a few minutes before slicing.
8. Serve immediately.

Citrus Pork Loin Roast

Prep time: 10 minutes | Cook time: 45 minutes | Serves 8

1 tablespoon lime juice	1 teaspoon dried lemongrass
1 tablespoon orange marmalade	2 pound (907 g) boneless pork loin roast
1 teaspoon coarse brown mustard	Salt and ground black pepper, to taste
1 teaspoon curry powder	Cooking spray

1. Insert the Crisper Basket and close the hood. Select AIR CRISP, set the temperature to 360ºF (182ºC), and set the time to 45 minutes. Select START/STOP to begin preheating.
2. Mix the lime juice, marmalade, mustard, curry powder, and lemongrass.
3. Rub mixture all over the surface of the pork loin. Season with salt and pepper.
4. Spray the Crisper Basket with cooking spray and place pork roast diagonally in the basket.
5. Close the hood and AIR CRISP for 45 minutes, until the internal temperature reaches at least 145ºF (63ºC).
6. Wrap roast in foil and let rest for 10 minutes before slicing.
7. Serve immediately.

Tonkatsu

Prep time: 5 minutes | Cook time: 10 minutes per batch | Serves 4

$2/_3$ cup all-purpose flour	4 (4-ounce / 113-g) center-cut boneless pork loin chops
2 large egg whites	(about ½ inch thick)
1 cup panko breadcrumbs	Cooking spray

1. Spritz the Crisper Basket with cooking spray.
2. Insert the Crisper Basket and close the hood. Select AIR CRISP, set the temperature to 375ºF (191ºC), and set the time to 10 minutes. Select START/STOP to begin preheating.
3. Pour the flour in a bowl. Whisk the egg whites in a separate bowl. Spread the breadcrumbs on a large plate.
4. Dredge the pork loin chops in the flour first, press to coat well, then shake the excess off and dunk the chops in the eggs whites, and then roll the chops over the breadcrumbs. Shake the excess off.
5. Arrange the pork chops in batches in a single layer in the basket and spritz with cooking spray.
6. Close the hood and AIR CRISP for 10 minutes or until the pork chops are lightly browned and crunchy. Flip the chops halfway through. Repeat with remaining chops.
7. Serve immediately.

Teriyaki Pork and Mushroom Rolls

Prep time: 10 minutes | Cook time: 8 minutes | Serves 6

4 tablespoons brown sugar	2-inch ginger, chopped
4 tablespoons mirin	6 (4-ounce / 113-g) pork belly slices
4 tablespoons soy sauce	6 ounces (170 g) Enoki mushrooms
1 teaspoon almond flour	

1. Mix the brown sugar, mirin, soy sauce, almond flour, and ginger together until brown sugar dissolves.
2. Take pork belly slices and wrap around a bundle of mushrooms. Brush each roll with teriyaki sauce. Chill for half an hour.
3. Insert the Crisper Basket and close the hood. Select AIR CRISP, set the temperature to 350ºF (177ºC), and set the time to 8 minutes. Select START/STOP to begin preheating.
4. Add marinated pork rolls to the basket.
5. Close the hood and AIR CRISP for 8 minutes. Flip the rolls halfway through.
6. Serve immediately.

Beef and Vegetable Cubes

Prep time: 15 minutes | Cook time: 17 minutes | Serves 4

2 tablespoons olive oil	¼ teaspoon ground cumin
1 tablespoon apple cider vinegar	1 pound (454 g) top round steak, cut into cubes
1 teaspoon fine sea salt	4 ounces (113 g) broccoli, cut into florets
½ teaspoons ground black pepper	4 ounces (113 g) mushrooms, sliced
1 teaspoon shallot powder	1 teaspoon dried basil
¾ teaspoon smoked cayenne pepper	1 teaspoon celery seeds
½ teaspoons garlic powder	

1. Massage the olive oil, vinegar, salt, black pepper, shallot powder, cayenne pepper, garlic powder, and cumin into the cubed steak, ensuring to coat each piece evenly.

2. Allow to marinate for a minimum of 3 hours.
3. Insert the Crisper Basket and close the hood. Select AIR CRISP, set the temperature to 365ºF (185ºC), and set the time to 12 minutes. Select START/STOP to begin preheating.
4. Put the beef cubes in the Crisper Basket. Close the hood and AIR CRISP for 12 minutes.
5. When the steak is cooked through, place it in a bowl.
6. Wipe the grease from the basket and pour in the vegetables. Season them with basil and celery seeds.
7. Increase the temperature of the grill to 400ºF (204ºC) and AIR CRISP for 5 to 6 minutes. When the vegetables are hot, serve them with the steak.

Potato and Prosciutto Salad

Prep time: 10 minutes | Cook time: 7 minutes | Serves 8

Salad:

4 pounds (1.8 kg) potatoes, boiled and cubed	diced
	2 cups shredded Cheddar cheese
15 slices prosciutto,	

Dressing:

15 ounces (425 g) sour cream	1 teaspoon black pepper
2 tablespoons mayonnaise	1 teaspoon dried basil
1 teaspoon salt	

1. Select AIR CRISP, set the temperature to 350ºF (177ºC), and set the time to 7 minutes. Select START/STOP to begin preheating.
2. Put the potatoes, prosciutto, and Cheddar in a baking pan. Place the pan directly in the pot. Close the hood and AIR CRISP for 7 minutes.
3. In a separate bowl, mix the sour cream, mayonnaise, salt, pepper, and basil using a whisk.
4. Coat the salad with the dressing and serve.

Lamb Rack with Pistachio

Prep time: 10 minutes | Cook time: 20 minutes | Serves 2

½ cup finely chopped pistachios
1 teaspoon chopped fresh rosemary
3 tablespoons panko breadcrumbs
2 teaspoons chopped fresh oregano

1 tablespoon olive oil
Salt and freshly ground black pepper, to taste
1 lamb rack, bones fat trimmed and frenched
1 tablespoon Dijon mustard

1. Insert the Crisper Basket and close the hood. Select AIR CRISP, set the temperature to 380ºF (193ºC), and set the time to 12 minutes. Select START/STOP to begin preheating.
2. Put the pistachios, rosemary, breadcrumbs, oregano, olive oil, salt, and black pepper in a food processor. Pulse to combine until smooth.
3. Rub the lamb rack with salt and black pepper on a clean work surface, then place it in the basket.
4. Close the hood and AIR CRISP for 12 minutes or until lightly browned. Flip the lamb halfway through the cooking time.
5. Transfer the lamb to a plate and brush with Dijon mustard on the fat side, then sprinkle with the pistachios mixture over the lamb rack to coat well.
6. Put the lamb rack back to the basket. Close the hood and AIR CRISP for 8 more minutes or until the internal temperature of the rack reaches at least 145ºF (63ºC).
7. Remove the lamb rack from the grill with tongs and allow to cool for 5 minutes before sling to serve.

Apple-Glazed Pork

Prep time: 15 minutes | Cook time: 19 minutes | Serves 4

1 sliced apple
1 small onion, sliced
2 tablespoons apple cider vinegar, divided
½ teaspoon thyme
½ teaspoon rosemary

¼ teaspoon brown sugar
3 tablespoons olive oil, divided
¼ teaspoon smoked paprika
4 pork chops
Salt and ground black pepper, to taste

1. Select BAKE, set the temperature to 350ºF (177ºC), and set the time to 4 minutes. Select START/STOP to begin preheating.
2. Combine the apple slices, onion, 1 tablespoon of vinegar, thyme, rosemary, brown sugar, and 2 tablespoons of olive oil in a baking pan. Stir to mix well.
3. Place the pan directly in the pot. Close the hood and BAKE for 4 minutes.
4. Meanwhile, combine the remaining vinegar and olive oil, and paprika in a large bowl. Sprinkle with salt and ground black pepper. Stir to mix well. Dredge the pork in the mixture and toss to coat well.
5. Remove the baking pan from the grill and put in the pork. Place the pan directly in the pot. Close the hood and AIR CRISP for 10 minutes to lightly brown the pork. Flip the pork chops halfway through.
6. Remove the pork from the grill and baste with baked apple mixture on both sides. Put the pork back to the grill and AIR CRISP for an additional 5 minutes. Flip halfway through.
7. Serve immediately.

Bacon-Wrapped Sausage with Tomato Relish

Prep time: 1 hour 15 minutes | Cook time: 32 minutes | Serves 4

8 pork sausages

8 bacon strips

Relish:

8 large tomatoes, chopped
1 small onion, peeled
1 clove garlic, peeled
1 tablespoon white wine vinegar

3 tablespoons chopped parsley
1 teaspoon smoked paprika
2 tablespoons sugar
Salt and ground black pepper, to taste

1. Purée the tomatoes, onion, and garlic in a food processor until well mixed and smooth.
2. Pour the purée in a saucepan and drizzle with white wine vinegar. Sprinkle with salt and ground black pepper. Simmer over medium heat for 10 minutes.
3. Add the parsley, paprika, and sugar to the saucepan and cook for 10 more minutes or until it has a thick consistency. Keep stirring during the cooking. Refrigerate for an hour to chill.
4. Insert the Crisper Basket and close the hood. Select AIR CRISP, set the temperature to 350ºF (177ºC), and set the time to 12 minutes. Select START/STOP to begin preheating.
5. Wrap the sausage with bacon strips and secure with toothpicks, then place them in the basket.
6. Close the hood and AIR CRISP for 12 minutes or until the bacon is crispy and browned. Flip the bacon-wrapped sausage halfway through.
7. Transfer the bacon-wrapped sausage on a plate and baste with the relish or just serve with the relish alongside.

Simple Pork Meatballs with Red Chili

Prep time: 5 minutes | Cook time: 15 minutes | Serves 4

1 pound (454 g) ground pork
2 cloves garlic, finely minced
1 cup scallions, finely chopped
1½ tablespoons Worcestershire sauce
½ teaspoon freshly grated ginger root

1 teaspoon turmeric powder
1 tablespoon oyster sauce
1 small sliced red chili, for garnish
Cooking spray

1. Spritz the Crisper Basket with cooking spray.
2. Insert the Crisper Basket and close the hood. Select AIR CRISP, set the temperature to 350ºF (177ºC), and set the time to 15 minutes. Select START/STOP to begin preheating.
3. Combine all the ingredients, except for the red chili in a large bowl. Toss to mix well.
4. Shape the mixture into equally sized balls, then arrange them in the basket and spritz with cooking spray.
5. Close the hood and AIR CRISP for 15 minutes or until the balls are lightly browned. Flip the balls halfway through.
6. Serve the pork meatballs with red chili on top.

Smoky Paprika Pork and Vegetable Kabobs

Prep time: 25 minutes | Cook time: 15 minutes | Serves 4

1 pound (454 g) pork tenderloin, cubed
1 teaspoon smoked paprika
Salt and ground black pepper, to taste
1 green bell pepper, cut into chunks

1 zucchini, cut into chunks
1 red onion, sliced
1 tablespoon oregano
Cooking spray

Special Equipment:
Small bamboo skewers, soaked in water for 20 minutes to keep them from burning while cooking

1. Spritz the Crisper Basket with cooking spray.
2. Insert the Crisper Basket and close the hood. Select AIR CRISP, set the temperature to 350ºF (177ºC), and set the time to 15 minutes. Select START/STOP to begin preheating.
3. Add the pork to a bowl and season with the smoked paprika, salt and black pepper. Thread the seasoned pork cubes and vegetables alternately onto the soaked skewers.
4. Arrange the skewers in the prepared Crisper Basket and spray with cooking spray.
5. Close the hood and AIR CRISP for 15 minutes, or until the pork is well browned and the vegetables are tender, flipping once halfway through.
6. Transfer the skewers to the serving dishes and sprinkle with oregano. Serve hot.

Spicy Pork Chops with Carrots and Mushrooms

Prep time: 10 minutes | Cook time: 15 to 18 minutes | Serves 4

2 carrots, cut into sticks
1 cup mushrooms, sliced
2 garlic cloves, minced
2 tablespoons olive oil
1 pound (454 g) boneless pork chops

1 teaspoon dried oregano
1 teaspoon dried thyme
1 teaspoon cayenne pepper
Salt and ground black pepper, to taste
Cooking spray

1. Spritz the Crisper Basket with cooking spray.
2. Insert the Crisper Basket and close the hood. Select AIR CRISP, set the temperature to 360ºF (182ºC), and set the time to 18 minutes. Select START/STOP to begin preheating.
3. In a mixing bowl, toss together the carrots, mushrooms, garlic, olive oil and salt until well combined.
4. Add the pork chops to a different bowl and season with oregano, thyme, cayenne pepper, salt and black pepper.
5. Lower the vegetable mixture in the prepared Crisper Basket. Place the seasoned pork chops on top. Close the hood and AIR CRISP for 15 to 18 minutes, or until the pork is well browned and the vegetables are tender, flipping the pork and shaking the basket once halfway through.
6. Transfer the pork chops to the serving dishes and let cool for 5 minutes. Serve warm with vegetable on the side.

Chapter 7 Fish and Seafood

Miso-Glazed Cod with Bok Choy

Prep time: 5 minutes | Cook time: 17 minutes | Serves 4

4 (6-ounce / 170-g) cod fillets
¼ cup miso
3 tablespoons brown sugar
1 teaspoon sesame oil, divided
1 tablespoon white wine or mirin
2 tablespoons soy sauce
¼ teaspoon red pepper flakes
1 pound (454 g) baby bok choy, halved lengthwise

1. Place the cod, miso, brown sugar, ¾ teaspoon of sesame oil, and white wine in a large resealable plastic bag or container. Move the fillets around to coat evenly with the marinade. Refrigerate for 30 minutes.
2. Insert the Grill Grate and close the hood. Select GRILL, set the temperature to MAX, and set the time to 8 minutes. Select START/STOP to begin preheating.
3. When the unit beeps to signify it has preheated, place the fillets on the Grill Grate. Gently press them down to maximize grill marks. Close the hood and GRILL for 8 minutes. (There is no need to flip the fish during grilling.)
4. While the cod grills, in a small bowl, whisk together the remaining ¼ teaspoon of sesame oil, soy sauce, and red pepper flakes. Brush the bok choy halves with the soy sauce mixture on all sides.
5. Remove the cod from the grill and set aside on a cutting board to rest. Tent with aluminum foil to keep warm.
6. Close the hood of the grill. Select GRILL, set the temperature to MAX, and set the time to 9 minutes. Select START/STOP to begin preheating to grill the bok choy.
7. When the unit beeps to signify it has preheated, place the bok choy on the Grill Grate, cut-side down. Close the hood and GRILL for 9 minutes. (There is no need to flip the bok choy during grilling.)
8. Remove the bok choy from the grill, plate with the cod, and serve.

Lime-Honey Salmon with Mango Salsa

Prep time: 10 minutes | Cook time: 8 minutes | Serves 4

2 tablespoons unsalted butter, melted
⅓ cup honey
1 tablespoon soy sauce
Juice of 3 limes, divided
Grated zest of ½ lime
3 garlic cloves, minced and divided
4 (6-ounce / 170-g) skinless salmon fillets
1 mango, peeled and diced
1 avocado, peeled and diced
½ tomato, diced
½ red onion, diced
1 jalapeño pepper, seeded, stemmed, and diced
1 tablespoon extra-virgin olive oil
Sea salt, to taste
Freshly ground black pepper, to taste

1. Place the butter, honey, soy sauce, juice of 2 limes, lime zest, and 2 minced garlic cloves in a large resealable plastic bag or container. Add the salmon fillets and coat evenly with the marinade. Refrigerate for 30 minutes.
2. While the salmon is marinating, in a large bowl, combine the mango, avocado, tomato, onion, remaining minced garlic clove, jalapeño, remaining juice of 1 lime, oil, salt, and pepper. Cover and refrigerate.
3. Insert the Grill Grate and close the hood. Select GRILL, set the temperature to MAX, and set the time to 8 minutes. Select START/STOP to begin preheating.
4. When the unit beeps to signify it has preheated, place the fillets on the Grill Grate, gently pressing them down to maximize grill marks. Close the hood and GRILL for 6 minutes. (There is no need to flip the fish during grilling.)
5. After 6 minutes, check the fillets for doneness; the internal temperature should read at least 140ºF (60ºC) on a food thermometer. If necessary, close the hood and continue cooking up to 2 minutes more.
6. When cooking is complete, top the fillets with salsa and serve immediately.

Garlic Scallops

Prep time: 10 minutes | Cook time: 10 to 15 minutes | Serves 4

2 teaspoons olive oil	16 ounces (454 g)
1 packet dry zesty Italian dressing mix	small scallops, patted dry
1 teaspoon minced garlic	Cooking spray

1. Insert the Crisper Basket and close the hood. Select AIR CRISP, set the temperature to 400°F (204°C), and set the time to 15 minutes. Select START/STOP to begin preheating.
2. Spray the Crisper Basket lightly with cooking spray.
3. In a large zip-top plastic bag, combine the olive oil, Italian dressing mix, and garlic.
4. Add the scallops, seal the zip-top bag, and coat the scallops in the seasoning mixture.
5. Place the scallops in the Crisper Basket and lightly spray with cooking spray.
6. Close the hood and AIR CRISP for 5 minutes, shake the basket, and AIR CRISP for 5 to 10 more minutes, or until the scallops reach an internal temperature of 120°F (49°C).
7. Serve immediately.

Spanish Garlic Shrimp

Prep time: 10 minutes | Cook time: 10 to 15 minutes | Serves 4

2 teaspoons minced garlic	crushed red pepper
2 teaspoons lemon juice	12 ounces (340 g) medium shrimp, deveined, with tails on
2 teaspoons olive oil	
½ to 1 teaspoon	Cooking spray

1. In a medium bowl, mix together the garlic, lemon juice, olive oil, and crushed red pepper to make a marinade.
2. Add the shrimp and toss to coat in the marinade. Cover with plastic wrap and place the bowl in the refrigerator for 30 minutes.
3. Spray the Crisper Basket lightly with cooking spray.

4. Insert the Crisper Basket and close the hood. Select AIR CRISP, set the temperature to 400°F (204°C), and set the time to 15 minutes. Select START/STOP to begin preheating.
5. Place the shrimp in the Crisper Basket. Close the hood and AIR CRISP for 5 minutes. Shake the basket and AIR CRISP until the shrimp are cooked through and nicely browned, for an additional 5 to 10 minutes. Cool for 5 minutes before serving.

Lime-Chili Shrimp Bowl

Prep time: 10 minutes | Cook time: 10 to 15 minutes | Serves 4

2 teaspoons lime juice	peeled and deveined
1 teaspoon olive oil	2 cups cooked brown rice
1 teaspoon honey	1 (15-ounce / 425-g) can seasoned black beans, warmed
1 teaspoon minced garlic	
1 teaspoon chili powder	1 large avocado, chopped
Salt, to taste	1 cup sliced cherry tomatoes
12 ounces (340 g) medium shrimp,	Cooking spray

1. Insert the Crisper Basket and close the hood. Select AIR CRISP, set the temperature to 400°F (204°C), and set the time to 15 minutes. Select START/STOP to begin preheating.
2. Spray the Crisper Basket lightly with cooking spray.
3. In a medium bowl, mix together the lime juice, olive oil, honey, garlic, chili powder, and salt to make a marinade.
4. Add the shrimp and toss to coat evenly in the marinade.
5. Place the shrimp in the Crisper Basket. Close the hood and AIR CRISP for 5 minutes. Shake the basket and AIR CRISP until the shrimp are cooked through and starting to brown, an additional 5 to 10 minutes.
6. To assemble the bowls, spoon ¼ of the rice, black beans, avocado, and cherry tomatoes into each of four bowls. Top with the shrimp and serve.

Spicy Orange Shrimp

Prep time: 20 minutes | Cook time: 10 to 15 minutes | Serves 4

⅓ cup orange juice	cayenne pepper
3 teaspoons minced garlic	1 pound (454 g) medium shrimp,
1 teaspoon Old Bay seasoning	peeled and deveined, with tails off
¼ to ½ teaspoon	Cooking spray

1. In a medium bowl, combine the orange juice, garlic, Old Bay seasoning, and cayenne pepper.
2. Dry the shrimp with paper towels to remove excess water.
3. Add the shrimp to the marinade and stir to evenly coat. Cover with plastic wrap and place in the refrigerator for 30 minutes so the shrimp can soak up the marinade.
4. Insert the Crisper Basket and close the hood. Select AIR CRISP, set the temperature to 400ºF (204ºC), and set the time to 15 minutes. Select START/STOP to begin preheating.
5. Spray the Crisper Basket lightly with cooking spray.
6. Place the shrimp into the Crisper Basket. Close the hood and AIR CRISP for 5 minutes. Shake the basket and lightly spray with olive oil. AIR CRISP until the shrimp are opaque and crisp, 5 to 10 more minutes.
7. Serve immediately.

Green Curry Shrimp

Prep time: 15 minutes | Cook time: 5 minutes | Serves 4

1 to 2 tablespoons Thai green curry paste	fresh ginger
	1 clove garlic, minced
2 tablespoons coconut oil, melted	1 pound (454 g) jumbo raw shrimp, peeled and deveined
1 tablespoon half-and-half or coconut milk	¼ cup chopped fresh Thai basil or sweet basil
1 teaspoon fish sauce	¼ cup chopped fresh cilantro
1 teaspoon soy sauce	
1 teaspoon minced	

1. In a baking pan, combine the curry paste, coconut oil, half-and-half, fish sauce, soy sauce, ginger, and garlic. Whisk until well combined.
2. Add the shrimp and toss until well coated. Marinate at room temperature for 15 to 30 minutes.
3. Insert the Crisper Basket and close the hood. Select AIR CRISP, set the temperature to 400ºF (204ºC), and set the time to 5 minutes. Select START/STOP to begin preheating.
4. Place the pan directly in the pot. Close the hood and AIR CRISP for 5 minutes, stirring halfway through the cooking time.
5. Transfer the shrimp to a serving bowl or platter. Garnish with the basil and cilantro. Serve immediately.

Cajun-Style Fish Tacos

Prep time: 5 minutes | Cook time: 10 to 15 minutes | Serves 6

2 teaspoons avocado oil	1 (14-ounce / 397-g) package coleslaw mix
1 tablespoon Cajun seasoning	12 corn tortillas
4 tilapia fillets	2 limes, cut into wedges

1. Insert the Crisper Basket and close the hood. Select AIR CRISP, set the temperature to 380ºF (193ºC), and set the time to 15 minutes. Select START/STOP to begin preheating.
2. Line the Crisper Basket with parchment paper.
3. In a medium, shallow bowl, mix the avocado oil and the Cajun seasoning to make a marinade. Add the tilapia fillets and coat evenly.
4. Place the fillets in the basket in a single layer, leaving room between each fillet. You may need to cook in batches.
5. Close the hood and AIR CRISP for 10 to 15 minutes until the fish is cooked and easily flakes with a fork.
6. Assemble the tacos by placing some of the coleslaw mix in each tortilla. Add ⅓ of a tilapia fillet to each tortilla. Squeeze some lime juice over the top of each taco and serve.

Blackened Shrimp Tacos

Prep time: 10 minutes | Cook time: 10 to 15 minutes | Serves 4

12 ounces (340 g) medium shrimp, deveined, with tails off
1 teaspoon olive oil
1 to 2 teaspoons Blackened seasoning
8 corn tortillas, warmed
1 (14-ounce / 397-g) bag coleslaw mix
2 limes, cut in half
Cooking spray

1. Insert the Crisper Basket and close the hood. Select AIR CRISP, set the temperature to 400ºF (204ºC), and set the time to 15 minutes. Select START/STOP to begin preheating.
2. Spray the Crisper Basket lightly with cooking spray.
3. Dry the shrimp with a paper towel to remove excess water.
4. In a medium bowl, toss the shrimp with olive oil and Blackened seasoning.
5. Place the shrimp in the Crisper Basket. Close the hood and AIR CRISP for 5 minutes. Shake the basket, lightly spray with cooking spray, and cook until the shrimp are cooked through and starting to brown, 5 to 10 more minutes.
6. Fill each tortilla with the coleslaw mix and top with the blackened shrimp. Squeeze fresh lime juice over top and serve.

Crispy Catfish Strips

Prep time: 5 minutes | Cook time: 16 to 18 minutes | Serves 4

1 cup buttermilk
5 catfish fillets, cut into 1½-inch strips
Cooking spray
1 cup cornmeal
1 tablespoon Creole, Cajun, or Old Bay seasoning

1. Pour the buttermilk into a shallow baking pan. Place the catfish in the dish and refrigerate for at least 1 hour to help remove any fishy taste.
2. Insert the Crisper Basket and close the hood. Select AIR CRISP, set the temperature to 400ºF (204ºC), and set the time to 18 minutes. Select START/STOP to begin preheating.
3. Spray the Crisper Basket lightly with cooking spray.
4. In a shallow bowl, combine cornmeal and Creole seasoning.
5. Shake any excess buttermilk off the catfish. Place each strip in the cornmeal mixture and coat completely. Press the cornmeal into the catfish gently to help it stick.
6. Place the strips in the Crisper Basket in a single layer. Lightly spray the catfish with cooking spray. You may need to cook the catfish in more than one batch.
7. Close the hood and AIR CRISP for 8 minutes. Turn the catfish strips over and lightly spray with cooking spray. AIR CRISP until golden brown and crispy, for 8 to 10 more minutes.
8. Serve warm.

Goat Cheese Shrimp

Prep time: 15 minutes | Cook time: 7 to 8 minutes | Serves 2

1 pound (454 g) shrimp, deveined
1½ tablespoons olive oil
1½ tablespoons balsamic vinegar
1 tablespoon coconut aminos
½ tablespoon fresh parsley, roughly chopped
Sea salt flakes, to
taste
1 teaspoon Dijon mustard
½ teaspoon smoked cayenne pepper
½ teaspoon garlic powder
Salt and ground black peppercorns, to taste
1 cup shredded goat cheese

1. Insert the Crisper Basket and close the hood. Select AIR CRISP, set the temperature to 385ºF (196ºC), and set the time to 8 minutes. Select START/STOP to begin preheating.
2. Except for the cheese, stir together all the ingredients in a large bowl until the shrimp are evenly coated.
3. Arrange the shrimp in the Crisper Basket. Close the hood and AIR CRISP for 7 to 8 minutes, shaking the basket halfway through, or until the shrimp are pink and cooked through.
4. Serve the shrimp with the shredded goat cheese sprinkled on top.

Roasted Cod with Sesame Seeds

Prep time: 5 minutes | Cook time: 7 to 9 minutes | Makes 1 fillet

1 tablespoon reduced-sodium soy sauce
2 teaspoons honey
Cooking spray

6 ounces (170 g) fresh cod fillet
1 teaspoon sesame seeds

1. Insert the Crisper Basket and close the hood. Select ROAST, set the temperature to 360ºF (182ºC), and set the time to 10 minutes. Select START/STOP to begin preheating.
2. In a small bowl, combine the soy sauce and honey.
3. Spray the Crisper Basket with cooking spray, then place the cod in the basket, brush with the soy mixture, and sprinkle sesame seeds on top.
4. Close the hood and ROAST for 7 to 9 minutes, or until opaque.
5. Remove the fish and allow to cool on a wire rack for 5 minutes before serving.

Cajun-Style Salmon Burgers

Prep time: 10 minutes | Cook time: 10 to 15 minutes | Serves 4

4 (5-ounce / 142-g) cans pink salmon in water, any skin and bones removed, drained
2 eggs, beaten
1 cup whole-wheat bread crumbs

4 tablespoons light mayonnaise
2 teaspoons Cajun seasoning
2 teaspoons dry mustard
4 whole-wheat buns
Cooking spray

1. In a medium bowl, mix the salmon, egg, bread crumbs, mayonnaise, Cajun seasoning, and dry mustard. Cover with plastic wrap and refrigerate for 30 minutes.
2. Insert the Crisper Basket and close the hood. Select AIR CRISP, set the temperature to 360ºF (182ºC), and set the time to 15 minutes. Select START/STOP to begin preheating.
3. Spray the Crisper Basket lightly with cooking spray.
4. Shape the mixture into four ½-inch-thick patties about the same size as the buns.
5. Place the salmon patties in the Crisper Basket in a single layer and lightly spray the tops with cooking spray. You may need to cook them in batches.
6. Close the hood and AIR CRISP for 6 to 8 minutes. Turn the patties over and lightly spray with cooking spray. AIR CRISP until crispy on the outside, for 4 to 7 more minutes.
7. Serve on whole-wheat buns.

Air-Fried Scallops

Prep time: 10 minutes | Cook time: 12 minutes | Serves 2

⅓ cup shallots, chopped
1½ tablespoons olive oil
1½ tablespoons coconut aminos
1 tablespoon Mediterranean seasoning mix
½ tablespoon

balsamic vinegar
½ teaspoon ginger, grated
1 clove garlic, chopped
1 pound (454 g) scallops, cleaned
Cooking spray
Belgian endive, for garnish

1. Place all the ingredients except the scallops and Belgian endive in a small skillet over medium heat and stir to combine. Let this mixture simmer for about 2 minutes.
2. Remove the mixture from the skillet to a large bowl and set aside to cool.
3. Add the scallops, coating them all over, then transfer to the refrigerator to marinate for at least 2 hours.
4. Insert the Crisper Basket and close the hood. Select AIR CRISP, set the temperature to 345ºF (174ºC), and set the time to 10 minutes. Select START/STOP to begin preheating.
5. Arrange the scallops in the Crisper Basket in a single layer and spray with cooking spray.
6. Close the hood and AIR CRISP for 10 minutes, flipping the scallops halfway through, or until the scallops are tender and opaque.
7. Serve garnished with the Belgian endive.

Vegetable and Fish Tacos

Prep time: 10 minutes | Cook time: 9 to 12 minutes | Serves 4

1 pound (454 g) white fish fillets
2 teaspoons olive oil
3 tablespoons freshly squeezed lemon juice, divided
1½ cups chopped red cabbage
1 large carrot, grated
½ cup low-sodium salsa
⅓ cup low-fat Greek yogurt
4 soft low-sodium whole-wheat tortillas

1. Insert the Crisper Basket and close the hood. Select AIR CRISP, set the temperature to 400ºF (204ºC), and set the time to 12 minutes. Select START/ STOP to begin preheating.
2. Brush the fish with the olive oil and sprinkle with 1 tablespoon of lemon juice. Close the hood and AIR CRISP for 9 to 12 minutes, or until the fish just flakes when tested with a fork.
3. Meanwhile, in a medium bowl, stir together the remaining 2 tablespoons of lemon juice, the red cabbage, carrot, salsa, and yogurt.
4. When the fish is cooked, remove it from the Crisper Basket and break it up into large pieces.
5. Offer the fish, tortillas, and the cabbage mixture, and let each person assemble a taco.
6. Serve immediately.

Garlic-Lemon Tilapia

Prep time: 5 minutes | Cook time: 10 to 15 minutes | Serves 4

1 tablespoon lemon juice
1 tablespoon olive oil
1 teaspoon minced garlic
½ teaspoon chili powder
4 (6-ounce / 170-g) tilapia fillets

1. Insert the Crisper Basket and close the hood. Select AIR CRISP, set the temperature to 380ºF (193ºC), and set the time to 15 minutes. Select START/ STOP to begin preheating.
2. Line the Crisper Basket with parchment paper.

3. In a large, shallow bowl, mix together the lemon juice, olive oil, garlic, and chili powder to make a marinade. Place the tilapia fillets in the bowl and coat evenly.
4. Place the fillets in the basket in a single layer, leaving space between each fillet. You may need to cook in more than one batch.
5. Close the hood and AIR CRISP for 10 to 15 minutes until the fish is cooked and flakes easily with a fork.
6. Serve hot.

Tuna and Cucumber Salad

Prep time: 10 minutes | Cook time: 6 minutes | Serves 4

2 tablespoons rice wine vinegar
¼ teaspoon sea salt, plus additional for seasoning
½ teaspoon freshly ground black pepper, plus additional for seasoning
6 tablespoons extra-
virgin olive oil
1½ pounds (680 g) ahi tuna, cut into four strips
2 tablespoons sesame oil
1 (10-ounce / 284-g) bag baby greens
½ English cucumber, sliced

1. Insert the Grill Grate, and close the hood. Select GRILL, set the temperature to MAX, and set the time to 6 minutes. Select START/STOP to begin preheating.
2. Meanwhile, in a small bowl, whisk together the rice vinegar, ¼ teaspoon of salt, and ½ teaspoon of pepper. Slowly pour in the oil while whisking, until the vinaigrette is fully combined.
3. Season the tuna with salt and pepper, and drizzle with the sesame oil.
4. When the unit beeps to signify it has preheated, place the tuna strips on the Grill Grate. Close the hood, and GRILL for 4 to 6 minutes. (There is no need to flip during cooking.)
5. While the tuna cooks, divide the baby greens and cucumber slices evenly among four plates or bowls.
6. When cooking is complete, top each salad with one tuna strip. Drizzle the vinaigrette over the top, and serve immediately.

Baked Flounder Fillets

Prep time: 8 minutes | Cook time: 12 minutes | Serves 2

2 flounder fillets, patted dry
1 egg
½ teaspoon Worcestershire sauce
¼ cup almond flour
¼ cup coconut flour
½ teaspoon coarse sea salt
½ teaspoon lemon pepper
¼ teaspoon chili powder
Cooking spray

1. Insert the Crisper Basket and close the hood. Select BAKE, set the temperature to 390ºF (199ºC), and set the time to 12 minutes. Select START/STOP to begin preheating.
2. Spritz the Crisper Basket with cooking spray.
3. In a shallow bowl, beat together the egg with Worcestershire sauce until well incorporated.
4. In another bowl, thoroughly combine the almond flour, coconut flour, sea salt, lemon pepper, and chili powder.
5. Dredge the fillets in the egg mixture, shaking off any excess, then roll in the flour mixture to coat well.
6. Place the fillets in the Crisper Basket. Close the hood and BAKE for 7 minutes. Flip the fillets and spray with cooking spray. Continue cooking for 5 minutes, or until the fish is flaky.
7. Serve warm.

Simple Salmon Patty Bites

Prep time: 15 minutes | Cook time: 10 to 15 minutes | Serves 4

4 (5-ounce / 142-g) cans pink salmon, skinless, boneless in water, drained
2 eggs, beaten
1 cup whole-wheat panko bread crumbs
4 tablespoons finely
minced red bell pepper
2 tablespoons parsley flakes
2 teaspoons Old Bay seasoning
Cooking spray

1. Insert the Crisper Basket and close the hood. Select AIR CRISP, set the temperature to 360ºF (182ºC), and set the time to 15 minutes. Select START/STOP to begin preheating.
2. Spray the Crisper Basket lightly with cooking spray.
3. In a medium bowl, mix the salmon, eggs, panko bread crumbs, red bell pepper, parsley flakes, and Old Bay seasoning.
4. Using a small cookie scoop, form the mixture into 20 balls.
5. Place the salmon bites in the Crisper Basket in a single layer and spray lightly with cooking spray. You may need to cook them in batches.
6. Close the hood and AIR CRISP for 10 to 15 minutes until crispy, shaking the basket a couple of times for even cooking.
7. Serve immediately.

Crispy Cod Cakes with Salad Greens

Prep time: 15 minutes | Cook time: 12 minutes | Serves 4

1 pound (454 g) cod fillets, cut into chunks
⅓ cup packed fresh basil leaves
3 cloves garlic, crushed
½ teaspoon smoked paprika
¼ teaspoon salt
¼ teaspoon pepper
1 large egg, beaten
1 cup panko bread crumbs
Cooking spray
Salad greens, for serving

1. In a food processor, pulse cod, basil, garlic, smoked paprika, salt, and pepper until cod is finely chopped, stirring occasionally. Form into 8 patties, about 2 inches in diameter. Dip each first into the egg, then into the panko, patting to adhere. Spray with oil on one side.
2. Insert the Crisper Basket and close the hood. Select AIR CRISP, set the temperature to 400ºF (204ºC), and set the time to 12 minutes. Select START/STOP to begin preheating.
3. Working in batches, place half the cakes in the basket, oil-side down; spray with oil. Close the hood and AIR CRISP for 12 minutes, until golden brown and cooked through.
4. Serve cod cakes with salad greens.

Coconut Chili Fish Curry

Prep time: 10 minutes | Cook time: 20 to 22 minutes | Serves 4

2 tablespoons sunflower oil, divided
1 pound (454 g) fish, chopped
1 ripe tomato, pureéd
2 red chilies, chopped
1 shallot, minced
1 garlic clove, minced
1 cup coconut milk
1 tablespoon coriander powder
1 teaspoon red curry paste
½ teaspoon fenugreek seeds
Salt and white pepper, to taste

1. Insert the Crisper Basket and close the hood. Select AIR CRISP, set the temperature to 380ºF (193ºC), and set the time to 10 minutes. Select START/STOP to begin preheating.
2. Coat the Crisper Basket with 1 tablespoon of sunflower oil.
3. Place the fish in the basket. Close the hood and AIR CRISP for 10 minutes. Flip the fish halfway through the cooking time.
4. When done, transfer the cooked fish to a baking pan greased with the remaining 1 tablespoon of sunflower oil. Stir in the remaining ingredients and return to the grill.
5. Reduce the temperature to 350ºF (177ºC) and AIR CRISP for another 10 to 12 minutes until heated through.
6. Cool for 5 to 8 minutes before serving.

Garlic Shrimp with Parsley

Prep time: 10 minutes | Cook time: 5 minutes | Serves 4

18 shrimp, shelled and deveined
2 garlic cloves, peeled and minced
2 tablespoons extra-virgin olive oil
2 tablespoons freshly squeezed lemon juice
½ cup fresh parsley, coarsely chopped
1 teaspoon onion powder
1 teaspoon lemon-pepper seasoning
½ teaspoon hot paprika
½ teaspoon salt
¼ teaspoon cumin powder

1. Toss all the ingredients in a mixing bowl until the shrimp are well coated.

2. Cover and allow to marinate in the refrigerator for 30 minutes.
3. Insert the Crisper Basket and close the hood. Select AIR CRISP, set the temperature to 400ºF (204ºC), and set the time to 5 minutes. Select START/STOP to begin preheating.
4. Arrange the shrimp in the Crisper Basket. Close the hood and AIR CRISP for 5 minutes, or until the shrimp are pink on the outside and opaque in the center.
5. Remove from the basket and serve warm.

Fired Shrimp with Mayonnaise Sauce

Prep time: 5 minutes | Cook time: 7 minutes | Serves 4

Shrimp:
12 jumbo shrimp
½ teaspoon garlic salt
¼ teaspoon freshly cracked mixed peppercorns

Sauce:
4 tablespoons mayonnaise
1 teaspoon grated lemon rind
1 teaspoon Dijon mustard
1 teaspoon chipotle powder
½ teaspoon cumin powder

1. Insert the Crisper Basket and close the hood. Select AIR CRISP, set the temperature to 395ºF (202ºC), and set the time to 7 minutes. Select START/STOP to begin preheating.
2. In a medium bowl, season the shrimp with garlic salt and cracked mixed peppercorns.
3. Place the shrimp in the Crisper Basket. Close the hood and AIR CRISP for 5 minutes. Flip the shrimp and cook for another 2 minutes until they are pink and no longer opaque.
4. Meanwhile, stir together all the ingredients for the sauce in a small bowl until well mixed.
5. Remove the shrimp from the basket and serve alongside the sauce.

Breaded Calamari with Lemon

Prep time: 5 minutes | Cook time: 12 minutes | Serves 4

2 large eggs
2 garlic cloves, minced
½ cup cornstarch
1 cup bread crumbs

1 pound (454 g) calamari rings
Cooking spray
1 lemon, sliced

1.
2. In a small bowl, whisk the eggs with minced garlic. Place the cornstarch and bread crumbs into separate shallow dishes.
3. Dredge the calamari rings in the cornstarch, then dip in the egg mixture, shaking off any excess, finally roll them in the bread crumbs to coat well. Let the calamari rings sit for 10 minutes in the refrigerator.
4. Insert the Crisper Basket and close the hood. Select AIR CRISP, set the temperature to 390ºF (199ºC), and set the time to 12 minutes. Select START/STOP to begin preheating.
5. Spritz the Crisper Basket with cooking spray.
6. Put the calamari rings in the basket. Close the hood and AIR CRISP for 12 minutes until cooked through. Shake the basket halfway through the cooking time.
7. Serve the calamari rings with the lemon slices sprinkled on top.

Piri-Piri King Prawn

Prep time: 10 minutes | Cook time: 8 minutes | Serves 2

12 king prawns, rinsed
1 tablespoon coconut oil
Salt and ground black pepper, to taste
1 teaspoon onion powder

1 teaspoon garlic paste
1 teaspoon curry powder
½ teaspoon piri piri powder
½ teaspoon cumin powder

1. Insert the Crisper Basket and close the hood. Select AIR CRISP, set the temperature to 360ºF (182ºC), and set the time to 8 minutes. Select START/STOP to begin preheating.

2. Combine all the ingredients in a large bowl and toss until the prawns are completely coated.
3. Place the prawns in the Crisper Basket. Close the hood and AIR CRISP for 8 minutes, shaking the basket halfway through, or until the prawns turn pink.
4. Serve hot.

Southwest Shrimp and Cabbage Tacos

Prep time: 15 minutes | Cook time: 10 minutes | Serves 4

4 corn tortillas
Nonstick cooking spray
1 pound (454 g) fresh jumbo shrimp
Juice of ½ lemon
1 teaspoon chili powder
1 teaspoon ground cumin

1 teaspoon Southwestern seasoning
¼ teaspoon cayenne pepper
2 cups shredded green cabbage
1 avocado, peeled and sliced

1. Insert the Grill Grate and close the hood. Select GRILL, set the temperature to MAX, and set the time to 10 minutes. Select START/STOP to begin preheating.
2. While the unit is preheating, spray both sides of the tortillas with cooking spray, and in a large bowl, toss the shrimp with the lemon juice, chili powder, cumin, Southwestern seasoning, and cayenne pepper, until evenly coated. Let marinate while grilling the tortillas in the next step.
3. When the unit beeps to signify it has preheated, place 1 tortilla on the Grill Grate. Close the hood and GRILL for 1 minute. After 1 minute, open the hood and remove the tortilla; set aside. Repeat with the remaining 3 tortillas.
4. After removing the final tortilla, carefully place the shrimp on the Grill Grate. Close the hood and GRILL for 5 minutes. (There is no need to flip the shrimp during grilling.)
5. Remove the shrimp from the grill, arrange on the grilled tortillas, and top with cabbage and avocado. Feel free to include other toppings, such as cotija cheese, cilantro, and lime wedges.

Paprika Shrimp

Prep time: 5 minutes | Cook time: 10 minutes | Serves 4

1 pound (454 g) tiger shrimp
2 tablespoons olive oil
½ tablespoon old bay seasoning
¼ tablespoon smoked paprika
¼ teaspoon cayenne pepper
A pinch of sea salt

1. Insert the Crisper Basket and close the hood. Select AIR CRISP, set the temperature to 380ºF (193ºC), and set the time to 10 minutes. Select START/STOP to begin preheating.
2. Toss all the ingredients in a large bowl until the shrimp are evenly coated.
3. Arrange the shrimp in the Crisper Basket. Close the hood and AIR CRISP for 10 minutes, shaking the basket halfway through, or until the shrimp are pink and cooked through.
4. Serve hot.

Easy Shrimp and Vegetable Paella

Prep time: 5 minutes | Cook time: 14 to 17 minutes | Serves 4

1 (10-ounce / 284-g) package frozen cooked rice, thawed
1 (6-ounce / 170-g) jar artichoke hearts, drained and chopped
¼ cup vegetable broth
½ teaspoon dried thyme
½ teaspoon turmeric
1 cup frozen cooked small shrimp
½ cup frozen baby peas
1 tomato, diced

1. Select BAKE, set the temperature to 340ºF (171ºC), and set the time to 17 minutes. Select START/STOP to begin preheating.
2. Mix together the cooked rice, chopped artichoke hearts, vegetable broth, thyme, and turmeric in a baking pan and stir to combine.
3. Place the pan directly in the pot. Close the hood and BAKE for 9 minutes, or until the rice is heated through.
4. Remove the pan from the grill and fold in the shrimp, baby peas, and diced tomato and mix well.

5. Return to the grill and continue baking for 5 to 8 minutes, or until the shrimp are done and the paella is bubbling.
6. Cool for 5 minutes before serving.

Crispy Crab and Fish Cakes

Prep time: 20 minutes | Cook time: 10 to 12 minutes | Serves 4

8 ounces (227 g) imitation crab meat
4 ounces (113 g) leftover cooked fish (such as cod, pollock, or haddock)
2 tablespoons minced celery
2 tablespoons minced green onion
2 tablespoons light mayonnaise
1 tablespoon plus 2 teaspoons Worcestershire sauce
¾ cup crushed saltine cracker crumbs
2 teaspoons dried parsley flakes
1 teaspoon prepared yellow mustard
½ teaspoon garlic powder
½ teaspoon dried dill weed, crushed
½ teaspoon Old Bay seasoning
½ cup panko bread crumbs
Cooking spray

1. Insert the Crisper Basket and close the hood. Select BAKE, set the temperature to 390ºF (199ºC), and set the time to 12 minutes. Select START/STOP to begin preheating.
2. Pulse the crab meat and fish in a food processor until finely chopped.
3. Transfer the meat mixture to a large bowl, along with the celery, green onion, mayo, Worcestershire sauce, cracker crumbs, parsley flakes, mustard, garlic powder, dill weed, and Old Bay seasoning. Stir to mix well.
4. Scoop out the meat mixture and form into 8 equal-sized patties with your hands.
5. Place the panko bread crumbs on a plate. Roll the patties in the bread crumbs until they are evenly coated on both sides. Spritz the patties with cooking spray.
6. Put the patties in the Crisper Basket. Close the hood and BAKE for 10 to 12 minutes, flipping them halfway through, or until they are golden brown and cooked through.
7. Divide the patties among four plates and serve.

Crab Ratatouille with Eggplant and Tomatoes

Prep time: 15 minutes | Cook time: 11 to 14 minutes | Serves 4

1½ cups peeled and cubed eggplant
2 large tomatoes, chopped
1 red bell pepper, chopped
1 onion, chopped
1 tablespoon olive oil
½ teaspoon dried

basil
½ teaspoon dried thyme
Pinch salt
Freshly ground black pepper, to taste
1½ cups cooked crab meat

1. Select ROAST, set the temperature to 400ºF (204ºC)., and set the time to 15 minutes. Select START/STOP to begin preheating.
2. In the pot, stir together the eggplant, tomatoes, bell pepper, onion, olive oil, basil and thyme. Season with salt and pepper.
3. Close the hood and ROAST for 9 minutes.
4. Add the crab meat and stir well and roast for another 2 to 5 minutes, or until the vegetables are softened and the ratatouille is bubbling.
5. Serve warm.

Herbed Scallops with Vegetables

Prep time: 15 minutes | Cook time: 8 to 11 minutes | Serves 4

1 cup frozen peas
1 cup green beans
1 cup frozen chopped broccoli
2 teaspoons olive oil
½ teaspoon dried

oregano
½ teaspoon dried basil
12 ounces (340 g) sea scallops, rinsed and patted dry

1. Insert the Crisper Basket and close the hood. Select AIR CRISP, set the temperature to 400ºF (204ºC), and set the time to 6 minutes. Select START/STOP to begin preheating.
2. Put the peas, green beans, and broccoli in a large bowl. Drizzle with the olive oil and toss to coat well. Transfer the vegetables to the Crisper Basket. Close the hood and AIR CRISP for 4 to 6 minutes, or until they are fork-tender.

3. Remove the vegetables from the basket to a serving bowl. Scatter with the oregano and basil and set aside.
4. Place the scallops in the Crisper Basket. Close the hood and AIR CRISP for 4 to 5 minutes, or until the scallops are firm and just opaque in the center.
5. Transfer the cooked scallops to the bowl of vegetables and toss well. Serve warm.

Grilled Swordfish Steaks

Prep time: 5 minutes | Cook time: 8 minutes | Serves 4

1 tablespoon freshly squeezed lemon juice
1 tablespoon extra-virgin olive oil
Sea salt, to taste
Freshly ground black pepper, to taste
4 (8-ounce / 227-g) fresh swordfish

steaks, about 1-inch thick
4 tablespoons unsalted butter
1 lemon, sliced crosswise into 8 slices
2 tablespoons capers, drained

1. In a large shallow bowl, whisk together the lemon juice and oil. Season the swordfish steaks with salt and pepper on each side, and place them in the oil mixture. Turn to coat both sides. Refrigerate for 15 minutes.
2. Insert the Grill Grate and close the hood. Select GRILL, set the temperature to MAX, and set the time to 8 minutes. Select START/STOP to begin preheating.
3. When the unit beeps to signify it has preheated, place the swordfish on the Grill Grate. Close the hood and GRILL for 9 minutes. (There is no need to flip the swordfish during cooking.)
4. While the swordfish grills, melt the butter in a small saucepan over medium heat. Stir and GRILL for about 3 minutes, until the butter has slightly browned. Add the lemon slices and capers to the pan, and GRILL for 1 minute. Turn off the heat.
5. Remove the swordfish from the grill and transfer it to a cutting board. Slice the fish into thick strips, transfer to serving platter, pour the caper sauce over the top, and serve immediately.

Breaded Scallops

Prep time: 5 minutes | Cook time: 6 to 8 minutes | Serves 4

1 egg
3 tablespoons flour
1 cup bread crumbs
1 pound (454 g) fresh scallops

2 tablespoons olive oil
Salt and black pepper, to taste

1. Insert the Crisper Basket and close the hood. Select AIR CRISP, set the temperature to 360ºF (182ºC), and set the time to 8 minutes. Select START/STOP to begin preheating.
2. In a bowl, lightly beat the egg. Place the flour and bread crumbs into separate shallow dishes.
3. Dredge the scallops in the flour and shake off any excess. Dip the flour-coated scallops in the beaten egg and roll in the bread crumbs.
4. Brush the scallops generously with olive oil and season with salt and pepper, to taste.
5. Arrange the scallops in the Crisper Basket. Close the hood and AIR CRISP for 6 to 8 minutes, or until the scallops are firm and reach an internal temperature of just 145ºF (63ºC) on a meat thermometer. Shake the basket halfway through the cooking time.
6. Let the scallops cool for 5 minutes and serve.

Bacon-Wrapped Scallops

Prep time: 5 minutes | Cook time: 10 minutes | Serves 4

8 slices bacon, cut in half
16 sea scallops, patted dry
Cooking spray
Salt and freshly

ground black pepper, to taste
16 toothpicks, soaked in water for at least 30 minutes

1. Insert the Crisper Basket and close the hood. Select AIR CRISP, set the temperature to 370ºF (188ºC), and set the time to 10 minutes. Select START/STOP to begin preheating.
2. On a clean work surface, wrap half of a slice of bacon around each scallop and secure with a toothpick.
3. Lay the bacon-wrapped scallops in the Crisper Basket in a single layer. You may need to work in batches to avoid overcrowding.
4. Spritz the scallops with cooking spray and sprinkle the salt and pepper to season.
5. Close the hood and AIR CRISP for 10 minutes, flipping the scallops halfway through, or until the bacon is cooked through and the scallops are firm.
6. Remove the scallops from the basket to a plate and repeat with the remaining scallops. Serve warm.

Garlicky Shrimp Caesar Salad

Prep time: 10 minutes | Cook time: 5 minutes | Serves 4

1 pound (454 g) fresh jumbo shrimp
Juice of ½ lemon
3 garlic cloves, minced
Sea salt, to taste
Freshly ground black

pepper, to taste
2 heads romaine lettuce, chopped
¾ cup Caesar dressing
½ cup grated Parmesan cheese

1. Insert the Grill Grate and close the hood. Select GRILL, set the temperature to MAX, and set the time to 5 minutes. Select START/STOP to begin preheating.
2. In a large bowl, toss the shrimp with the lemon juice, garlic, salt, and pepper. Let marinate while the grill is preheating.
3. When the unit beeps to signify it has preheated, carefully place the shrimp on the Grill Grate. Close the hood and GRILL for 5 minutes. (There is no need to flip the shrimp during grilling.)
4. While the shrimp grills, toss the romaine lettuce with the Caesar dressing, then divide evenly among four plates or bowls.
5. When cooking is complete, use tongs to remove the shrimp from the grill and place on top of each salad. Sprinkle with the Parmesan cheese and serve.

Crispy Fish Sticks

Prep time: 10 minutes | Cook time: 10 minutes | Serves 4

1 pound (454 g) cod fillets
¼ cup all-purpose flour
1 large egg
1 teaspoon Dijon mustard
½ cup bread crumbs

1 tablespoon dried parsley
1 teaspoon paprika
½ teaspoon freshly ground black pepper
Nonstick cooking spray

1. Insert the Crisper Basket, and close the hood. Select AIR CRISP, set the temperature to 390ºF (199ºC), and set the time to 10 minutes. Select START/STOP to begin preheating.
2. While the unit is preheating, cut the fish fillets into ¾- to 1-inch-wide strips.
3. Place the flour on a plate. In a medium shallow bowl, whisk together the egg and Dijon mustard. In a separate medium shallow bowl, combine the bread crumbs, dried parsley, paprika, and black pepper.
4. One at a time, dredge the cod strips in the flour, shaking off any excess, then coat them in the egg mixture. Finally, dredge them in the bread crumb mixture, and coat on all sides.
5. When the unit beeps to signify it has preheated, spray the basket with the cooking spray. Place the cod fillet strips in the basket, and coat them with the cooking spray. Close the hood, and AIR CRISP for 10 minutes.
6. Remove the fish sticks from the basket and serve.

Blackened Salmon

Prep time: 10 minutes | Cook time: 5 to 7 minutes | Serves 4

Salmon:
1 tablespoon sweet paprika
½ teaspoon cayenne pepper
1 teaspoon garlic powder
1 teaspoon dried oregano
1 teaspoon dried thyme

¾ teaspoon kosher salt
⅛ teaspoon freshly ground black pepper
Cooking spray
4 (6 ounces / 170 g each) wild salmon fillets

Cucumber-Avocado Salsa:
2 tablespoons chopped red onion
1½ tablespoons fresh lemon juice
1 teaspoon extra-virgin olive oil
¼ teaspoon plus ⅛ teaspoon kosher salt

Freshly ground black pepper, to taste
4 Persian cucumbers, diced
6 ounces (170 g) Hass avocado, diced

1. For the salmon: In a small bowl, combine the paprika, cayenne, garlic powder, oregano, thyme, salt, and black pepper. Spray both sides of the fish with oil and rub all over. Coat the fish all over with the spices.
2. For the cucumber-avocado salsa: In a medium bowl, combine the red onion, lemon juice, olive oil, salt, and pepper. Let stand for 5 minutes, then add the cucumbers and avocado.
3. Insert the Crisper Basket and close the hood. Select AIR CRISP, set the temperature to 400ºF (204ºC), and set the time to 7 minutes. Select START/STOP to begin preheating.
4. Working in batches, arrange the salmon fillets skin side down in the Crisper Basket. Close the hood and AIR CRISP for 5 to 7 minutes, or until the fish flakes easily with a fork, depending on the thickness of the fish.
5. Serve topped with the salsa.

Lemony Shrimp and Zucchini

Prep time: 15 minutes | Cook time: 7 to 8 minutes | Serves 4

1¼ pounds (567 g) extra-large raw shrimp, peeled and deveined
2 medium zucchini (about 8 ounces / 227 g each), halved lengthwise and cut into ½-inch-thick slices
1½ tablespoons olive oil
½ teaspoon garlic salt

1½ teaspoons dried oregano
⅛ teaspoon crushed red pepper flakes (optional)
Juice of ½ lemon
1 tablespoon chopped fresh mint
1 tablespoon chopped fresh dill

1. Insert the Crisper Basket and close the hood. Select AIR CRISP, set the temperature to 350ºF (177ºC), and set the time to 8 minutes. Select START/STOP to begin preheating.
2. In a large bowl, combine the shrimp, zucchini, oil, garlic salt, oregano, and pepper flakes (if using) and toss to coat.
3. Working in batches, arrange a single layer of the shrimp and zucchini in the Crisper Basket. Close the hood and AIR CRISP for 7 to 8 minutes, shaking the basket halfway, until the zucchini is golden and the shrimp are cooked through.
4. Transfer to a serving dish and tent with foil while you AIR CRISP the remaining shrimp and zucchini.
5. Top with the lemon juice, mint, and dill and serve.

Spiced Crab Cakes

Prep time: 10 minutes | Cook time: 10 minutes | Serves 4

1 egg
½ cup mayonnaise, plus 3 tablespoons
Juice of ½ lemon
1 tablespoon minced scallions (green parts only)
1 teaspoon Old Bay seasoning
8 ounces (227 g) lump crab meat
⅓ cup bread crumbs

Nonstick cooking spray
½ teaspoon cayenne pepper
¼ teaspoon paprika
¼ teaspoon garlic powder
¼ teaspoon chili powder
¼ teaspoon onion powder
¼ teaspoon freshly ground black pepper
⅛ teaspoon ground nutmeg

1. Insert the Crisper Basket and close the hood. Select AIR CRISP, set the temperature to 375ºF (191ºC), and set the time to 10 minutes. Select START/STOP to begin preheating.
2. While the unit is preheating, in a medium bowl, whisk together the egg, 3 tablespoons of mayonnaise, lemon juice, scallions, and Old Bay seasoning. Gently stir in the crab meat, making sure not to break up the meat into small pieces. Add the bread crumbs, and gradually mix them in. Form the mixture into four patties.
3. When the unit beeps to signify it has preheated, place the crab cakes in the basket and coat them with the cooking spray. Close the hood and AIR CRISP for 10 minutes.
4. While the crab cakes are cooking, in a small bowl, mix the remaining ½ cup of mayonnaise, cayenne pepper, paprika, garlic powder, chili powder, onion powder, black pepper, and nutmeg until fully combined.
5. When cooking is complete, serve the crab cakes with the Cajun aioli spooned on top.

Grilled Salmon in Lemony Sriracha Glaze

Prep time: 10 minutes | Cook time: 8 minutes | Serves 4

1 cup sriracha
Juice of 2 lemons
¼ cup honey

4 (6-ounce / 170-g) skinless salmon fillets
Chives, chopped, for garnish

1. Place the sriracha, lemon juice, and honey in a large resealable plastic bag or container. Add the salmon fillets and coat evenly. Refrigerate for 30 minutes.
2. Insert the Grill Grate and close the hood. Select GRILL, set the temperature to MAX, and set the time to 8 minutes. Select START/STOP to begin preheating.
3. When the unit beeps to signify it has preheated, place the fillets on the Grill Grate, gently pressing them down to maximize grill marks. Close the hood and GRILL for 6 minutes. (There is no need to flip the fish during cooking.)
4. After 6 minutes, check the fillets for doneness; the internal temperature should read at least 140ºF (60ºC) on a food thermometer. If necessary, close the hood and continue cooking up to 2 minutes more.
5. When cooking is complete, remove the fillets from the grill. Plate, and garnish with the chives.

Crispy Cod Sandwich

Prep time: 10 minutes | Cook time: 15 minutes | Serves 4

2 large eggs
10 ounces (284 g) beer (an ale, IPA, or any type you have on hand will work)
1½ teaspoons hot sauce
1½ cups cornstarch
1½ cups all-purpose flour
1 teaspoon sea salt
1 teaspoon freshly ground black pepper

4 (5- or 6-ounce / 142- or 170-g) fresh cod fillets
Nonstick cooking spray
4 soft rolls, sliced
Tartar sauce
Lettuce leaves
Lemon wedges

1. Insert the Crisper Basket and close the hood. Select AIR CRISP, set the temperature to 375ºF (191ºC), and set the time to 15 minutes. Select START/STOP to begin preheating.
2. While the unit is preheating, whisk together the eggs, beer, and hot sauce in a large shallow bowl. In a separate large bowl, whisk together the cornstarch, flour, salt, and pepper.
3. One at a time, coat the cod fillets in the egg mixture, then dredge them in the flour mixture and coat on all sides. Repeat with the remaining cod fillets.
4. When the unit beeps to signify it has preheated, spray the Crisper Basket with the cooking spray. Place the fish fillets in the basket and coat them with the cooking spray. Close the hood and AIR CRISP for 15 minutes.
5. After 15 minutes, check the fish for desired crispiness. Remove from the basket.
6. Assemble the sandwiches by spreading tartar sauce on one half of each of the sliced rolls. Add one fish fillet and lettuce leaves, and serve with lemon wedges.

Chapter 8 Desserts

Ultimate Skillet Brownies

Prep time: 15 minutes | Cook time: 40 minutes | Serves 6

½ cup all-purpose flour
¼ cup unsweetened cocoa powder
¾ teaspoon sea salt
2 large eggs
1 tablespoon water
½ cup granulated sugar
½ cup dark brown sugar
1 tablespoon vanilla extract
8 ounces (227 g) semisweet chocolate chips, melted
¾ cup unsalted butter, melted
Nonstick cooking spray

1. In a medium bowl, whisk together the flour, cocoa powder, and salt.
2. In a large bowl, whisk together the eggs, water, sugar, brown sugar, and vanilla until smooth.
3. In a microwave-safe bowl, melt the chocolate in the microwave. In a separate microwave-safe bowl, melt the butter.
4. In a separate medium bowl, stir together the chocolate and butter until evenly combined. Whisk into the egg mixture. Then slowly add the dry ingredients, stirring just until incorporated.
5. Remove the Grill Grate from the unit. Select BAKE, set the temperature to 350ºF (177ºC), and set the time to 40 minutes. Select START/STOP to begin preheating.
6. Meanwhile, lightly grease the baking pan with cooking spray. Pour the batter into the pan, spreading evenly.
7. When the unit beeps to signify it has preheated, place the pan directly in the pot. Close the hood and BAKE for 40 minutes.
8. After 40 minutes, check that baking is complete. A wooden toothpick inserted into the center of the brownies should come out clean.

Strawberry Pizza

Prep time: 10 minutes | Cook time: 6 minutes | Serves 4

2 tablespoons all-purpose flour, plus more as needed
½ store-bought pizza dough (about 8 ounces / 227 g)
1 tablespoon canola oil
1 cup sliced fresh strawberries
1 tablespoon sugar
½ cup chocolate-hazelnut spread

1. Insert the Grill Grate and close the hood. Select GRILL, set the temperature to MAX, and set the time to 6 minutes. Select START/STOP to begin preheating.
2. While the unit is preheating, dust a clean work surface with the flour. Place the dough on the floured surface, and roll it out to a 9-inch round of even thickness. Dust your rolling pin and work surface with additional flour, as needed, to ensure the dough does not stick.
3. Brush the surface of the rolled-out dough evenly with half the oil. Flip the dough over, and brush with the remaining oil. Poke the dough with a fork 5 or 6 times across its surface to prevent air pockets from forming during cooking.
4. When the unit beeps to signify it has preheated, place the dough on the Grill Grate. Close the hood and GRILL for 3 minutes.
5. After 3 minutes, flip the dough. Close the hood and continue grilling for the remaining 3 minutes.
6. Meanwhile, in a medium mixing bowl, combine the strawberries and sugar.
7. Transfer the pizza to a cutting board and let cool. Top with the chocolate-hazelnut spread and strawberries. Cut into pieces and serve.

Pound Cake with Mixed Berries

Prep time: 10 minutes | Cook time: 8 minutes | Serves 6

3 tablespoons unsalted butter, at room temperature
6 slices pound cake, sliced about 1-inch thick
1 cup fresh

raspberries
1 cup fresh blueberries
3 tablespoons sugar
½ tablespoon fresh mint, minced

1. Insert the Grill Grate and close the hood. Select GRILL, set the temperature to MAX, and set the time to 8 minutes. Select START/STOP to begin preheating.
2. While the unit is preheating, evenly spread the butter on both sides of each slice of pound cake.
3. When the unit beeps to signify it has preheated, place the pound cake on the Grill Grate. Close the hood and GRILL for 2 minutes.
4. After 2 minutes, flip the pound cake and GRILL for 2 minutes more, until golden brown. Repeat steps 3 and 4 for all of the pound cake slices.
5. While the pound cake grills, in a medium mixing bowl, combine the raspberries, blueberries, sugar, and mint.
6. When cooking is complete, plate the cake slices and serve topped with the berry mixture.

Fresh Blueberry Cobbler

Prep time: 15 minutes | Cook time: 30 minutes | Serves 6

4 cups fresh blueberries
1 teaspoon grated lemon zest
1 cup sugar, plus 2 tablespoons
1 cup all-purpose flour, plus 2 tablespoons

Juice of 1 lemon
2 teaspoons baking powder
¼ teaspoon salt
6 tablespoons unsalted butter
¾ cup whole milk
⅛ teaspoon ground cinnamon

1. In a medium bowl, combine the blueberries, lemon zest, 2 tablespoons of sugar, 2 tablespoons of flour, and lemon juice.

2. In a medium bowl, combine the remaining 1 cup of flour and 1 cup of sugar, baking powder, and salt. Cut the butter into the flour mixture until it forms an even crumb texture. Stir in the milk until a dough forms.
3. Select BAKE, set the temperature to 350ºF (177ºC), and set the time to 30 minutes. Select START/STOP to begin preheating.
4. Meanwhile, pour the blueberry mixture into the baking pan, spreading it evenly across the pan. Gently pour the batter over the blueberry mixture, then sprinkle the cinnamon over the top.
5. When the unit beeps to signify it has preheated, place the pan directly in the pot. Close the hood and BAKE for 30 minutes, until lightly golden.
6. When cooking is complete, serve warm.

Marshmallow Banana Boat

Prep time: 10 minutes | Cook time: 6 minutes | Serves 4

4 ripe bananas
1 cup mini marshmallows
½ cup chocolate

chips
½ cup peanut butter chips

1. Insert the Grill Grate and close the hood. Select GRILL, set the temperature to MEDIUM, and set the time to 6 minutes. Select START/STOP to begin preheating.
2. While the unit is preheating, slice each banana lengthwise while still in its peel, making sure not to cut all the way through. Using both hands, pull the banana peel open like you would a book, revealing the banana inside. Divide the marshmallows, chocolate chips, and peanut butter chips among the bananas, stuffing them inside the skin.
3. When the unit beeps to signify it has preheated, place the stuffed banana on the Grill Grate. Close the hood and GRILL for 4 to 6 minutes, until the chocolate is melted and the marshmallows are toasted.

Churros with Chocolate-Yogurt Sauce

Prep time: 15 minutes | Cook time: 30 minutes | Serves 8

1 cup water
1 stick unsalted butter, cut into 8 pieces
½ cup sugar, plus 1 tablespoon
1 cup all-purpose flour
1 teaspoon vanilla extract
3 large eggs
2 teaspoons ground cinnamon
Nonstick cooking spray
4 ounces (113 g) dark chocolate, chopped
¼ cup Greek yogurt

1. In a medium saucepan over medium-high heat, combine the water, butter, and the 1 tablespoon of sugar. Bring to a simmer. Add the flour, stirring it in quickly. Continue to cook, stirring constantly, until the mixture is thick, about 3 minutes. Transfer to a large bowl.
2. Using a spoon, beat the flour mixture for about 1 minute, until cooled slightly. Stir in the vanilla, then the eggs, one at a time.
3. Transfer the dough to a plastic bag or a piping bag. Let the dough rest for 1 hour at room temperature.
4. Insert the Crisper Basket and close the hood. Select AIR CRISP, set the temperature to 375ºF (191ºC), and set the time to 30 minutes. Select START/STOP to begin preheating.
5. Meanwhile, in a medium shallow bowl, combine the cinnamon and remaining ½ cup of sugar.
6. When the unit beeps to signify it has preheated, spray the basket with the nonstick cooking spray. Take the plastic bag with your dough and cut off one corner. Pipe the batter directly into the Crisper Basket, making 6 (3-inch-long) churros, placed at least ½ inch apart. Close the hood and AIR CRISP for 10 minutes.
7. Meanwhile, in a small microwave-safe mixing bowl, melt the chocolate in the microwave, stirring it after every 30 seconds, until completely melted and smooth. Add the yogurt and whisk until smooth.
8. After 10 minutes, carefully transfer the churros to the sugar mixture and toss to coat evenly. Repeat piping and air crisping with the remaining batter, adding time as needed.
9. Serve the churros with the warm chocolate dipping sauce.

Chocolate and Peanut Butter Lava Cupcakes

Prep time: 10 minutes | Cook time: 10 to 13 minutes | Serves 8

Nonstick baking spray with flour
1⅓ cups chocolate cake mix
1 egg
1 egg yolk
¼ cup safflower oil
¼ cup hot water
⅓ cup sour cream
3 tablespoons peanut butter
1 tablespoon powdered sugar

1. Select BAKE, set the temperature to 350ºF (177ºC), and set the time to 13 minutes. Select START/STOP to begin preheating.
2. Double up 16 foil muffin cups to make 8 cups. Spray each lightly with nonstick spray; set aside.
3. In a medium bowl, combine the cake mix, egg, egg yolk, safflower oil, water, and sour cream, and beat until combined.
4. In a small bowl, combine the peanut butter and powdered sugar and mix well. Form this mixture into 8 balls.
5. Spoon about ¼ cup of the chocolate batter into each muffin cup and top with a peanut butter ball. Spoon remaining batter on top of the peanut butter balls to cover them.
6. Arrange the cups in the pot, leaving some space between each. Place the pan directly in the pot. Close the hood and BAKE for 10 to 13 minutes or until the tops look dry and set.
7. Let the cupcakes cool for about 10 minutes, then serve warm.

Sugar-Glazed Biscuit Bites

Prep time: 15 minutes | Cook time: 12 minutes | Serves 8

²/₃ cup all-purpose flour, plus additional for dusting
²/₃ cup whole-wheat flour
2 tablespoons granulated sugar
1 teaspoon baking powder
¼ teaspoon ground cinnamon

¼ teaspoon sea salt
4 tablespoons salted butter, cold and cut into small pieces
⅓ cup whole milk
Nonstick cooking spray
2 cups powdered sugar
3 tablespoons water

1. In a large bowl, combine the all-purpose flour, whole-wheat flour, sugar, baking powder, cinnamon, and salt. Add the cold butter pieces, and cut them into the flour mixture using a pastry cutter or a fork, until well-combined and the mixture resembles a course meal. Add the milk to the mixture, and stir together until the dough comes together into a ball.
2. Insert the Crisper Basket and close the hood. Select AIR CRISP, set the temperature to 350ºF (177ºC), and set the time to 12 minutes. Select START/STOP to begin preheating.
3. While the unit is preheating, dust a clean work surface with the all-purpose flour. Place the dough on the floured surface, and knead until the dough is smooth and forms a cohesive ball, about 30 seconds. Cut the dough into 16 equal pieces. Gently roll each piece into a smooth ball.
4. When the unit beeps to signify it has preheated, coat the basket well with cooking spray. Place 8 biscuit bites in the basket, leaving room between each, and spray each with cooking spray. Close the hood and AIR CRISP for 10 to 12 minutes, until golden brown.
5. Meanwhile, in a medium mixing bowl, whisk together the powdered sugar and water until it forms a smooth glaze.
6. Gently remove the bites from the basket, and place them on a wire rack covered with aluminum foil. Repeat step 4 with the remaining biscuit bites.
7. Spoon half the glaze over the bites and let cool 5 minutes, then spoon over the remaining glaze.

Lemony Blackberry Crisp

Prep time: 5 minutes | Cook time: 20 minutes | Serves 1

2 tablespoons lemon juice
⅓ cup powdered erythritol
¼ teaspoon xantham

gum
2 cup blackberries
1 cup crunchy granola

1. Select BAKE, set the temperature to 350ºF (177ºC), and set the time to 15 minutes. Select START/STOP to begin preheating.
2. In a bowl, combine the lemon juice, erythritol, xantham gum, and blackberries. Transfer to a round baking pan and cover with aluminum foil.
3. Place the pan directly in the pot. Close the hood and BAKE for 12 minutes.
4. Take care when removing the pan from the grill. Give the blackberries a stir and top with the granola.
5. Return the pan to the grill and bake at 320ºF (160ºC) for an additional 3 minutes. Serve once the granola has turned brown and enjoy.

Chocolate Molten Cake

Prep time: 5 minutes | Cook time: 10 minutes | Serves 4

3.5 ounces (99 g) butter, melted
3½ tablespoons sugar

3.5 ounces (99 g) chocolate, melted
1½ tablespoons flour
2 eggs

1. Select BAKE, set the temperature to 375ºF (191ºC), and set the time to 10 minutes. Select START/STOP to begin preheating.
2. Grease four ramekins with a little butter.
3. Rigorously combine the eggs, butter, and sugar before stirring in the melted chocolate.
4. Slowly fold in the flour.
5. Spoon an equal amount of the mixture into each ramekin.
6. Put them in the pot. Close the hood and BAKE for 10 minutes.
7. Put the ramekins upside-down on plates and let the cakes fall out. Serve hot.

Pumpkin Pudding

Prep time: 10 minutes | Cook time: 15 minutes | Serves 4

3 cups pumpkin purée	1 teaspoon clove
3 tablespoons honey	1 teaspoon nutmeg
1 tablespoon ginger	1 cup full-fat cream
1 tablespoon cinnamon	2 eggs
	1 cup sugar

1. Select BAKE, set the temperature to 390°F (199°C), and set the time to 15 minutes. Select START/STOP to begin preheating.
2. In a bowl, stir all the ingredients together to combine.
3. Scrape the mixture into a greased baking pan. Place the pan directly in the pot. Close the hood and BAKE for 15 minutes.
4. Serve warm.

Simple Corn Biscuits

Prep time: 15 minutes | Cook time: 15 minutes | Serves 6

1½ cups all-purpose flour, plus additional for dusting	½ teaspoon sea salt
½ cup yellow cornmeal	$1/_3$ cup vegetable shortening
2½ teaspoons baking powder	$2/_3$ cup buttermilk
	Nonstick cooking spray

1. In a large bowl, combine the flour, cornmeal, baking powder, and salt.
2. Add the shortening, and cut it into the flour mixture, until well combined and the dough resembles a coarse meal. Add the buttermilk and stir together just until moistened.
3. Insert the Crisper Basket and close the hood. Select AIR CRISP, set the temperature to 350°F (177°C), and set the time to 15 minutes. Select START/STOP to begin preheating.
4. While the unit is preheating, dust a clean work surface with flour. Knead the mixture on the floured surface until a cohesive dough forms. Roll out the dough to an even thickness, then cut into biscuits with a 2-inch biscuit cutter.
5. When the unit beeps to signify it has preheated, coat the basket with cooking spray. Place 6 to 8 biscuits in the basket, well spaced, and spray each with cooking spray. Close the hood and AIR CRISP for 12 to 15 minutes, until golden brown.
6. Gently remove the biscuits from the basket, and place them on a wire rack to cool. Repeat with the remaining dough.

Graham Cracker Cheesecake

Prep time: 10 minutes | Cook time: 20 minutes | Serves 8

1 cup graham cracker crumbs	$1/_3$ cup sugar
3 tablespoons softened butter	2 eggs
1½ (8-ounce / 227-g) packages cream cheese, softened	1 tablespoon flour
	1 teaspoon vanilla
	¼ cup chocolate syrup

1. For the crust, combine the graham cracker crumbs and butter in a small bowl and mix well. Press into the bottom of a baking pan and put in the freezer to set.
2. For the filling, combine the cream cheese and sugar in a medium bowl and mix well. Beat in the eggs, one at a time. Add the flour and vanilla.
3. Select BAKE, set the temperature to 450°F (232°C), and set the time to 20 minutes. Select START/STOP to begin preheating.
4. Remove $2/_3$ cup of the filling to a small bowl and stir in the chocolate syrup until combined.
5. Pour the vanilla filling into the pan with the crust. Drop the chocolate filling over the vanilla filling by the spoonful. With a clean butter knife, stir the fillings in a zigzag pattern to marbleize them.
6. Place the pan directly in the pot. Close the hood and BAKE for 20 minutes or until the cheesecake is just set.
7. Cool on a wire rack for 1 hour, then chill in the refrigerator until the cheesecake is firm.
8. Serve immediately.

Rich Chocolate Cookie

Prep time: 10 minutes | Cook time: 9 minutes | Serves 4

Nonstick baking spray with flour
3 tablespoons softened butter
1/3 cup plus 1 tablespoon brown sugar
1 egg yolk
½ cup flour
2 tablespoons ground white chocolate
¼ teaspoon baking soda
½ teaspoon vanilla
¾ cup chocolate chips

1. Select BAKE, set the temperature to 350ºF (177ºC), and set the time to 9 minutes. Select START/STOP to begin preheating.
2. In a medium bowl, beat the butter and brown sugar together until fluffy. Stir in the egg yolk.
3. Add the flour, white chocolate, baking soda, and vanilla, and mix well. Stir in the chocolate chips.
4. Line a baking pan with parchment paper. Spray the parchment paper with nonstick baking spray with flour.
5. Spread the batter into the prepared pan, leaving a ½-inch border on all sides.
6. Place the pan directly in the pot. Close the hood and BAKE for 9 minutes or until the cookie is light brown and just barely set.
7. Remove the pan from the grill and let cool for 10 minutes. Remove the cookie from the pan, remove the parchment paper, and let cool on a wire rack.
8. Serve immediately.

Orange Cake

Prep time: 10 minutes | Cook time: 23 minutes | Serves 8

Nonstick baking spray with flour
1¼ cups all-purpose flour
1/3 cup yellow cornmeal
¾ cup white sugar
1 teaspoon baking soda
¼ cup safflower oil
1¼ cups orange juice, divided
1 teaspoon vanilla
¼ cup powdered sugar

1. Select BAKE, set the temperature to 350ºF (177ºC), and set the time to 23 minutes. Select START/STOP to begin preheating.
2. Spray a baking pan with nonstick spray and set aside.
3. In a medium bowl, combine the flour, cornmeal, sugar, baking soda, safflower oil, 1 cup of the orange juice, and vanilla, and mix well.
4. Pour the batter into the baking pan. Place the pan directly in the pot. Close the hood and BAKE for 23 minutes or until a toothpick inserted in the center of the cake comes out clean.
5. Remove the cake from the grill and place on a cooling rack. Using a toothpick, make about 20 holes in the cake.
6. In a small bowl, combine remaining ¼ cup of orange juice and the powdered sugar and stir well. Drizzle this mixture over the hot cake slowly so the cake absorbs it.
7. Cool completely, then cut into wedges to serve.

Apple, Peach, and Cranberry Crisp

Prep time: 10 minutes | Cook time: 12 minutes | Serves 8

1 apple, peeled and chopped
2 peaches, peeled and chopped
1/3 cup dried cranberries
2 tablespoons honey
1/3 cup brown sugar
¼ cup flour
½ cup oatmeal
3 tablespoons softened butter

1. Select BAKE, set the temperature to 370ºF (188ºC), and set the time to 12 minutes. Select START/STOP to begin preheating.
2. In a baking pan, combine the apple, peaches, cranberries, and honey, and mix well.
3. In a medium bowl, combine the brown sugar, flour, oatmeal, and butter, and mix until crumbly. Sprinkle this mixture over the fruit in the pan.
4. Place the pan directly in the pot. Close the hood and BAKE for 10 to 12 minutes or until the fruit is bubbly and the topping is golden brown. Serve warm.

Oatmeal and Carrot Cookie Cups

Prep time: 10 minutes | Cook time: 8 minutes | Makes 16 cups

3 tablespoons unsalted butter, at room temperature
¼ cup packed brown sugar
1 tablespoon honey
1 egg white
½ teaspoon vanilla extract

⅓ cup finely grated carrot
½ cup quick-cooking oatmeal
⅓ cup whole-wheat pastry flour
½ teaspoon baking soda
¼ cup dried cherries

1. Select BAKE, set the temperature to 350ºF (177ºC), and set the time to 8 minutes. Select START/STOP to begin preheating.
2. In a medium bowl, beat the butter, brown sugar, and honey until well combined.
3. Add the egg white, vanilla, and carrot. Beat to combine.
4. Stir in the oatmeal, pastry flour, and baking soda.
5. Stir in the dried cherries.
6. Double up 32 mini muffin foil cups to make 16 cups. Fill each with about 4 teaspoons of dough. Place the cookie cups directly in the pot.
7. Close the hood and BAKE for 8 minutes, 8 at a time, or until light golden brown and just set. Serve warm.

Curry Peaches, Pears, and Plums

Prep time: 5 minutes | Cook time: 5 minutes | Serves 6 to 8

2 peaches
2 firm pears
2 plums
2 tablespoons melted

butter
1 tablespoon honey
2 to 3 teaspoons curry powder

1. Insert the Crisper Basket and close the hood. Select BAKE, set the temperature to 325ºF (163ºC), and set the time to 8 minutes. Select START/STOP to begin preheating.
2. Cut the peaches in half, remove the pits, and cut each half in half again. Cut the pears in half, core them, and remove the stem. Cut each half in half again. Do the same with the plums.
3. Spread a large sheet of heavy-duty foil on the work surface. Arrange the fruit on the foil and drizzle with the butter and honey. Sprinkle with the curry powder.
4. Wrap the fruit in the foil, making sure to leave some air space in the packet.
5. Put the foil package in the basket. Close the hood and BAKE for 5 to 8 minutes, shaking the basket once during the cooking time, until the fruit is soft.
6. Serve immediately.

Orange and Anise Cake

Prep time: 5 minutes | Cook time: 20 minutes | Serves 6

1 stick butter, at room temperature
5 tablespoons liquid monk fruit
2 eggs plus 1 egg yolk, beaten
⅓ cup hazelnuts, roughly chopped
3 tablespoons sugar-free orange marmalade
6 ounces (170 g)

unbleached almond flour
1 teaspoon baking soda
½ teaspoon baking powder
½ teaspoon ground cinnamon
½ teaspoon ground allspice
½ ground anise seed
Cooking spray

1. Select BAKE, set the temperature to 310ºF (154ºC), and set the time to 20 minutes. Select START/STOP to begin preheating.
2. Lightly spritz a baking pan with cooking spray.
3. In a mixing bowl, whisk the butter and liquid monk fruit until the mixture is pale and smooth. Mix in the beaten eggs, hazelnuts, and marmalade and whisk again until well incorporated.
4. Add the almond flour, baking soda, baking powder, cinnamon, allspice, anise seed and stir to mix well.
5. Scrape the batter into the prepared baking pan. Place the pan directly in the pot. Close the hood and BAKE for 20 minutes, or until the top of the cake springs back when gently pressed with your fingers.
6. Transfer to a wire rack and let the cake cool to room temperature. Serve immediately.

Black Forest Pies

Prep time: 10 minutes | Cook time: 15 minutes | Serves 6

3 tablespoons milk or dark chocolate chips
2 tablespoons thick, hot fudge sauce
2 tablespoons chopped dried cherries

1 (10-by-15-inch) sheet frozen puff pastry, thawed
1 egg white, beaten
2 tablespoons sugar
½ teaspoon cinnamon

1. Insert the Crisper Basket and close the hood. Select BAKE, set the temperature to 350ºF (177ºC), and set the time to 15 minutes. Select START/STOP to begin preheating.
2. In a small bowl, combine the chocolate chips, fudge sauce, and dried cherries.
3. Roll out the puff pastry on a floured surface. Cut into 6 squares with a sharp knife.
4. Divide the chocolate chip mixture into the center of each puff pastry square. Fold the squares in half to make triangles. Firmly press the edges with the tines of a fork to seal.
5. Brush the triangles on all sides sparingly with the beaten egg white. Sprinkle the tops with sugar and cinnamon.
6. Put in the Crisper Basket. Close the hood and BAKE for 15 minutes or until the triangles are golden brown. The filling will be hot, so cool for at least 20 minutes before serving.

Banana and Walnut Cake

Prep time: 10 minutes | Cook time: 25 minutes | Serves 6

1 pound (454 g) bananas, mashed
8 ounces (227 g) flour
6 ounces (170 g) sugar
3.5 ounces (99 g)

walnuts, chopped
2.5 ounces (71 g) butter, melted
2 eggs, lightly beaten
¼ teaspoon baking soda

1. Select BAKE, set the temperature to 355ºF (179ºC), and set the time to 10 minutes. Select START/STOP to begin preheating.

2. In a bowl, combine the sugar, butter, egg, flour, and baking soda with a whisk. Stir in the bananas and walnuts.
3. Transfer the mixture to a greased baking pan. Place the pan directly in the pot. Close the hood and BAKE for 10 minutes.
4. Reduce the temperature to 330ºF (166ºC) and bake for another 15 minutes. Serve hot.

Grilled Peaches with Bourbon Butter Sauce

Prep time: 10 minutes | Cook time: 12 minutes | Serves 4

4 tablespoons salted butter
¼ cup bourbon
½ cup brown sugar

4 ripe peaches, halved and pitted
¼ cup candied pecans

1. Insert the Grill Grate and close the hood. Select GRILL, set the temperature to MAX, and set the time to 12 minutes. Select START/STOP to begin preheating.
2. While the unit is preheating, in a saucepan over medium heat, melt the butter for about 5 minutes. Once the butter is browned, remove the pan from the heat and carefully add the bourbon.
3. Return the saucepan to medium-high heat and add the brown sugar. Bring to a boil and let the sugar dissolve for 5 minutes, stirring occasionally.
4. Pour the bourbon butter sauce into a medium shallow bowl and arrange the peaches cut-side down to coat in the sauce.
5. When the unit beeps to signify it has preheated, place the fruit on the Grill Grate in a single layer (you may need to do this in multiple batches). Gently press the fruit down to maximize grill marks. Close the hood and GRILL for 10 to 12 minutes without flipping. If working in batches, repeat this step for all the peaches.
6. When cooking is complete, remove the peaches and top each with the pecans. Drizzle with the remaining bourbon butter sauce and serve immediately.

Pineapple and Chocolate Cake

Prep time: 10 minutes | Cook time: 35 to 40 minutes | Serves 4

2 cups flour	juice
4 ounces (113 g) butter, melted	1 ounce (28 g) dark chocolate, grated
¼ cup sugar	1 large egg
½ pound (227 g) pineapple, chopped	2 tablespoons skimmed milk
½ cup pineapple	

1. Select BAKE, set the temperature to 370ºF (188ºC), and set the time to 40 minutes. Select START/STOP to begin preheating.
2. Grease a cake tin with a little oil or butter.
3. In a bowl, combine the butter and flour to create a crumbly consistency.
4. Add the sugar, chopped pineapple, juice, and grated dark chocolate and mix well.
5. In a separate bowl, combine the egg and milk. Add this mixture to the flour mixture and stir well until a soft dough forms.
6. Pour the mixture into the cake tin and transfer to the grill.
7. Close the hood and BAKE for 35 to 40 minutes.
8. Serve immediately.

Chocolate Coconut Brownies

Prep time: 15 minutes | Cook time: 15 minutes | Serves 8

½ cup coconut oil	anise star
2 ounces (57 g) dark chocolate	¼ teaspoon coconut extract
1 cup sugar	½ teaspoons vanilla extract
2½ tablespoons water	1 tablespoon honey
4 whisked eggs	½ cup flour
¼ teaspoon ground cinnamon	½ cup desiccated coconut
½ teaspoons ground	Sugar, for dusting

1. Select BAKE, set the temperature to 355ºF (179ºC), and set the time to 15 minutes. Select START/STOP to begin preheating.

2. Melt the coconut oil and dark chocolate in the microwave.
3. Combine with the sugar, water, eggs, cinnamon, anise, coconut extract, vanilla, and honey in a large bowl.
4. Stir in the flour and desiccated coconut. Incorporate everything well.
5. Lightly grease a baking pan with butter. Transfer the mixture to the pan.
6. Place the pan directly in the pot. Close the hood and BAKE for 15 minutes.
7. Remove from the grill and allow to cool slightly.
8. Take care when taking it out of the baking pan. Slice it into squares.
9. Dust with sugar before serving.

Pear and Apple Crisp

Prep time: 10 minutes | Cook time: 20 minutes | Serves 6

½ pound (227 g) apples, cored and chopped	cinnamon
	¼ teaspoon ground cloves
½ pound (227 g) pears, cored and chopped	1 teaspoon vanilla extract
1 cup flour	¼ cup chopped walnuts
1 cup sugar	Whipped cream, for serving
1 tablespoon butter	
1 teaspoon ground	

1. Select BAKE, set the temperature to 340ºF (171ºC), and set the time to 20 minutes. Select START/STOP to begin preheating.
2. Lightly grease a baking pan and place the apples and pears inside.
3. Combine the rest of the ingredients, minus the walnuts and the whipped cream, until a coarse, crumbly texture is achieved.
4. Pour the mixture over the fruits and spread it evenly. Top with the chopped walnuts.
5. Place the pan directly in the pot. Close the hood and BAKE for 20 minutes or until the top turns golden brown.
6. Serve at room temperature with whipped cream.

Chocolate S'mores

Prep time: 5 minutes | Cook time: 3 minutes | Serves 12

12 whole cinnamon graham crackers
2 (1.55-ounce / 44-g) chocolate bars, broken into 12 pieces
12 marshmallows

1. Insert the Crisper Basket and close the hood. Select BAKE, set the temperature to 350ºF (177ºC), and set the time to 3 minutes. Select START/STOP to begin preheating.
2. Halve each graham cracker into 2 squares.
3. Put 6 graham cracker squares in the basket. Do not stack. Put a piece of chocolate into each. Close the hood and BAKE for 2 minutes.
4. Open the grill and add a marshmallow onto each piece of melted chocolate. Bake for 1 additional minute.
5. Remove the cooked s'mores from the grill, then repeat steps 2 and 3 for the remaining 6 s'mores.
6. Top with the remaining graham cracker squares and serve.

Chocolate and Coconut Cake

Prep time: 5 minutes | Cook time: 15 minutes | Serves 6

½ cup unsweetened chocolate, chopped
½ stick butter, at room temperature
1 tablespoon liquid stevia
1½ cups coconut flour
2 eggs, whisked
½ teaspoon vanilla extract
A pinch of fine sea salt
Cooking spray

1. Place the chocolate, butter, and stevia in a microwave-safe bowl. Microwave for about 30 seconds until melted.
2. Let the chocolate mixture cool for 5 to 10 minutes.
3. Add the remaining ingredients to the bowl of chocolate mixture and whisk to incorporate.
4. Select BAKE, set the temperature to 330ºF (166ºC), and set the time to 15 minutes. Select START/STOP to begin preheating.
5. Lightly spray a baking pan with cooking spray.
6. Scrape the chocolate mixture into the prepared baking pan.
7. Place the pan directly in the pot. Close the hood and BAKE for 15 minutes, or until the top springs back lightly when gently pressed with your fingers.
8. Let the cake cool for 5 minutes and serve.

Orange Coconut Cake

Prep time: 5 minutes | Cook time: 17 minutes | Serves 6

1 stick butter, melted
¾ cup granulated Swerve
2 eggs, beaten
¾ cup coconut flour
¼ teaspoon salt
1/3 teaspoon grated nutmeg
1/3 cup coconut milk
1¼ cups almond flour
½ teaspoon baking powder
2 tablespoons unsweetened orange jam
Cooking spray

1. Select BAKE, set the temperature to 355ºF (179ºC), and set the time to 17 minutes. Select START/STOP to begin preheating.
2. Coat a baking pan with cooking spray. Set aside.
3. In a large mixing bowl, whisk together the melted butter and granulated Swerve until fluffy.
4. Mix in the beaten eggs and whisk again until smooth. Stir in the coconut flour, salt, and nutmeg and gradually pour in the coconut milk. Add the remaining ingredients and stir until well incorporated.
5. Scrape the batter into the baking pan.
6. Place the pan directly in the pot. Close the hood and BAKE for 17 minutes until the top of the cake springs back when gently pressed with your fingers.
7. Remove from the grill to a wire rack to cool. Serve chilled.

Ultimate Coconut Chocolate Cake

Prep time: 5 minutes | Cook time: 15 minutes | Serves 10

1¼ cups unsweetened bakers' chocolate
1 stick butter
1 teaspoon liquid stevia

⅓ cup shredded coconut
2 tablespoons coconut milk
2 eggs, beaten
Cooking spray

1. Select BAKE, set the temperature to 330ºF (166ºC), and set the time to 15 minutes. Select START/STOP to begin preheating.
2. Lightly spritz a baking pan with cooking spray.
3. Place the chocolate, butter, and stevia in a microwave-safe bowl. Microwave for about 30 seconds until melted. Let the chocolate mixture cool to room temperature.
4. Add the remaining ingredients to the chocolate mixture and stir until well incorporated. Pour the batter into the prepared baking pan.
5. Place the pan directly in the pot. Close the hood and BAKE for 15 minutes, or until a toothpick inserted in the center comes out clean.
6. Remove from the pan and allow to cool for about 10 minutes before serving.

Classic Pound Cake

Prep time: 5 minutes | Cook time: 30 minutes | Serves 8

1 stick butter, at room temperature
1 cup Swerve
4 eggs
1½ cups coconut flour
½ cup buttermilk
½ teaspoon baking soda
½ teaspoon baking

powder
¼ teaspoon salt
1 teaspoon vanilla essence
A pinch of ground star anise
A pinch of freshly grated nutmeg
Cooking spray

1. Select BAKE, set the temperature to 320ºF (160ºC), and set the time to 30 minutes. Select START/STOP to begin preheating.

2. Spray a baking pan with cooking spray.
3. With an electric mixer or hand mixer, beat the butter and Swerve until creamy. One at a time, mix in the eggs and whisk until fluffy. Add the remaining ingredients and stir to combine.
4. Transfer the batter to the prepared baking pan. Place the pan directly in the pot. Close the hood and BAKE for 30 minutes until the center of the cake is springy. Rotate the pan halfway through the cooking time.
5. Allow the cake to cool in the pan for 10 minutes before removing and serving.

Blackberry Chocolate Cake

Prep time: 10 minutes | Cook time: 22 minutes | Serves 8

½ cup butter, at room temperature
2 ounces (57 g) Swerve
4 eggs
1 cup almond flour
1 teaspoon baking soda

⅓ teaspoon baking powder
½ cup cocoa powder
1 teaspoon orange zest
⅓ cup fresh blackberries

1. Select BAKE, set the temperature to 335ºF (168ºC), and set the time to 22 minutes. Select START/STOP to begin preheating.
2. With an electric mixer or hand mixer, beat the butter and Swerve until creamy.
3. One at a time, mix in the eggs and beat again until fluffy.
4. Add the almond flour, baking soda, baking powder, cocoa powder, orange zest and mix well. Add the butter mixture to the almond flour mixture and stir until well blended. Fold in the blackberries.
5. Scrape the batter to a baking pan. Place the pan directly in the pot. Close the hood and BAKE for 22 minutes. Check the cake for doneness: If a toothpick inserted into the center of the cake comes out clean, it's done.
6. Allow the cake cool on a wire rack to room temperature. Serve immediately.

Lemon Ricotta Cake

Prep time: 5 minutes | Cook time: 25 minutes | Serves 6

17.5 ounces (496 g) ricotta cheese
5.4 ounces (153 g) sugar
3 eggs, beaten

3 tablespoons flour
1 lemon, juiced and zested
2 teaspoons vanilla extract

1. Select BAKE, set the temperature to 320ºF (160ºC), and set the time to 25 minutes. Select START/STOP to begin preheating.
2. In a large mixing bowl, stir together all the ingredients until the mixture reaches a creamy consistency.
3. Pour the mixture into a baking pan. Place the pan directly in the pot.
4. Close the hood and BAKE for 25 minutes until a toothpick inserted in the center comes out clean.
5. Allow to cool for 10 minutes on a wire rack before serving.

Cinnamon Candied Apples

Prep time: 15 minutes | Cook time: 12 minutes | Serves 4

1 cup packed light brown sugar
2 teaspoons ground cinnamon

2 medium Granny Smith apples, peeled and diced

1. Select BAKE, set the temperature to 350ºF (177ºC), and set the time to 12 minutes. Select START/STOP to begin preheating.
2. Thoroughly combine the brown sugar and cinnamon in a medium bowl.
3. Add the apples to the bowl and stir until well coated. Transfer the apples to a baking pan.
4. Place the pan directly in the pot. Close the hood and BAKE for 9 minutes. Stir the apples once and bake for an additional 3 minutes until softened.
5. Serve warm.

Coffee Chocolate Cake

Prep time: 5 minutes | Cook time: 30 minutes | Serves 8

Dry Ingredients:
1½ cups almond flour
½ cup coconut meal
⅔ cup Swerve

1 teaspoon baking powder
¼ teaspoon salt

Wet Ingredients:
1 egg
1 stick butter, melted

½ cup hot strongly brewed coffee

Topping:
½ cup confectioner's Swerve
¼ cup coconut flour
3 tablespoons coconut oil

1 teaspoon ground cinnamon
½ teaspoon ground cardamom

1. Select BAKE, set the temperature to 330ºF (166ºC), and set the time to 30 minutes. Select START/STOP to begin preheating.
2. In a medium bowl, combine the almond flour, coconut meal, Swerve, baking powder, and salt.
3. In a large bowl, whisk the egg, melted butter, and coffee until smooth.
4. Add the dry mixture to the wet and stir until well incorporated. Transfer the batter to a greased baking pan.
5. Stir together all the ingredients for the topping in a small bowl. Spread the topping over the batter and smooth the top with a spatula.
6. Place the pan directly in the pot. Close the hood and BAKE for 30 minutes, or until the cake springs back when gently pressed with your fingers.
7. Rest for 10 minutes before serving.

Chocolate Pecan Pie

Prep time: 20 minutes | Cook time: 25 minutes | Serves 8

1 (9-inch) unbaked pie crust

Filling:

2 large eggs	chips
⅓ cup butter, melted	1½ cups coarsely
1 cup sugar	chopped pecans
½ cup all-purpose	2 tablespoons
flour	bourbon
1 cup milk chocolate	

1. Select BAKE, set the temperature to 350ºF (177ºC), and set the time to 25 minutes. Select START/STOP to begin preheating.
2. Whisk the eggs and melted butter in a large bowl until creamy.
3. Add the sugar and flour and stir to incorporate. Mix in the milk chocolate chips, pecans, and bourbon and stir until well combined.
4. Use a fork to prick holes in the bottom and sides of the pie crust. Pour the prepared filling into the pie crust. Place the pie crust in the pot.
5. Close the hood and BAKE for 25 minutes until a toothpick inserted in the center comes out clean.
6. Allow the pie cool for 10 minutes in the basket before serving.

Easy Blackberry Cobbler

Prep time: 15 minutes | Cook time: 25 to 30 minutes | Serves 6

3 cups fresh or frozen	extract
blackberries	8 tablespoons (1
1¾ cups sugar,	stick) butter, melted
divided	1 cup self-rising flour
1 teaspoon vanilla	Cooking spray

1. Select BAKE, set the temperature to 350ºF (177ºC), and set the time to 30 minutes. Select START/STOP to begin preheating.
2. Spritz a baking pan with cooking spray.
3. Mix the blackberries, 1 cup of sugar, and vanilla in a medium bowl and stir to combine.

4. Stir together the melted butter, remaining sugar, and flour in a separate medium bowl.
5. Spread the blackberry mixture evenly in the prepared pan and top with the butter mixture.
6. Place the pan directly in the pot. Close the hood and BAKE for 20 to 25 minutes. Check for doneness and bake for another 5 minutes, if needed.
7. Remove from the grill and place on a wire rack to cool to room temperature. Serve immediately.

Fudge Pie

Prep time: 15 minutes | Cook time: 25 to 30 minutes | Serves 8

1½ cups sugar	sticks) butter, melted
½ cup self-rising	1½ teaspoons vanilla
flour	extract
⅓ cup unsweetened	1 (9-inch) unbaked
cocoa powder	pie crust
3 large eggs, beaten	¼ cup confectioners'
12 tablespoons (1½	sugar (optional)

1. Select BAKE, set the temperature to 350ºF (177ºC), and set the time to 30 minutes. Select START/STOP to begin preheating.
2. Thoroughly combine the sugar, flour, and cocoa powder in a medium bowl. Add the beaten eggs and butter and whisk to combine. Stir in the vanilla.
3. Pour the prepared filling into the pie crust and transfer to the pot.
4. Close the hood and BAKE for 25 to 30 minutes until just set.
5. Allow the pie to cool for 5 minutes. Sprinkle with the confectioners' sugar, if desired. Serve warm.

Black and White Brownies

Prep time: 10 minutes | Cook time: 20 minutes | Makes 1 dozen brownies

1 egg
¼ cup brown sugar
2 tablespoons white sugar
2 tablespoons safflower oil
1 teaspoon vanilla
⅓ cup all-purpose flour
¼ cup cocoa powder
¼ cup white chocolate chips
Nonstick cooking spray

1. Select BAKE, set the temperature to 340ºF (171ºC), and set the time to 20 minutes. Select START/STOP to begin preheating.
2. Spritz a baking pan with nonstick cooking spray.
3. Whisk together the egg, brown sugar, and white sugar in a medium bowl. Mix in the safflower oil and vanilla and stir to combine.
4. Add the flour and cocoa powder and stir just until incorporated. Fold in the white chocolate chips.
5. Scrape the batter into the prepared baking pan.
6. Place the pan directly in the pot. Close the hood and BAKE for 20 minutes, or until the brownie springs back when touched lightly with your fingers.
7. Transfer to a wire rack and let cool for 30 minutes before slicing to serve.

Peanut Butter-Chocolate Bread Pudding

Prep time: 10 minutes | Cook time: 10 to 12 minutes | Serves 8

1 egg
1 egg yolk
¾ cup chocolate milk
3 tablespoons brown sugar
3 tablespoons peanut butter
2 tablespoons cocoa powder
1 teaspoon vanilla
5 slices firm white bread, cubed
Nonstick cooking spray

1. Select BAKE, set the temperature to 330ºF (166ºC), and set the time to 12 minutes. Select START/STOP to begin preheating.
2. Spritz a baking pan with nonstick cooking spray.
3. Whisk together the egg, egg yolk, chocolate milk, brown sugar, peanut butter, cocoa powder, and vanilla until well combined.
4. Fold in the bread cubes and stir to mix well. Allow the bread soak for 10 minutes.
5. When ready, transfer the egg mixture to the prepared baking pan.
6. Place the pan directly in the pot. Close the hood and BAKE for 10 to 12 minutes, or until the pudding is just firm to the touch.
7. Serve at room temperature.

Chia Pudding

Prep time: 5 minutes | Cook time: 4 minutes | Serves 2

1 cup chia seeds
1 cup unsweetened coconut milk
1 teaspoon liquid stevia
1 tablespoon coconut oil
1 teaspoon butter, melted

1. Select BAKE, set the temperature to 360ºF (182ºC), and set the time to 4 minutes. Select START/STOP to begin preheating.
2. Mix together the chia seeds, coconut milk, and stevia in a large bowl. Add the coconut oil and melted butter and stir until well blended.
3. Divide the mixture evenly between the ramekins, filling only about ⅔ of the way. Transfer to the pot.
4. Close the hood and BAKE for 4 minutes.
5. Allow to cool for 5 minutes and serve warm.

Chapter 9 Holiday Specials

Bourbon Monkey Bread

Prep time: 15 minutes | Cook time: 25 minutes | Serves 6 to 8

1 (16.3-ounce / 462-g) can store-bought refrigerated biscuit dough
¼ cup packed light brown sugar
1 teaspoon ground cinnamon
½ teaspoon freshly grated nutmeg
½ teaspoon ground ginger
½ teaspoon kosher salt
¼ teaspoon ground allspice
⅛ teaspoon ground cloves
4 tablespoons (½ stick) unsalted butter, melted
½ cup powdered sugar
2 teaspoons bourbon
2 tablespoons chopped candied cherries
2 tablespoons chopped pecans

1. Select BAKE, set the temperature to 310ºF (154ºC), and set the time to 25 minutes. Select START/STOP to begin preheating.
2. Open the can and separate the biscuits, then cut each into quarters. Toss the biscuit quarters in a large bowl with the brown sugar, cinnamon, nutmeg, ginger, salt, allspice, and cloves until evenly coated.
3. Transfer the dough pieces and any sugar left in the bowl to a round cake pan, metal cake pan, or foil pan and drizzle evenly with the melted butter.
4. Place the pan directly in the pot. Close the hood and BAKE for 25 minutes until the monkey bread is golden brown and cooked through in the middle. Transfer the pan to a wire rack and let cool completely. Unmold from the pan.
5. In a small bowl, whisk the powdered sugar and the bourbon into a smooth glaze. Drizzle the glaze over the cooled monkey bread and, while the glaze is still wet, sprinkle with the cherries and pecans to serve.

Golden Nuggets

Prep time: 15 minutes | Cook time: 4 minutes per batch | Makes 20 nuggets

1 cup all-purpose flour, plus more for dusting
1 teaspoon baking powder
½ teaspoon butter, at room temperature, plus more for brushing
¼ teaspoon salt
¼ cup water
⅛ teaspoon onion powder
¼ teaspoon garlic powder
⅛ teaspoon seasoning salt
Cooking spray

1. Insert the Crisper Basket and close the hood. Select AIR CRISP, set the temperature to 370ºF (188ºC), and set the time to 4 minutes. Select START/STOP to begin preheating.
2. Line the Crisper Basket with parchment paper.
3. Mix the flour, baking powder, butter, and salt in a large bowl. Stir to mix well. Gradually whisk in the water until a sanity dough forms.
4. Put the dough on a lightly floured work surface, then roll it out into a ½-inch thick rectangle with a rolling pin.
5. Cut the dough into about twenty 1- or 2-inch squares, then arrange the squares in a single layer in the basket. Spritz with cooking spray. You need to work in batches to avoid overcrowding.
6. Combine onion powder, garlic powder, and seasoning salt in a small bowl. Stir to mix well, then sprinkle the squares with the powder mixture.
7. Close the hood and AIR CRISP for 4 minutes or until golden brown. Flip the squares halfway through the cooking time.
8. Remove the golden nuggets from the grill and brush with more butter immediately. Serve warm.

Garlicky Olive Stromboli

Prep time: 25 minutes | Cook time: 25 minutes | Serves 8

4 large cloves garlic, unpeeled
3 tablespoons grated Parmesan cheese
½ cup packed fresh basil leaves
½ cup marinated, pitted green and black olives
¼ teaspoon crushed red pepper
½ pound (227 g) pizza dough, at room temperature
4 ounces (113 g) sliced provolone cheese (about 8 slices)
Cooking spray

1. Insert the Crisper Basket and close the hood. Select AIR CRISP, set the temperature to 370ºF (188ºC), and set the time to 10 minutes. Select START/STOP to begin preheating.
2. Spritz the Crisper Basket with cooking spray.
3. Put the unpeeled garlic in the Crisper Basket.
4. Close the hood and AIR CRISP for 10 minutes or until the garlic is softened completely. Remove them from the grill and allow to cool until you can handle.
5. Peel the garlic and place into a food processor with 2 tablespoons of Parmesan, basil, olives, and crushed red pepper. Pulse to mix well. Set aside.
6. Arrange the pizza dough on a clean work surface, then roll it out with a rolling pin into a rectangle. Cut the rectangle in half.
7. Sprinkle half of the garlic mixture over each rectangle half, and leave ½-inch edges uncover. Top them with the provolone cheese.
8. Brush one long side of each rectangle half with water, then roll them up. Spritz the Crisper Basket with cooking spray. Transfer the rolls to the basket. Spritz with cooking spray and scatter with remaining Parmesan.
9. Close the hood and AIR CRISP for 15 minutes or until golden brown. Flip the rolls halfway through.
10. Remove the rolls from the grill and allow to cool for a few minutes before serving.

Kale Salad Sushi Rolls with Sriracha Mayonnaise

Prep time: 10 minutes | Cook time: 10 minutes | Serves 12

Kale Salad:
1½ cups chopped kale
1 tablespoon sesame seeds
¾ teaspoon soy sauce
¾ teaspoon toasted
sesame oil
½ teaspoon rice vinegar
¼ teaspoon ginger
⅛ teaspoon garlic powder

Sushi Rolls:
3 sheets sushi nori
1 batch cauliflower rice
½ avocado, sliced
Sriracha Mayonnaise:
¼ cup Sriracha sauce
¼ cup vegan mayonnaise

Coating:
½ cup panko breadcrumbs

1. Insert the Crisper Basket and close the hood. Select AIR CRISP, set the temperature to 390ºF (199ºC), and set the time to 10 minutes. Select START/STOP to begin preheating.
2. In a medium bowl, toss all the ingredients for the salad together until well coated and set aside.
3. Place a sheet of nori on a clean work surface and spread the cauliflower rice in an even layer on the nori. Scoop 2 to 3 tablespoon of kale salad on the rice and spread over. Place 1 or 2 avocado slices on top. Roll up the sushi, pressing gently to get a nice, tight roll. Repeat to make the remaining 2 rolls.
4. In a bowl, stir together the Sriracha sauce and mayonnaise until smooth. Add breadcrumbs to a separate bowl.
5. Dredge the sushi rolls in Sriracha Mayonnaise, then roll in breadcrumbs till well coated.
6. Place the coated sushi rolls in the Crisper Basket. Close the hood and AIR CRISP for 10 minutes, or until golden brown and crispy. Flip the sushi rolls gently halfway through to ensure even cooking..
7. Transfer to a platter and rest for 5 minutes before slicing each roll into 8 pieces. Serve warm.

Milky Pecan Tart

Prep time: 2hours 25 minutes | Cook time: 30 minutes | Serves 8

Tart Crust:

¼ cup firmly packed brown sugar
⅓ cup butter, softened

1 cup all-purpose flour
¼ teaspoon kosher salt

Filling:

¼ cup whole milk
4 tablespoons butter, diced
½ cup packed brown sugar
¼ cup pure maple

syrup
1½ cups finely chopped pecans
¼ teaspoon pure vanilla extract
¼ teaspoon sea salt

1. Select BAKE, set the temperature to 350ºF (177ºC), and set the time to 25 minutes. Select START/STOP to begin preheating.
2. Line a baking pan with aluminum foil, then spritz the pan with cooking spray.
3. Stir the brown sugar and butter in a bowl with a hand mixer until puffed, then add the flour and salt and stir until crumbled.
4. Pour the mixture in the prepared baking pan and tilt the pan to coat the bottom evenly.
5. Place the pan directly in the pot. Close the hood and BAKE for 13 minutes or until the crust is golden brown.
6. Meanwhile, pour the milk, butter, sugar, and maple syrup in a saucepan. Stir to mix well. Bring to a simmer, then cook for 1 more minute. Stir constantly.
7. Turn off the heat and mix the pecans and vanilla into the filling mixture.
8. Pour the filling mixture over the golden crust and spread with a spatula to coat the crust evenly.
9. Bake in the grill for an additional 12 minutes or until the filling mixture is set and frothy.
10. Remove the baking pan from the grill and sprinkle with salt. Allow to sit for 10 minutes or until cooled.
11. Transfer the pan to the refrigerator to chill for at least 2 hours, then remove the aluminum foil and slice to serve.

Pão de Queijo

Prep time: 37 minutes | Cook time: 24 minutes | Makes 12 balls

2 tablespoons butter, plus more for greasing
½ cup milk
1½ cups tapioca flour

½ teaspoon salt
1 large egg
⅔ cup finely grated aged Asiago cheese

1. Put the butter in a saucepan and pour in the milk, heat over medium heat until the liquid boils. Keep stirring.
2. Turn off the heat and mix in the tapioca flour and salt to form a soft dough. Transfer the dough in a large bowl, then wrap the bowl in plastic and let sit for 15 minutes.
3. Break the egg in the bowl of dough and whisk with a hand mixer for 2 minutes or until a sanity dough forms. Fold the cheese in the dough. Cover the bowl in plastic again and let sit for 10 more minutes.
4. Select BAKE, set the temperature to 375ºF (191ºC), and set the time to 12 minutes. Select START/STOP to begin preheating.
5. Grease a cake pan with butter.
6. Scoop 2 tablespoons of the dough into the cake pan. Repeat with the remaining dough to make dough 12 balls. Keep a little distance between each two balls. You may need to work in batches to avoid overcrowding.
7. Place the pan directly in the pot. Close the hood and BAKE for 12 minutes or until the balls are golden brown and fluffy. Flip the balls halfway through the cooking time.
8. Remove the balls from the grill and allow to cool for 5 minutes before serving.

Hearty Honey Yeast Rolls

Prep time: 10 minutes | Cook time: 20 minutes | Makes 8 rolls

¼ cup whole milk, heated to 115ºF (46ºC) in the microwave
½ teaspoon active dry yeast
1 tablespoon honey
²/₃ cup all-purpose flour, plus more for dusting

½ teaspoon kosher salt
2 tablespoons unsalted butter, at room temperature, plus more for greasing
Flaky sea salt, to taste

1. In a large bowl, whisk together the milk, yeast, and honey and let stand until foamy, about 10 minutes.
2. Stir in the flour and salt until just combined. Stir in the butter until absorbed. Scrape the dough onto a lightly floured work surface and knead until smooth, about 6 minutes. Transfer the dough to a lightly greased bowl, cover loosely with a sheet of plastic wrap or a kitchen towel, and let sit until nearly doubled in size, about 1 hour.
3. Uncover the dough, lightly press it down to expel the bubbles, then portion it into 8 equal pieces. Prep the work surface by wiping it clean with a damp paper towel (if there is flour on the work surface, it will prevent the dough from sticking lightly to the surface, which helps it form a ball). Roll each piece into a ball by cupping the palm of the hand around the dough against the work surface and moving the heel of the hand in a circular motion while using the thumb to contain the dough and tighten it into a perfectly round ball. Once all the balls are formed, nestle them side by side in the Crisper Basket.
4. Cover the rolls loosely with a kitchen towel or a sheet of plastic wrap and let sit until lightly risen and puffed, 20 to 30 minutes.
5. Insert the Crisper Basket and close the hood. Select AIR CRISP, set the temperature to 270ºF (132ºC), and set the time to 12 minutes. Select START/STOP to begin preheating.
6. Uncover the rolls and gently brush with more butter, being careful not to press the rolls too hard. Close the hood and AIR CRISP for 12 minutes until the rolls are light golden brown and fluffy.
7. Remove the rolls from the grill and brush liberally with more butter, if you like, and sprinkle each roll with a pinch of sea salt. Serve warm.

Simple Butter Cake

Prep time: 25 minutes | Cook time: 20 minutes | Serves 8

1 cup all-purpose flour
1¼ teaspoons baking powder
¼ teaspoon salt
½ cup plus 1½ tablespoons granulated white sugar

9½ tablespoons butter, at room temperature
2 large eggs
1 large egg yolk
2½ tablespoons milk
1 teaspoon vanilla extract
Cooking spray

1. Select BAKE, set the temperature to 325ºF (163ºC), and set the time to 20 minutes. Select START/STOP to begin preheating.
2. Spritz a cake pan with cooking spray.
3. Combine the flour, baking powder, and salt in a large bowl. Stir to mix well.
4. Whip the sugar and butter in a separate bowl with a hand mixer on medium speed for 3 minutes.
5. Whip the eggs, egg yolk, milk, and vanilla extract into the sugar and butter mix with a hand mixer.
6. Pour in the flour mixture and whip with hand mixer until sanity and smooth.
7. Scrape the batter into the cake pan and level the batter with a spatula.
8. Place the pan directly in the pot. Close the hood and BAKE for 20 minutes or until a toothpick inserted in the center comes out clean. Check the doneness during the last 5 minutes of the baking.
9. Invert the cake on a cooling rack and allow to cool for 15 minutes before slicing to serve.

Pigs in a Blanket

Prep time: 10 minutes | Cook time: 8 minutes per batch | Makes 16 rolls

1 can refrigerated crescent roll dough
1 small package mini smoked sausages, patted dry

2 tablespoons melted butter
2 teaspoons sesame seeds
1 teaspoon onion powder

1. Select BAKE, set the temperature to 330ºF (166ºC), and set the time to 8 minutes. Select START/STOP to begin preheating.
2. Place the crescent roll dough on a clean work surface and separate into 8 pieces. Cut each piece in half and you will have 16 triangles.
3. Make the pigs in the blanket: Arrange each sausage on each dough triangle, then roll the sausages up.
4. Brush the pigs with melted butter and place half of the pigs in the blanket in the baking pan. Sprinkle with sesame seeds and onion powder.
5. Place the pan directly in the pot. Close the hood and BAKE for 8 minutes or until the pigs are fluffy and golden brown. Flip the pigs halfway through.
6. Serve immediately.

Hasselback Potatoes

Prep time: 5 minutes | Cook time: 50 minutes | Serves 4

4 russet potatoes, peeled
Salt and freshly ground black pepper, to taste

¼ cup grated Parmesan cheese
Cooking spray

1. Insert the Crisper Basket and close the hood. Select AIR CRISP, set the temperature to 400ºF (204ºC), and set the time to 50 minutes. Select START/STOP to begin preheating.
2. Spray the Crisper Basket lightly with cooking spray.
3. Make thin parallel cuts into each potato, ⅛-inch to ¼-inch apart, stopping at about ½ of the way through. The potato needs to stay intact along the bottom.
4. Spray the potatoes with cooking spray and use the hands or a silicone brush to completely coat the potatoes lightly in oil.
5. Put the potatoes, sliced side up, in the Crisper Basket in a single layer. Leave a little room between each potato. Sprinkle the potatoes lightly with salt and black pepper.
6. Close the hood and AIR CRISP for 20 minutes. Reposition the potatoes and spritz lightly with cooking spray again. AIR CRISP until the potatoes are fork-tender and crispy and browned, for another 20 to 30 minutes.
7. Sprinkle the potatoes with Parmesan cheese and serve.

Spicy Black Olives

Prep time: 10 minutes | Cook time: 5 minutes | Serves 4

12 ounces (340 g) pitted black extra-large olives
¼ cup all-purpose flour
1 cup panko bread crumbs
2 teaspoons dried thyme

1 teaspoon red pepper flakes
1 teaspoon smoked paprika
1 egg beaten with 1 tablespoon water
Vegetable oil for spraying

1. Insert the Crisper Basket and close the hood. Select AIR CRISP, set the temperature to 400ºF (204ºC), and set the time to 5 minutes. Select START/STOP to begin preheating.
2. Drain the olives and place them on a paper towel–lined plate to dry.
3. Put the flour on a plate. Combine the panko, thyme, red pepper flakes, and paprika on a separate plate. Dip an olive in the flour, shaking off any excess, then coat with egg mixture. Dredge the olive in the panko mixture, pressing to make the crumbs adhere, and place the breaded olive on a platter. Repeat with the remaining olives.
4. Spray the olives with oil and place them in a single layer in the Crisper Basket. Work in batches if necessary so as not to overcrowd the basket.
5. Close the hood and AIR CRISP for 5 minutes until the breading is browned and crispy. Serve warm

Shrimp with Sriracha and Worcestershire Sauce

Prep time: 15 minutes | Cook time: 10 minutes per batch | Serves 4

1 tablespoon Sriracha sauce
1 teaspoon Worcestershire sauce
2 tablespoons sweet chili sauce
¾ cup mayonnaise
1 egg, beaten

1 cup panko breadcrumbs
1 pound (454 g) raw shrimp, shelled and deveined, rinsed and drained
Lime wedges, for serving
Cooking spray

1. Insert the Crisper Basket and close the hood. Select AIR CRISP, set the temperature to 360ºF (182ºC), and set the time to 10 minutes. Select START/STOP to begin preheating.
2. Spritz the Crisper Basket with cooking spray.
3. Combine the Sriracha sauce, Worcestershire sauce, chili sauce, and mayo in a bowl. Stir to mix well. Reserve ⅓ cup of the mixture as the dipping sauce.
4. Combine the remaining sauce mixture with the beaten egg. Stir to mix well. Put the panko in a separate bowl.
5. Dredge the shrimp in the sauce mixture first, then into the panko. Roll the shrimp to coat well. Shake the excess off.
6. Place the shrimp in the basket, then spritz with cooking spray. You may need to work in batches to avoid overcrowding.
7. Close the hood and AIR CRISP for 10 minutes or until opaque. Flip the shrimp halfway through the cooking time.
8. Remove the shrimp from the grill and serve with reserve sauce mixture and squeeze the lime wedges over.

Jewish Blintzes

Prep time: 5 minutes | Cook time: 10 minutes | Makes 8 blintzes

2 (7½-ounce / 213-g) packages farmer cheese, mashed
¼ cup cream cheese
¼ teaspoon vanilla extract

¼ cup granulated white sugar
8 egg roll wrappers
4 tablespoons butter, melted

1. Insert the Crisper Basket and close the hood. Select AIR CRISP, set the temperature to 375ºF (191ºC), and set the time to 10 minutes. Select START/STOP to begin preheating.
2. Combine the farmer cheese, cream cheese, vanilla extract, and sugar in a bowl. Stir to mix well.
3. Unfold the egg roll wrappers on a clean work surface, spread ¼ cup of the filling at the edge of each wrapper and leave a ½-inch edge uncovering.
4. Wet the edges of the wrappers with water and fold the uncovered edge over the filling. Fold the left and right sides in the center, then tuck the edge under the filling and fold to wrap the filling.
5. Brush the wrappers with melted butter, then arrange the wrappers in a single layer in the basket, seam side down. Leave a little space between each two wrappers. Work in batches to avoid overcrowding.
6. Close the hood and AIR CRISP for 10 minutes or until golden brown.
7. Serve immediately.

Teriyaki Shrimp Skewers

Prep time: 10 minutes | Cook time: 6 minutes | Makes 12 skewered shrimp

1½ tablespoons mirin
1½ teaspoons ginger juice
1½ tablespoons soy sauce
12 large shrimp (about 20 shrimps per

pound), peeled and deveined
1 large egg
¾ cup panko breadcrumbs
Cooking spray

1. Combine the mirin, ginger juice, and soy sauce in a large bowl. Stir to mix well.
2. Dunk the shrimp in the bowl of mirin mixture, then wrap the bowl in plastic and refrigerate for 1 hour to marinate.
3. Insert the Crisper Basket and close the hood. Select AIR CRISP, set the temperature to 400ºF (204ºC), and set the time to 6 minutes. Select START/STOP to begin preheating.
4. Spritz the Crisper Basket with cooking spray.
5. Run twelve 4-inch skewers through each shrimp.
6. Whisk the egg in the bowl of marinade to combine well. Pour the breadcrumbs on a plate.
7. Dredge the shrimp skewers in the egg mixture, then shake the excess off and roll over the breadcrumbs to coat well.
8. Arrange the shrimp skewers in the basket and spritz with cooking spray. You need to work in batches to avoid overcrowding.
9. Close the hood and AIR CRISP for 6 minutes or until the shrimp are opaque and firm. Flip the shrimp skewers halfway through.
10. Serve immediately.

Supplì al Telefono (Risotto Croquettes)

Prep time: 1 hour 40 minutes | Cook time: 1 hour | Serves 6

Risotto Croquettes:
4 tablespoons unsalted butter
1 small yellow onion, minced
1 cup Arborio rice
3½ cups chicken stock
½ cup dry white wine
3 eggs
Zest of 1 lemon
½ cup grated Parmesan cheese

2 ounces (57 g) fresh Mozzarella cheese
¼ cup peas
2 tablespoons water
½ cup all-purpose flour
1½ cups panko breadcrumbs
Kosher salt and ground black pepper, to taste
Cooking spray

Tomato Sauce:
2 tablespoons extra-virgin olive oil
4 cloves garlic, minced
¼ teaspoon red pepper flakes

1 (28-ounce / 794-g) can crushed tomatoes
2 teaspoons granulated sugar
Kosher salt and ground black pepper, to taste

1. Melt the butter in a pot over medium heat, then add the onion and salt to taste. Sauté for 5 minutes or until the onion in translucent.
2. Add the rice and stir to coat well. Cook for 3 minutes or until the rice is lightly browned. Pour in the chicken stock and wine.
3. Bring to a boil. Then cook for 20 minutes or until the rice is tender and liquid is almost absorbed.
4. Make the risotto: When the rice is cooked, break the egg into the pot. Add the lemon zest and Parmesan cheese. Sprinkle with salt and ground black pepper. Stir to mix well.
5. Pour the risotto in a baking pan, then level with a spatula to spread the risotto evenly. Wrap the baking pan in plastic and refrigerate for1 hour.
6. Meanwhile, heat the olive oil in a saucepan over medium heat until shimmering.
7. Add the garlic and sprinkle with red pepper flakes. Sauté for a minute or until fragrant.
8. Add the crushed tomatoes and sprinkle with sugar. Stir to mix well. Bring to a boil. Reduce the heat to low and simmer for 15 minutes or until lightly thickened. Sprinkle with salt and pepper to taste. Set aside until ready to serve.
9. Remove the risotto from the refrigerator. Scoop the risotto into twelve 2-inch balls, then flatten the balls with your hands.
10. Arrange a about ½-inch piece of Mozzarella and 5 peas in the center of each flattened ball, then wrap them back into balls.
11. Transfer the balls in a baking pan lined with parchment paper, then refrigerate for 15 minutes or until firm.
12. Insert the Crisper Basket and close the hood. Select BAKE, set the temperature to 400ºF (204ºC), and set the time to 10 minutes. Select START/STOP to begin preheating.
13. Whisk the remaining 2 eggs with 2 tablespoons of water in a bowl. Pour the flour in a second bowl and pour the panko in a third bowl.
14. Dredge the risotto balls in the bowl of flour first, then into the eggs, and then into the panko. Shake the excess off.
15. Transfer the balls to the basket and spritz with cooking spray. You may need to work in batches to avoid overcrowding.
16. Close the hood and BAKE for 10 minutes or until golden brown. Flip the balls halfway through.
17. Serve the risotto balls with the tomato sauce.

Chapter 10 Fast and Easy Everyday Favorites

Bacon-Wrapped Jalapeño Poppers

Prep time: 5 minutes | Cook time: 12 minutes | Serves 6

6 large jalapeños
4 ounces (113 g)
⅓-less-fat cream cheese
¼ cup shredded reduced-fat sharp
Cheddar cheese
2 scallions, green tops only, sliced
6 slices center-cut bacon, halved

1. Insert the Crisper Basket and close the hood. Select BAKE, set the temperature to 325ºF (163ºC), and set the time to 12 minutes. Select START/STOP to begin preheating.
2. Wearing rubber gloves, halve the jalapeños lengthwise to make 12 pieces. Scoop out the seeds and membranes and discard.
3. In a medium bowl, combine the cream cheese, Cheddar, and scallions. Using a small spoon or spatula, fill the jalapeños with the cream cheese filling. Wrap a bacon strip around each pepper and secure with a toothpick.
4. Working in batches, place the stuffed peppers in a single layer in the Crisper Basket. Close the hood and BAKE for 12 minutes, until the peppers are tender, the bacon is browned and crisp, and the cheese is melted.
5. Serve warm.

Indian-Style Sweet Potato Fries

Prep time: 5 minutes | Cook time: 8 minutes | Makes 20 fries

Seasoning Mixture:
¾ teaspoon ground coriander
½ teaspoon garam masala
½ teaspoon garlic
powder
½ teaspoon ground cumin
¼ teaspoon ground cayenne pepper

Fries:
2 large sweet potatoes, peeled
2 teaspoons olive oil

1. Insert the Crisper Basket and close the hood. Select AIR CRISP, set the temperature to 400ºF (204ºC), and set the time to 8 minutes. Select START/STOP to begin preheating.
2. In a small bowl, combine the coriander, garam masala, garlic powder, cumin, and cayenne pepper.
3. Slice the sweet potatoes into ¼-inch-thick fries.
4. In a large bowl, toss the sliced sweet potatoes with the olive oil and the seasoning mixture.
5. Transfer the seasoned sweet potatoes to the Crisper Basket. Close the hood and AIR CRISP for 8 minutes, until crispy.
6. Serve warm.

Easy Devils on Horseback

Prep time: 5 minutes | Cook time: 7 minutes | Serves 12

24 petite pitted prunes (4½ ounces / 128 g)
¼ cup crumbled blue
cheese, divided
8 slices center-cut bacon, cut crosswise into thirds

1. Insert the Crisper Basket and close the hood. Select AIR CRISP, set the temperature to 400ºF (204ºC), and set the time to 7 minutes. Select START/STOP to begin preheating.
2. Halve the prunes lengthwise, but don't cut them all the way through. Place ½ teaspoon of cheese in the center of each prune. Wrap a piece of bacon around each prune and secure the bacon with a toothpick.
3. Working in batches, arrange a single layer of the prunes in the Crisper Basket. Close the hood and AIR CRISP for about 7 minutes, flipping halfway, until the bacon is cooked through and crisp.
4. Let cool slightly and serve warm.

Cheesy Chile Toast

Prep time: 5 minutes | Cook time: 5 minutes | Serves 1

2 tablespoons grated Parmesan cheese	10 to 15 thin slices serrano chile or jalapeño
2 tablespoons grated Mozzarella cheese	2 slices sourdough bread
2 teaspoons salted butter, at room temperature	½ teaspoon black pepper

1. Insert the Crisper Basket and close the hood. Select BAKE, set the temperature to 325ºF (163ºC), and set the time to 5 minutes. Select START/STOP to begin preheating.
2. In a small bowl, stir together the Parmesan, Mozzarella, butter, and chiles.
3. Spread half the mixture onto one side of each slice of bread. Sprinkle with the pepper. Place the slices, cheese-side up, in the Crisper Basket.
4. Close the hood and BAKE for 5 minutes, or until the cheese has melted and started to brown slightly.
5. Serve immediately.

Baked Cheese Sandwich

Prep time: 5 minutes | Cook time: 8 minutes | Serves 2

2 tablespoons mayonnaise	4 thick slices Brie cheese
4 thick slices sourdough bread	8 slices hot capicola

1. Insert the Crisper Basket and close the hood. Select BAKE, set the temperature to 350ºF (177ºC), and set the time to 8 minutes. Select START/STOP to begin preheating.
2. Spread the mayonnaise on one side of each slice of bread. Place 2 slices of bread in the Crisper Basket, mayonnaise-side down.
3. Place the slices of Brie and capicola on the bread and cover with the remaining two slices of bread, mayonnaise-side up.
4. Close the hood and BAKE for 8 minutes, or until the cheese has melted.
5. Serve immediately.

Hot Wings

Prep time: 5 minutes | Cook time: 30 minutes | Makes 16 wings

16 chicken wings	sauce
3 tablespoons hot	Cooking spray

1. Insert the Crisper Basket and close the hood. Select AIR CRISP, set the temperature to 360ºF (182ºC), and set the time to 15 minutes. Select START/STOP to begin preheating.
2. Spritz the Crisper Basket with cooking spray.
3. Arrange the chicken wings in the basket. You need to work in batches to avoid overcrowding.
4. Close the hood and AIR CRISP for 15 minutes or until well browned. Shake the basket at lease three times during the cooking.
5. Transfer the wings on a plate and serve with hot sauce.

Lemony and Garlicky Asparagus

Prep time: 5 minutes | Cook time: 10 minutes | Makes 10 spears

10 spears asparagus (about ½ pound / 227 g in total), snap the ends off	2 teaspoons minced garlic
1 tablespoon lemon juice	½ teaspoon salt
	¼ teaspoon ground black pepper
	Cooking spray

1. Insert the Crisper Basket and close the hood. Select AIR CRISP, set the temperature to 400ºF (204ºC), and set the time to 10 minutes. Select START/STOP to begin preheating.
2. Line the Crisper Basket with parchment paper.
3. Put the asparagus spears in a large bowl. Drizzle with lemon juice and sprinkle with minced garlic, salt, and ground black pepper. Toss to coat well.
4. Transfer the asparagus in the basket and spritz with cooking spray. Close the hood and AIR CRISP for 10 minutes or until wilted and soft. Flip the asparagus halfway through.
5. Serve immediately.

Parsnip Fries with Garlic-Yogurt Dip

Prep time: 10 minutes | Cook time: 10 minutes | Serves 4

3 medium parsnips, peeled, cut into sticks
¼ teaspoon kosher salt

Dip:
¼ cup plain Greek yogurt
⅛ teaspoon garlic powder
1 tablespoon sour

1 teaspoon olive oil
1 garlic clove, unpeeled
Cooking spray

cream
¼ teaspoon kosher salt
Freshly ground black pepper, to taste

1. Insert the Crisper Basket and close the hood. Select AIR CRISP, set the temperature to 360ºF (182ºC), and set the time to 10 minutes. Select START/STOP to begin preheating.
2. Spritz the Crisper Basket with cooking spray.
3. Put the parsnip sticks in a large bowl, then sprinkle with salt and drizzle with olive oil.
4. Transfer the parsnip into the basket and add the garlic.
5. Close the hood and AIR CRISP for 5 minutes, then remove the garlic from the grill and shake the basket. AIR CRISP for 5 more minutes or until the parsnip sticks are crisp.
6. Meanwhile, peel the garlic and crush it. Combine the crushed garlic with the ingredients for the dip. Stir to mix well.
7. When the frying is complete, remove the parsnip fries from the grill and serve with the dipping sauce.

Roasted Carrot Chips

Prep time: 5 minutes | Cook time: 15 minutes | Makes 3 cups

3 large carrots, peeled and sliced into long and thick chips diagonally
1 tablespoon granulated garlic
1 teaspoon salt

¼ teaspoon ground black pepper
1 tablespoon olive oil
1 tablespoon finely chopped fresh parsley

1. Select ROAST, set the temperature to 360ºF (182ºC), and set the time to 15 minutes. Select START/STOP to begin preheating.
2. Toss the carrots with garlic, salt, ground black pepper, and olive oil in a large bowl to coat well.
3. Place the carrots in the pot. Close the hood and ROAST for 15 minutes or until the carrot chips are soft. Shake the basket halfway through.
4. Serve the carrot chips with parsley on top.

Southwest Corn and Bell Pepper Roast

Prep time: 10 minutes | Cook time: 10 minutes | Serves 4

For the Corn:
1½ cups thawed frozen corn kernels
1 cup mixed diced bell peppers
1 jalapeño, diced
1 cup diced yellow onion
½ teaspoon ancho

chile powder
1 tablespoon fresh lemon juice
1 teaspoon ground cumin
½ teaspoon kosher salt
Cooking spray

For Serving:
¼ cup feta cheese
¼ cup chopped fresh cilantro

1 tablespoon fresh lemon juice

1. Insert the Crisper Basket and close the hood. Select AIR CRISP, set the temperature to 375ºF (191ºC), and set the time to 10 minutes. Select START/STOP to begin preheating.
2. Spritz the basket with cooking spray.
3. Combine the ingredients for the corn in a large bowl. Stir to mix well.
4. Pout the mixture into the basket. Close the hood and AIR CRISP for 10 minutes or until the corn and bell peppers are soft. Shake the basket halfway through the cooking time.
5. Transfer them onto a large plate, then spread with feta cheese and cilantro. Drizzle with lemon juice and serve.

Crispy Brussels Sprouts

Prep time: 5 minutes | Cook time: 20 minutes | Serves 4

¼ teaspoon salt
⅛ teaspoon ground black pepper
1 tablespoon extra-virgin olive oil

1 pound (454 g) Brussels sprouts, trimmed and halved
Lemon wedges, for garnish

1. Insert the Crisper Basket and close the hood. Select AIR CRISP, set the temperature to 350ºF (177ºC), and set the time to 20 minutes. Select START/ STOP to begin preheating.
2. Combine the salt, black pepper, and olive oil in a large bowl. Stir to mix well.
3. Add the Brussels sprouts to the bowl of mixture and toss to coat well.
4. Arrange the Brussels sprouts in the basket. Close the hood and AIR CRISP for 20 minutes or until lightly browned and wilted. Shake the basket two times during the cooking.
5. Transfer the cooked Brussels sprouts to a large plate and squeeze the lemon wedges on top to serve.

Sweet and Sour Peanuts

Prep time: 5 minutes | Cook time: 5 minutes | Serves 9

3 cups shelled raw peanuts
1 tablespoon hot red pepper sauce

3 tablespoons granulated white sugar

1. Insert the Crisper Basket and close the hood. Select AIR CRISP, set the temperature to 400ºF (204ºC), and set the time to 5 minutes. Select START/ STOP to begin preheating.
2. Put the peanuts in a large bowl, then drizzle with hot red pepper sauce and sprinkle with sugar. Toss to coat well.
3. Pour the peanuts in the basket. Close the hood and AIR CRISP for 5 minutes or until the peanuts are crispy and browned. Shake the basket halfway through.
4. Serve immediately.

Simple Baked Green Beans

Prep time: 5 minutes | Cook time: 10 minutes | Makes 2 cups

½ teaspoon lemon pepper
2 teaspoons granulated garlic
½ teaspoon salt

1 tablespoon olive oil
2 cups fresh green beans, trimmed and snapped in half

1. Insert the Crisper Basket and close the hood. Select BAKE, set the temperature to 370ºF (188ºC), and set the time to 10 minutes. Select START/STOP to begin preheating.
2. Combine the lemon pepper, garlic, salt, and olive oil in a bowl. Stir to mix well.
3. Add the green beans to the bowl of mixture and toss to coat well.
4. Arrange the green beans in the basket. Close the hood and BAKE for 10 minutes or until tender and crispy. Shake the basket halfway through to make sure the green beans are cooked evenly.
5. Serve immediately.

Spicy Old Bay Shrimp

Prep time: 7 minutes | Cook time: 10 minutes | Makes 2 cups

½ teaspoon Old Bay Seasoning
1 teaspoon ground cayenne pepper
½ teaspoon paprika
1 tablespoon olive oil

⅛ teaspoon salt
½ pound (227 g) shrimps, peeled and deveined
Juice of half a lemon

1. Insert the Crisper Basket and close the hood. Select AIR CRISP, set the temperature to 390ºF (199ºC), and set the time to 10 minutes. Select START/ STOP to begin preheating.
2. Combine the Old Bay Seasoning, cayenne pepper, paprika, olive oil, and salt in a large bowl, then add the shrimps and toss to coat well.
3. Put the shrimps in the basket. Close the hood and AIR CRISP for 10 minutes or until opaque. Flip the shrimps halfway through.
4. Serve the shrimps with lemon juice on top.

Simple Sweet Potato Soufflé

Prep time: 10 minutes | Cook time: 30 minutes | Serves 4

1 sweet potato, baked and mashed	1 large egg, separated
2 tablespoons unsalted butter, divided	¼ cup whole milk
	½ teaspoon kosher salt

1. Select BAKE, set the temperature to 330ºF (166ºC), and set the time to 15 minutes. Select START/STOP to begin preheating.
2. In a medium bowl, combine the sweet potato, 1 tablespoon of melted butter, egg yolk, milk, and salt. Set aside.
3. In a separate medium bowl, whisk the egg white until stiff peaks form.
4. Using a spatula, gently fold the egg white into the sweet potato mixture.
5. Coat the inside of four 3-inch ramekins with the remaining 1 tablespoon of butter, then fill each ramekin halfway full. Place 2 ramekins in the pot.
6. Close the hood and BAKE for 15 minutes. Repeat this process with the remaining ramekins.
7. Remove the ramekins from the grill and allow to cool on a wire rack for 10 minutes before serving

Beet Salad with Lemon Vinaigrette

Prep time: 10 minutes | Cook time: 12 to 15 minutes | Serves 4

6 medium red and golden beets, peeled and sliced	salt
	½ cup crumbled feta cheese
1 teaspoon olive oil	8 cups mixed greens
¼ teaspoon kosher	Cooking spray

Vinaigrette:

2 teaspoons olive oil	chopped fresh chives
2 tablespoons	Juice of 1 lemon

1. Insert the Crisper Basket and close the hood. Select AIR CRISP, set the temperature to 360ºF (182ºC), and set the time to 15 minutes. Select START/STOP to begin preheating.
2. In a large bowl, toss the beets, olive oil, and kosher salt.
3. Spray the Crisper Basket with cooking spray, then place the beets in the basket. Close the hood and AIR CRISP for 12 to 15 minutes or until tender.
4. While the beets cook, make the vinaigrette in a large bowl by whisking together the olive oil, lemon juice, and chives.
5. Remove the beets from the grill, toss in the vinaigrette, and allow to cool for 5 minutes. Add the feta and serve on top of the mixed greens.

Golden Salmon and Carrot Croquettes

Prep time: 15 minutes | Cook time: 10 minutes | Serves 6

2 egg whites	2 tablespoons minced garlic cloves
1 cup almond flour	½ cup chopped onion
1 cup panko breadcrumbs	2 tablespoons chopped chives
1 pound (454 g) chopped salmon fillet	Cooking spray
⅔ cup grated carrots	

1. Insert the Crisper Basket and close the hood. Select AIR CRISP, set the temperature to 350ºF (177ºC), and set the time to 10 minutes. Select START/STOP to begin preheating.
2. Spritz the Crisper Basket with cooking spray.
3. Whisk the egg whites in a bowl. Put the flour in a second bowl. Pour the breadcrumbs in a third bowl. Set aside.
4. Combine the salmon, carrots, garlic, onion, and chives in a large bowl. Stir to mix well.
5. Form the mixture into balls with your hands. Dredge the balls into the flour, then egg, and then breadcrumbs to coat well.
6. Arrange the salmon balls in the basket and spritz with cooking spray.
7. Close the hood and AIR CRISP for 10 minutes or until crispy and browned. Shake the basket halfway through.
8. Serve immediately.

Garlicky Baked Cherry Tomatoes

Prep time: 5 minutes | Cook time: 4 to 6 minutes | Serves 2

2 cups cherry tomatoes
1 clove garlic, thinly sliced
1 teaspoon olive oil
⅛ teaspoon kosher
salt
1 tablespoon freshly chopped basil, for topping
Cooking spray

1. Select BAKE, set the temperature to 360ºF (182ºC), and set the time to 6 minutes. Select START/STOP to begin preheating.
2. Spritz a baking pan with cooking spray and set aside.
3. In a large bowl, toss together the cherry tomatoes, sliced garlic, olive oil, and kosher salt. Spread the mixture in an even layer in the prepared pan.
4. Place the pan directly in the pot. Close the hood and BAKE for 4 to 6 minutes, or until the tomatoes become soft and wilted.
5. Transfer to a bowl and rest for 5 minutes. Top with the chopped basil and serve warm.

Herb-Roasted Veggies

Prep time: 10 minutes | Cook time: 14 to 18 minutes | Serves 4

1 red bell pepper, sliced
1 (8-ounce / 227-g) package sliced mushrooms
1 cup green beans, cut into 2-inch pieces
⅓ cup diced red
onion
3 garlic cloves, sliced
1 teaspoon olive oil
½ teaspoon dried basil
½ teaspoon dried tarragon

1. Insert the Crisper Basket and close the hood. Select ROAST, set the temperature to 350ºF (177ºC), and set the time to 18 minutes. Select START/STOP to begin preheating.
2. In a medium bowl, mix the red bell pepper, mushrooms, green beans, red onion, and garlic. Drizzle with the olive oil. Toss to coat.
3. Add the herbs and toss again.

4. Place the vegetables in the Crisper Basket. Close the hood and ROAST for 14 to 18 minutes, or until tender. Serve immediately.

South Carolina Shrimp and Corn Bake

Prep time: 10 minutes | Cook time: 18 minutes | Serves 2

1 ear corn, husk and silk removed, cut into 2-inch rounds
8 ounces (227 g) red potatoes, unpeeled, cut into 1-inch pieces
2 teaspoons Old Bay Seasoning, divided
2 teaspoons vegetable oil, divided
¼ teaspoon ground black pepper
8 ounces (227 g) large shrimps (about 12 shrimps), deveined
6 ounces (170 g) andouille or chorizo sausage, cut into 1-inch pieces
2 garlic cloves, minced
1 tablespoon chopped fresh parsley

1. Select BAKE, set the temperature to 400ºF (204ºC), and set the time to 12 minutes. Select START/STOP to begin preheating.
2. Put the corn rounds and potatoes in a large bowl. Sprinkle with 1 teaspoon of Old Bay seasoning and drizzle with vegetable oil. Toss to coat well.
3. Transfer the corn rounds and potatoes to a baking pan.
4. Place the pan directly in the pot. Close the hood and BAKE for 12 minutes or until soft and browned. Flip halfway through the cooking time.
5. Meanwhile, cut slits into the shrimps but be careful not to cut them through. Combine the shrimps, sausage, remaining Old Bay seasoning, and remaining vegetable oil in the large bowl. Toss to coat well.
6. When the baking of the potatoes and corn rounds is complete, add the shrimps and sausage and bake for 6 more minutes or until the shrimps are opaque. Flip halfway through the cooking time.
7. When the baking is finished, serve them on a plate and spread with parsley before serving.

Classic Mexican Street Corn

Prep time: 5 minutes | Cook time: 7 minutes | Serves 4

4 medium ears corn, husked
Cooking spray
2 tablespoons mayonnaise
1 tablespoon fresh lime juice
½ teaspoon ancho chile powder

¼ teaspoon kosher salt
2 ounces (57 g) crumbled Cotija or feta cheese
2 tablespoons chopped fresh cilantro

1. Insert the Crisper Basket and close the hood. Select AIR CRISP, set the temperature to 375ºF (191ºC), and set the time to 7 minutes. Select START/STOP to begin preheating.
2. Spritz the corn with cooking spray. Working in batches, arrange the ears of corn in the Crisper Basket in a single layer. Close the hood and AIR CRISP for about 7 minutes, flipping halfway, until the kernels are tender when pierced with a paring knife. When cool enough to handle, cut the corn kernels off the cob.
3. In a large bowl, mix together mayonnaise, lime juice, ancho powder, and salt. Add the corn kernels and mix to combine. Transfer to a serving dish and top with the Cotija and cilantro. Serve immediately.

Scalloped Veggie Mix

Prep time: 10 minutes | Cook time: 15 minutes | Serves 4

1 Yukon Gold potato, thinly sliced
1 small sweet potato, peeled and thinly sliced
1 medium carrot, thinly sliced
¼ cup minced onion

3 garlic cloves, minced
¾ cup 2 percent milk
2 tablespoons cornstarch
½ teaspoon dried thyme

1. Select BAKE, set the temperature to 380ºF (193ºC), and set the time to 15 minutes. Select START/STOP to begin preheating.
2. In a baking pan, layer the potato, sweet potato, carrot, onion, and garlic.
3. In a small bowl, whisk the milk, cornstarch, and thyme until blended. Pour the milk mixture evenly over the vegetables in the pan.
4. Place the pan directly in the pot. Close the hood and BAKE for 15 minutes. Check the casserole—it should be golden brown on top, and the vegetables should be tender.
5. Serve immediately.

Peppery Brown Rice Fritters

Prep time: 10 minutes | Cook time: 8 to 10 minutes | Serves 4

1 (10-ounce / 284-g) bag frozen cooked
brown rice, thawed
1 egg
3 tablespoons brown rice flour
⅓ cup finely grated carrots

⅓ cup minced red bell pepper
2 tablespoons minced fresh basil
3 tablespoons grated Parmesan cheese
2 teaspoons olive oil

1. Insert the Crisper Basket and close the hood. Select AIR CRISP, set the temperature to 380ºF (193ºC), and set the time to 10 minutes. Select START/STOP to begin preheating.
2. In a small bowl, combine the thawed rice, egg, and flour and mix to blend.
3. Stir in the carrots, bell pepper, basil, and Parmesan cheese.
4. Form the mixture into 8 fritters and drizzle with the olive oil.
5. Put the fritters carefully into the Crisper Basket. Close the hood and AIR CRISP for 8 to 10 minutes, or until the fritters are golden brown and cooked through.
6. Serve immediately.

Indian Masala Omelet

Prep time: 10 minutes | Cook time: 12 minutes | Serves 2

4 large eggs
½ cup diced onion
½ cup diced tomato
¼ cup chopped fresh cilantro
1 jalapeño, deseeded and finely chopped

½ teaspoon ground turmeric
½ teaspoon kosher salt
½ teaspoon cayenne pepper
Olive oil, for greasing the pan

1. Select BAKE, set the temperature to 250ºF (121ºC), and set the time to 12 minutes. Select START/STOP to begin preheating.
2. Generously grease a 3-cup Bundt pan.
3. In a large bowl, beat the eggs. Stir in the onion, tomato, cilantro, jalapeño, turmeric, salt, and cayenne.
4. Pour the egg mixture into the prepared pan. Place the pan directly in the pot. Close the hood and BAKE for 12 minutes, or until the eggs are cooked through. Carefully unmold and cut the omelet into four pieces.
5. Serve immediately.

Chapter 11 Casseroles, Frittatas, and Quiches

Easy Mac and Cheese

Prep time: 10 minutes | Cook time: 10 minutes | Serves 2

1 cup cooked macaroni
1 cup grated Cheddar cheese
½ cup warm milk
Salt and ground black pepper, to taste
1 tablespoon grated Parmesan cheese

1. Select BAKE, set the temperature to 350°F (177°C), and set the time to 10 minutes. Select START/STOP to begin preheating.
2. In a baking pan, mix all the ingredients, except for Parmesan.
3. Place the pan directly in the pot. Close the hood and BAKE for 10 minutes.
4. Add the Parmesan cheese on top and serve.

Mini Quiche Cups

Prep time: 15 minutes | Cook time: 16 minutes | Makes 10 quiche cups

4 ounces (113 g) ground pork sausage
3 eggs
¾ cup milk
Cooking spray
4 ounces (113 g) sharp Cheddar cheese, grated

Special Equipment:
20 foil muffin cups

1. Insert the Crisper Basket and close the hood. Select AIR CRISP, set the temperature to 390°F (199°C), and set the time to 6 minutes. Select START/STOP to begin preheating.
2. Spritz the Crisper Basket with cooking spray.
3. Divide sausage into 3 portions and shape each into a thin patty.
4. Put patties in the Crisper Basket. Close the hood and AIR CRISP for 6 minutes.
5. While sausage is cooking, prepare the egg mixture. Combine the eggs and milk in a large bowl and whisk until well blended. Set aside.
6. When sausage has cooked fully, remove patties from the basket, drain well, and use a fork to crumble the meat into small pieces.
7. Double the foil cups into 10 sets. Remove paper liners from the top muffin cups and spray the foil cups lightly with cooking spray.
8. Divide crumbled sausage among the 10 muffin cup sets.
9. Top each with grated cheese, divided evenly among the cups.
10. Put 5 cups in the Crisper Basket.
11. Pour egg mixture into each cup, filling until each cup is at least ⅔ full.
12. Close the hood and BAKE for 8 minutes. Check for doneness. A knife inserted into the center shouldn't have any raw egg on it when removed.
13. Repeat steps 8 through 11 for the remaining quiches.
14. Serve warm.

Shrimp Green Casserole

Prep time: 15 minutes | Cook time: 22 minutes | Serves 4

1 pound (454 g) shrimp, cleaned and deveined
2 cups cauliflower, cut into florets
2 green bell pepper, sliced
1 shallot, sliced
2 tablespoons sesame oil
1 cup tomato paste
Cooking spray

1. Select BAKE, set the temperature to 360°F (182°C), and set the time to 22 minutes. Select START/STOP to begin preheating.
2. Spritz a baking pan with cooking spray.
3. Arrange the shrimp and vegetables in the baking pan. Then, drizzle the sesame oil over the vegetables. Pour the tomato paste over the vegetables.
4. Place the pan directly in the pot. Close the hood and BAKE for 10 minutes. Stir with a large spoon and bake for a further 12 minutes.
5. Serve warm.

Ritzy Vegetable Frittata

Prep time: 15 minutes | Cook time: 21 minutes | Serves 2

4 eggs
¼ cup milk
Sea salt and ground black pepper, to taste
1 zucchini, sliced
½ bunch asparagus, sliced
½ cup mushrooms, sliced
½ cup spinach, shredded
½ cup red onion, sliced
½ tablespoon olive oil
5 tablespoons feta cheese, crumbled
4 tablespoons Cheddar cheese, grated
¼ bunch chives, minced

1. In a bowl, mix the eggs, milk, salt and pepper.
2. Over a medium heat, sauté the vegetables for 6 minutes with the olive oil in a nonstick pan.
3. Put some parchment paper in the base of a baking pan. Pour in the vegetables, followed by the egg mixture. Top with the feta and grated Cheddar.
4. Select BAKE, set the temperature to 320ºF (160ºC), and set the time to 15 minutes. Select START/STOP to begin preheating.
5. Place the pan directly in the pot. Close the hood and BAKE for 15 minutes. Remove the frittata from the grill and leave to cool for 5 minutes.
6. Top with the minced chives and serve.

Western Prosciutto Casserole

Prep time: 5 minutes | Cook time: 10 minutes | Serves 2

1 cup day-old whole grain bread, cubed
3 large eggs, beaten
2 tablespoons water
⅛ teaspoon kosher salt
1 ounce (28 g) prosciutto, roughly chopped
1 ounce (28 g) Pepper Jack cheese, roughly chopped
1 tablespoon chopped fresh chives
Nonstick cooking spray

1. Select BAKE, set the temperature to 360ºF (182ºC), and set the time to 10 minutes. Select START/STOP to begin preheating.
2. Spray a baking pan with nonstick cooking spray, then place the bread cubes in the pan.
3. In a medium bowl, stir together the beaten eggs and water, then stir in the kosher salt, prosciutto, cheese, and chives. Pour the egg mixture over the bread cubes.
4. Place the pan directly in the pot. Close the hood and BAKE for 10 minutes, or until the eggs are set and the top is golden brown.
5. Serve warm.

Goat Cheese and Asparagus Frittata

Prep time: 5 minutes | Cook time: 25 minutes | Serves 2 to 4

1 cup asparagus spears, cut into 1-inch pieces
1 teaspoon vegetable oil
1 tablespoon milk
6 eggs, beaten
2 ounces (57 g) goat cheese, crumbled
1 tablespoon minced chives, optional
Kosher salt and pepper, to taste

1. Select BAKE, set the temperature to 400ºF (204ºC), and set the time to 5 minutes. Select START/STOP to begin preheating.
2. Add the asparagus spears to a small bowl and drizzle with the vegetable oil. Toss until well coated and transfer to a cake pan.
3. Place the pan directly in the pot. Close the hood and BAKE for 5 minutes, or until the asparagus become tender and slightly wilted. Remove then pan from the grill.
4. Stir together the milk and eggs in a medium bowl. Pour the mixture over the asparagus in the pan. Sprinkle with the goat cheese and the chives (if using) over the eggs. Season with a pinch of salt and pepper.
5. Place the pan back to the grill and bake at 320ºF (160ºC) for 20 minutes or until the top is lightly golden and the eggs are set.
6. Transfer to a serving dish. Slice and serve.

Taco Beef and Chile Casserole

Prep time: 10 minutes | Cook time: 15 minutes | Serves 4

1 pound (454 g) 85% lean ground beef
1 tablespoon taco seasoning
1 (7-ounce / 198-g) can diced mild green chiles
½ cup milk
2 large eggs
1 cup shredded Mexican cheese blend
2 tablespoons all-purpose flour
½ teaspoon kosher salt
Cooking spray

1. Select BAKE, set the temperature to 350ºF (177ºC), and set the time to 15 minutes. Select START/STOP to begin preheating.
2. Spritz a baking pan with cooking spray.
3. Toss the ground beef with taco seasoning in a large bowl to mix well. Pour the seasoned ground beef in the prepared baking pan.
4. Combing the remaining ingredients in a medium bowl. Whisk to mix well, then pour the mixture over the ground beef.
5. Place the pan directly in the pot. Close the hood and BAKE for 15 minutes or until a toothpick inserted in the center comes out clean.
6. Remove the casserole from the grill and allow to cool for 5 minutes, then slice to serve.

Shrimp Spinach Frittata

Prep time: 6 minutes | Cook time: 14 minutes | Serves 4

4 whole eggs
1 teaspoon dried basil
½ cup shrimp, cooked and chopped
½ cup baby spinach
½ cup rice, cooked
½ cup Monterey Jack cheese, grated
Salt, to taste
Cooking spray

1. Select BAKE, set the temperature to 360ºF (182ºC), and set the time to 14 minutes. Select START/STOP to begin preheating.
2. Spritz a baking pan with cooking spray.
3. Whisk the eggs with basil and salt in a large bowl until bubbly, then mix in the shrimp, spinach, rice, and cheese.

4. Pour the mixture into the baking pan. Place the pan directly in the pot.
5. Close the hood and BAKE for 14 minutes or until the eggs are set and the frittata is golden brown.
6. Slice to serve.

Chicken Divan

Prep time: 5 minutes | Cook time: 24 minutes | Serves 4

4 chicken breasts
Salt and ground black pepper, to taste
1 head broccoli, cut into florets
½ cup cream of
mushroom soup
1 cup shredded Cheddar cheese
½ cup croutons
Cooking spray

1. Insert the Crisper Basket and close the hood. Select AIR CRISP, set the temperature to 390ºF (199ºC), and set the time to 14 minutes. Select START/STOP to begin preheating.
2. Spritz the Crisper Basket with cooking spray.
3. Put the chicken breasts in the basket and sprinkle with salt and ground black pepper.
4. Close the hood and AIR CRISP for 14 minutes or until well browned and tender. Flip the breasts halfway through the cooking time.
5. Remove the breasts from the grill and allow to cool for a few minutes on a plate, then cut the breasts into bite-size pieces.
6. Combine the chicken, broccoli, mushroom soup, and Cheddar cheese in a large bowl. Stir to mix well.
7. Spritz a baking pan with cooking spray. Pour the chicken mixture into the pan. Spread the croutons over the mixture.
8. Place the pan directly in the pot. Close the hood and BAKE for 10 minutes or until the croutons are lightly browned and the mixture is set.
9. Remove the baking pan from the grill and serve immediately.

Broccoli, Carrot, and Tomato Quiche

Prep time: 6 minutes | Cook time: 14 minutes | Serves 4

4 eggs
1 teaspoon dried thyme
1 cup whole milk
1 steamed carrots, diced
2 cups steamed broccoli florets
2 medium tomatoes, diced
¼ cup crumbled feta cheese
1 cup grated Cheddar cheese
1 teaspoon chopped parsley
Salt and ground black pepper, to taste
Cooking spray

1. Select BAKE, set the temperature to 350ºF (177ºC), and set the time to 14 minutes. Select START/STOP to begin preheating.
2. Spritz a baking pan with cooking spray.
3. Whisk together the eggs, thyme, salt, and ground black pepper in a bowl and fold in the milk while mixing.
4. Put the carrots, broccoli, and tomatoes in the prepared baking pan, then spread with feta cheese and ½ cup Cheddar cheese. Pour the egg mixture over, then scatter with remaining Cheddar on top.
5. Place the pan directly in the pot. Close the hood and BAKE for 14 minutes or until the eggs are set and the quiche is puffed.
6. Remove the quiche from the grill and top with chopped parsley, then slice to serve.

Herbed Cheddar Frittata

Prep time: 10 minutes | Cook time: 20 minutes | Serves 4

½ cup shredded Cheddar cheese
½ cup half-and-half
4 large eggs
2 tablespoons chopped scallion greens
2 tablespoons
chopped fresh parsley
½ teaspoon kosher salt
½ teaspoon ground black pepper
Cooking spray

1. Select BAKE, set the temperature to 300ºF (149ºC), and set the time to 20 minutes. Select START/STOP to begin preheating.

2. Spritz a baking pan with cooking spray.
3. Whisk together all the ingredients in a large bowl, then pour the mixture into the prepared baking pan.
4. Place the pan directly in the pot. Close the hood and BAKE for 20 minutes or until set.
5. Serve immediately.

Creamy Pork Gratin

Prep time: 15 minutes | Cook time: 21 minutes | Serves 4

2 tablespoons olive oil
2 pounds (907 g) pork tenderloin, cut into serving-size pieces
1 teaspoon dried marjoram
¼ teaspoon chili powder
1 teaspoon coarse sea salt
½ teaspoon freshly ground black pepper
1 cup Ricotta cheese
1½ cups chicken broth
1 tablespoon mustard
Cooking spray

1. Select BAKE, set the temperature to 350ºF (177ºC), and set the time to 15 minutes. Select START/STOP to begin preheating.
2. Spritz a baking pan with cooking spray.
3. Heat the olive oil in a nonstick skillet over medium-high heat until shimmering.
4. Add the pork and sauté for 6 minutes or until lightly browned.
5. Transfer the pork to the prepared baking pan and sprinkle with marjoram, chili powder, salt, and ground black pepper.
6. Combine the remaining ingredients in a large bowl. Stir to mix well. Pour the mixture over the pork in the pan.
7. Place the pan directly in the pot. Close the hood and BAKE for 15 minutes or until frothy and the cheese melts. Stir the mixture halfway through.
8. Serve immediately.

Chorizo, Corn, and Potato Frittata

Prep time: 8 minutes | Cook time: 12 minutes | Serves 4

2 tablespoons olive oil
1 chorizo, sliced
4 eggs
½ cup corn
1 large potato, boiled and cubed
1 tablespoon chopped parsley
½ cup feta cheese, crumbled
Salt and ground black pepper, to taste

1. Select BAKE, set the temperature to 330ºF (166ºC), and set the time to 8 minutes. Select START/STOP to begin preheating.
2. Heat the olive oil in a nonstick skillet over medium heat until shimmering.
3. Add the chorizo and cook for 4 minutes or until golden brown.
4. Whisk the eggs in a bowl, then sprinkle with salt and ground black pepper.
5. Mix the remaining ingredients in the egg mixture, then pour the chorizo and its fat into a baking pan. Pour in the egg mixture.
6. Place the pan directly in the pot. Close the hood and BAKE for 8 minutes or until the eggs are set.
7. Serve immediately.

Greek Frittata

Prep time: 7 minutes | Cook time: 8 minutes | Serves 2

1 cup chopped mushrooms
2 cups spinach, chopped
4 eggs, lightly beaten
3 ounces (85 g) feta cheese, crumbled
2 tablespoons heavy cream
A handful of fresh parsley, chopped
Salt and ground black pepper, to taste
Cooking spray

1. Select BAKE, set the temperature to 350ºF (177ºC), and set the time to 8 minutes. Select START/STOP to begin preheating.
2. Spritz a baking pan with cooking spray.
3. Whisk together all the ingredients in a large bowl. Stir to mix well.
4. Pour the mixture in the prepared baking pan. Place the pan directly in the pot.

5. Close the hood and BAKE for 8 minutes or until the eggs are set.
6. Serve immediately.

Sumptuous Beef and Bean Chili Casserole

Prep time: 15 minutes | Cook time: 31 minutes | Serves 4

1 tablespoon olive oil
½ cup finely chopped bell pepper
½ cup chopped celery
1 onion, chopped
2 garlic cloves, minced
1 pound (454 g) ground beef
1 can diced tomatoes
½ teaspoon parsley
½ tablespoon chili powder
1 teaspoon chopped cilantro
1½ cups vegetable broth
1 (8-ounce / 227-g) can cannellini beans
Salt and ground black pepper, to taste

1. Select BAKE, set the temperature to 350ºF (177ºC), and set the time to 10 minutes. Select START/STOP to begin preheating.
2. Heat the olive oil in a nonstick skillet over medium heat until shimmering.
3. Add the bell pepper, celery, onion, and garlic to the skillet and sauté for 5 minutes or until the onion is translucent.
4. Add the ground beef and sauté for an additional 6 minutes or until lightly browned.
5. Mix in the tomatoes, parsley, chili powder, cilantro and vegetable broth, then cook for 10 more minutes. Stir constantly.
6. Pour them in a baking pan, then mix in the beans and sprinkle with salt and ground black pepper.
7. Place the pan directly in the pot. Close the hood and BAKE for 10 minutes or until the vegetables are tender and the beef is well browned.
8. Remove the baking pan from the grill and serve immediately.

Smoked Trout and Crème Fraiche Frittata

Prep time: 8 minutes | Cook time: 17 minutes | Serves 4

2 tablespoons olive oil
1 onion, sliced
1 egg, beaten
½ tablespoon horseradish sauce
6 tablespoons crème

fraiche
1 cup diced smoked trout
2 tablespoons chopped fresh dill
Cooking spray

1. Select BAKE, set the temperature to 350ºF (177ºC), and set the time to 14 minutes. Select START/STOP to begin preheating.
2. Spritz a baking pan with cooking spray.
3. Heat the olive oil in a nonstick skillet over medium heat until shimmering.
4. Add the onion and sauté for 3 minutes or until translucent.
5. Combine the egg, horseradish sauce, and crème fraiche in a large bowl. Stir to mix well, then mix in the sautéed onion, smoked trout, and dill.
6. Pour the mixture in the prepared baking pan. Place the pan directly in the pot. Close the hood and BAKE for 14 minutes or until the egg is set and the edges are lightly browned.
7. Serve immediately.

Sumptuous Vegetable Frittata

Prep time: 15 minutes | Cook time: 20 minutes | Serves 2

4 eggs
⅓ cup milk
2 teaspoons olive oil
1 large zucchini, sliced
2 asparagus, sliced thinly
⅓ cup sliced mushrooms
1 cup baby spinach

1 small red onion, sliced
⅓ cup crumbled feta cheese
⅓ cup grated Cheddar cheese
¼ cup chopped chives
Salt and ground black pepper, to taste

1. Select BAKE, set the temperature to 380ºF (193ºC), and set the time to 15 minutes. Select START/STOP to begin preheating.
2. Line a baking pan with parchment paper.

3. Whisk together the eggs, milk, salt, and ground black pepper in a large bowl. Set aside.
4. Heat the olive oil in a nonstick skillet over medium heat until shimmering.
5. Add the zucchini, asparagus, mushrooms, spinach, and onion to the skillet and sauté for 5 minutes or until tender.
6. Pour the sautéed vegetables into the prepared baking pan, then spread the egg mixture over and scatter with cheeses.
7. Place the pan directly in the pot. Close the hood and BAKE for 15 minutes or until the eggs are set the edges are lightly browned.
8. Remove the frittata from the grill and sprinkle with chives before serving.

Kale Frittata

Prep time: 5 minutes | Cook time: 11 minutes | Serves 2

1 cup kale, chopped
1 teaspoon olive oil
4 large eggs, beaten
Kosher salt, to taste

2 tablespoons water
3 tablespoons crumbled feta
Cooking spray

1. Select BROIL, set the temperature to 360ºF (182ºC), and set the time to 3 minutes. Select START/STOP to begin preheating.
2. Spritz a baking pan with cooking spray.
3. Add the kale to the baking pan and drizzle with olive oil. Place the pan directly in the pot. Close the hood and BROIL for 3 minutes.
4. Meanwhile, combine the eggs with salt and water in a large bowl. Stir to mix well.
5. Make the frittata: When the broiling time is complete, pour the eggs into the baking pan and spread with feta cheese. Reduce the temperature to 300ºF (149ºC).
6. Place the pan directly in the pot. Close the hood and BAKE for 8 minutes or until the eggs are set and the cheese melts.
7. Remove the baking pan from the grill and serve the frittata immediately.

Keto Cheese Quiche

Prep time: 20 minutes | Cook time: 1 hour | Serves 8

Crust:

1¼ cups blanched almond flour
1 large egg, beaten

1¼ cups grated Parmesan cheese
¼ teaspoon fine sea salt

Filling:

4 ounces (113 g) cream cheese
1 cup shredded Swiss cheese
⅓ cup minced leeks
4 large eggs, beaten
½ cup chicken broth

⅛ teaspoon cayenne pepper
¾ teaspoon fine sea salt
1 tablespoon unsalted butter, melted
Chopped green onions, for garnish
Cooking spray

1. Select BAKE, set the temperature to 325ºF (163ºC), and set the time to 27 minutes. Select START/STOP to begin preheating.
2. Spritz a pie pan with cooking spray.
3. Combine the flour, egg, Parmesan, and salt in a large bowl. Stir to mix until a satiny and firm dough forms.
4. Arrange the dough between two grease parchment papers, then roll the dough into a ¹⁄₁₆-inch thick circle.
5. Make the crust: Transfer the dough into the prepared pie pan and press to coat the bottom. Place the pan directly in the pot.
6. Close the hood and BAKE for 12 minutes or until the edges of the crust are lightly browned.
7. Meanwhile, combine the ingredient for the filling, except for the green onions in a large bowl.
8. Pour the filling over the cooked crust and cover the edges of the crust with aluminum foil. Bake for 15 more minutes, then reduce the heat to 300ºF (149ºC) and bake for another 30 minutes or until a toothpick inserted in the center comes out clean.
9. Remove the pie pan from the grill and allow to cool for 10 minutes before serving.

Mediterranean Quiche

Prep time: 10 minutes | Cook time: 30 minutes | Serves 4

4 eggs
¼ cup chopped Kalamata olives
½ cup chopped tomatoes
¼ cup chopped onion
½ cup milk

1 cup crumbled feta cheese
½ tablespoon chopped oregano
½ tablespoon chopped basil
Salt and ground black pepper, to taste
Cooking spray

1. Select BAKE, set the temperature to 340ºF (171ºC), and set the time to 30 minutes. Select START/STOP to begin preheating.
2. Spritz a baking pan with cooking spray.
3. Whisk the eggs with remaining ingredients in a large bowl. Stir to mix well.
4. Pour the mixture into the prepared baking pan. Place the pan directly in the pot.
5. Close the hood and BAKE for 30 minutes or until the eggs are set and a toothpick inserted in the center comes out clean. Check the doneness of the quiche during the last 10 minutes of baking.
6. Serve immediately.

Chapter 12 Sauces, Dips, and Dressings

Balsamic Dressing

Prep time: 5 minutes | Cook time: 0 minutes | Makes 1 cup

2 tablespoons Dijon mustard
¼ cup balsamic vinegar
¾ cup olive oil

1. Put all ingredients in a jar with a tight-fitting lid. Put on the lid and shake vigorously until thoroughly combined. Refrigerate until ready to use and shake well before serving.

Cashew Vodka Sauce

Prep time: 15 minutes | Cook time: 5 minutes | Makes 3 cups

¾ cup raw cashews
¼ cup boiling water
1 tablespoon olive oil
4 garlic cloves, minced
1½ cups unsweetened almond milk
1 tablespoon arrowroot powder
1 teaspoon salt
1 tablespoon nutritional yeast
1¼ cups marinara sauce

1. Put the cashews in a heatproof bowl and add boiling water to cover. Let soak for 10 minutes. Drain the cashews and place them in a blender. Add ¼ cup boiling water and blend for 1 to 2 minutes or until creamy. Set aside.
2. In a small saucepan, heat the olive oil over medium heat. Add the garlic and sauté for 2 minutes until golden. Whisk in the almond milk, arrowroot powder, and salt. Bring to a simmer. Continue to simmer, whisking frequently, for about 5 minutes or until the sauce thickens.
3. Carefully transfer the hot almond milk mixture to the blender with the cashews. Blend for 30 seconds to combine, then add the nutritional yeast and marinara sauce. Blend for 1 minute or until creamy.

Lemon Dijon Vinaigrette

Prep time: 5 minutes | Cook time: 0 minutes | Makes about 6 tablespoons

¼ cup extra-virgin olive oil
1 garlic clove, minced
2 tablespoons freshly squeezed lemon juice
1 teaspoon Dijon mustard
½ teaspoon raw honey
¼ teaspoon salt
¼ teaspoon dried basil

1. Place all the ingredients in a mason jar. Cover and shake vigorously until thoroughly mixed and well emulsified.
2. Serve chilled.

Cashew Pesto

Prep time: 10 minutes | Cook time: 0 minutes | Makes 1 cup

¼ cup raw cashews
Juice of 1 lemon
2 garlic cloves
⅓ red onion (about 2 ounces / 56 g in total)
1 tablespoon olive oil
4 cups basil leaves, packed
1 cup wheatgrass
¼ cup water
¼ teaspoon salt

1. Put the cashews in a heatproof bowl and add boiling water to cover. Soak for 5 minutes and then drain.
2. Put all ingredients in a blender and blend for 2 to 3 minutes or until fully combined.

Hummus

Prep time: 5 minutes | Cook time: 0 minutes | Serves 2

1 (19-ounce / 539-g) can chickpeas, drained and rinsed
¼ cup tahini
3 tablespoons cold water
2 tablespoons freshly squeezed lemon juice
1 garlic clove
½ teaspoon turmeric powder
⅛ teaspoon black pepper
Pinch of pink Himalayan salt

1. Combine all the ingredients in a food processor and blend until smooth.

Fresh Mixed Berry Vinaigrette

Prep time: 15 minutes | Cook time: 0 minutes | Makes about 1½ cups

1 cup mixed berries, thawed if frozen
½ cup balsamic vinegar
1/3 cup extra-virgin olive oil
2 tablespoons freshly squeezed lemon or lime juice
1 tablespoon lemon or lime zest
1 tablespoon Dijon mustard
1 tablespoon raw honey or maple syrup
1 teaspoon salt
½ teaspoon freshly ground black pepper

1. Place all the ingredients in a blender and purée until thoroughly mixed and smooth.
2. You can serve it over a bed of greens, grilled meat, or fresh fruit salad.

Cashew Ranch Dressing

Prep time: 15 minutes | Cook time: 0 minutes | Serves 12

1 cup cashews, soaked in warm water for at least 1 hour
½ cup water
2 tablespoons freshly squeezed lemon juice
1 tablespoon vinegar
1 teaspoon garlic powder
1 teaspoon onion powder
2 teaspoons dried dill

1. In a food processor, combine the cashews, water, lemon juice, vinegar, garlic powder, and onion powder. Blend until creamy and smooth. Add the dill and pulse a few times until combined.

Ginger Sweet Sauce

Prep time: 5 minutes | Cook time: 5 minutes | Makes 2/3 cup

3 tablespoons ketchup
2 tablespoons water
2 tablespoons maple syrup
1 tablespoon rice vinegar
2 teaspoons peeled
minced fresh ginger root
2 teaspoons soy sauce (or tamari, which is a gluten-free option)
1 teaspoon cornstarch

1. In a small saucepan over medium heat, combine all the ingredients and stir continuously for 5 minutes, or until slightly thickened. Enjoy warm or cold.

Kale and Almond Pesto

Prep time: 15 minutes | Cook time: 0 minutes | Makes about 1 cup

2 cups chopped kale leaves, rinsed well and stemmed
½ cup toasted almonds
2 garlic cloves
3 tablespoons extra-virgin olive oil
3 tablespoons freshly
squeezed lemon juice
2 teaspoons lemon zest
1 teaspoon salt
½ teaspoon freshly ground black pepper
¼ teaspoon red pepper flakes

1. Place all the ingredients in a food processor and pulse until smoothly puréed.
2. It tastes great with the eggs, salads, soup, pasta, cracker, and sandwiches.

Chimichurri

Prep time: 15 minutes | Cook time: 0 minutes | Makes 2 cups

1 cup minced fresh parsley
½ cup minced fresh cilantro
¼ cup minced fresh mint leaves
¼ cup minced garlic (about 6 cloves)
2 tablespoons minced
fresh oregano leaves
1 teaspoon fine Himalayan salt
1 cup olive oil or avocado oil
½ cup red wine vinegar
Juice of 1 lemon

1. Thoroughly mix the parsley, cilantro, mint leaves, garlic, oregano leaves, and salt in a medium bowl. Add the olive oil, vinegar, and lemon juice and whisk to combine.
2. Store in an airtight container in the refrigerator and shake before using.
3. You can serve the chimichurri over vegetables, poultry, meats, and fish. It also can be used as a marinade, dipping sauce, or condiment.

Pico de Gallo

Prep time: 5 minutes | Cook time: 0 minutes | Serves 2

3 large tomatoes, chopped
½ small red onion, diced
⅛ cup chopped fresh cilantro
3 garlic cloves, chopped

2 tablespoons chopped pickled jalapeño pepper
1 tablespoon lime juice
¼ teaspoon pink Himalayan salt (optional)

1. In a medium bowl, combine all the ingredients and mix with a wooden spoon.

Peanut-Lime Dressing

Prep time: 5 minutes | Cook time: 0 minutes | Serves 8

1 cup lite coconut milk
¼ cup freshly squeezed lime juice
¼ cup creamy peanut butter
2 tablespoons low-

sodium soy sauce or tamari
3 garlic cloves, minced
1 tablespoon grated fresh ginger

1. Place all the ingredients in a food processor or blender and process until completely mixed and smooth.
2. It's delicious served over grilled chicken or tossed with noodles and green onions.

Creamy Ranch Dressing

Prep time: 5 minutes | Cook time: 0 minutes | Serves 8

1 cup plain Greek yogurt
¼ cup chopped fresh dill
2 tablespoons chopped fresh chives

Zest of 1 lemon
1 garlic clove, minced
½ teaspoon sea salt
⅛ teaspoon freshly cracked black pepper

1. Mix together the yogurt, dill, chives, lemon zest, garlic, sea salt, and pepper in a small bowl and whisk to combine.
2. Serve chilled.

Creamy Coconut Lime Dressing

Prep time: 5 minutes | Cook time: 0 minutes | Makes about 1 cup

8 ounces (227 g) plain coconut yogurt
2 tablespoons chopped fresh parsley
2 tablespoons freshly

squeezed lemon juice
1 tablespoon snipped fresh chives
½ teaspoon salt
Pinch freshly ground black pepper

1. Stir together the coconut yogurt, parsley, lemon juice, chives, salt, and pepper in a medium bowl until completely mixed.
2. Transfer to an airtight container and refrigerate until ready to use.
3. This dressing perfectly pairs with spring mix greens, grilled chicken, or even your favorite salad.

Garlic Lime Tahini Dressing

Prep time: 5 minutes | Cook time: 0 minutes | Makes about ¾ cup

⅓ cup tahini
3 tablespoons filtered water
2 tablespoons freshly squeezed lime juice
1 tablespoon apple cider vinegar

1 teaspoon lime zest
1½ teaspoons raw honey
¼ teaspoon garlic powder
¼ teaspoon salt

1. Whisk together the tahini, water, vinegar, lime juice, lime zest, honey, salt, and garlic powder in a small bowl until well emulsified.
2. Serve immediately, or refrigerate in an airtight container for to 1 week.

Appendix I: Measurement Conversion Chart

VOLUME EQUIVALENTS(DRY)

US STANDARD	METRIC (APPROXIMATE)
1/8 teaspoon	0.5 mL
1/4 teaspoon	1 mL
1/2 teaspoon	2 mL
3/4 teaspoon	4 mL
1 teaspoon	5 mL
1 tablespoon	15 mL
1/4 cup	59 mL
1/2 cup	118 mL
3/4 cup	177 mL
1 cup	235 mL
2 cups	475 mL
3 cups	700 mL
4 cups	1 L

VOLUME EQUIVALENTS(LIQUID)

US STANDARD	US STANDARD (OUNCES)	METRIC (APPROXIMATE)
2 tablespoons	1 fl.oz.	30 mL
1/4 cup	2 fl.oz.	60 mL
1/2 cup	4 fl.oz.	120 mL
1 cup	8 fl.oz.	240 mL
1 1/2 cup	12 fl.oz.	355 mL
2 cups or 1 pint	16 fl.oz.	475 mL
4 cups or 1 quart	32 fl.oz.	1 L
1 gallon	128 fl.oz.	4 L

TEMPERATURES EQUIVALENTS

FAHRENHEIT(F)	CELSIUS(C) (APPROXIMATE)
225 °F	107 °C
250 °F	120 °C
275 °F	135 °C
300 °F	150 °C
325 °F	160 °C
350 °F	180 °C
375 °F	190 °C
400 °F	205 °C
425 °F	220 °C
450 °F	235 °C
475 °F	245 °C
500 °F	260 °C

WEIGHT EQUIVALENTS

US STANDARD	METRIC (APPROXIMATE)
1 ounce	28 g
2 ounces	57 g
5 ounces	142 g
10 ounces	284 g
15 ounces	425 g
16 ounces (1 pound)	455 g
1.5 pounds	680 g
2 pounds	907 g